D1410267

A Living Tradition

†

STUDIES IN WORLD CATHOLICISM

Other Titles in This Series

Beyond the Borders of Baptism: Catholicity, Allegiances, and Lived Identities. Edited by Michael L. Budde. Vol. 1, 2016. ISBN 9781498204736

New World Pope: Pope Francis and the Future of the Church. Edited by Michael L. Budde. Vol. 2, 2017. ISBN 9781498283717

Scattered and Gathered: Catholics in Diaspora. Vol. 3, 2017. Edited by Michael L. Budde. ISBN 9781532607097

Forthcoming Titles in This Series

Fragile World: Ecology and the Church. Edited by William T. Cavanaugh

Love, Joy, and Sex: African Conversation on Pope Francis's Amoris Laetitia *and the Gospel of Family in a Divided World.* Edited by Stan Chu Ilo

A Church with the Indigenous Peoples: The Intercultural Theology and Ecclesiology of JTatik Samuel Ruiz García. Michel Elias Andraos

A Living Tradition

Catholic Social Doctrine and Holy See Diplomacy

A. Alexander Stummvoll

CASCADE *Books* • Eugene, Oregon

A LIVING TRADITION
Catholic Social Doctrine and Holy See Diplomacy

Studies in World Catholicism 4

Cascade Books
An Imprint of Wipf and Stock Publishers
199 W. 8th Ave., Suite 3
Eugene, OR 97401

www.wipfandstock.com

PAPERBACK ISBN: 978-1-5326-0511-6
HARDCOVER ISBN: 978-1-5326-0513-0
EBOOK ISBN: 978-1-5326-0512-3

Cataloguing-in-Publication data:

Names: Stummvoll, A. Alexander, author.

Title: A living tradition : Catholic social doctrine and holy see diplomacy / A. Alexander Stummvoll.

Description: Eugene, OR : Cascade Books, 2018. | Studies in World Catholicism 4 | Includes bibliographical references and index(es).

Identifiers: ISBN 978-1-5326-0511-6 (paperback) | ISBN 978-1-5326-0513-0 (hardcover) | ISBN 978-1-5326-0512-3 (ebook)

Subjects: LCSH: Catholic Church—Foreign relations. | Catholic Church—Doctrines. | Christianity and international relations—Catholic Church. | Church and social problems—Catholic Church.

Classification: KBU4076 .S78 2018 (print) | KBU4076 .S78 (ebook)

Manufactured in the U.S.A. APRIL 30, 2018

In loving memory of my grandfather,
Dr. Karl Schnürl (1924–2011)

Contents

Preface

The idea that academic research should be pursued strictly independent of personal motivation and interests is a powerful myth of positivist social science which is convenient for those who are unwilling to reflect on the multiple ways in which our personal background and interests color our academic research, whether we are willing to admit it nor not. Post-positivist scholars, on the other hand, encourage researchers to explicitly reflect on their own underlying interests and motivations. The "interest of the researcher should always be clearly stated," Jörg Friedrichs and Friedrich Kratochwil argue, to allow "the relevant evaluators and the peer community at large to establish whether and to what extent some research serves a legitimate, useful, and socially relevant purpose."[1] In this spirit, I hope this prologue will help the readers of this book to better understand the personal, academic, and ecclesial context out of which this book emerges as well as its larger underlying purposes.

My relevant Catholic childhood memories consist of listening to Bible stories read by my grandfather, being an altar server at our local Cistercian monastery in Baden-Baden and, in later years, reflecting on peace and justice issues during annual Lenten meditations. Loving God and your neighbors across the street as well as in far-away places made Christianity intuitively attractive to me. My exposure to the Cistercian monastic life also instilled a love for good liturgy and Latin Gregorian chant in me. I cannot recollect a single sermon on hot-button issues such as abortion or contraception which will play an important role in Chapter 6. Having devoured the theological work of Hans Küng as a teenager, I once thought that such controversial teaching was nothing more than fading remnants of a distant past.

1. Friedrichs and Kratochwil, "On Acting and Knowing," 716.

A high-school exchange semester in Texas where my host family attended a Southern Baptist parish in Austin came as a spiritual culture shock. Moving from Gregorian chant to "Jesus, you are my all in all" was made easier, however, by becoming part of a large and vibrant youth program. The Baptist conception of faith as a personal decision with radical consequences was very different from my own European Catholic experience of faith as something that is culturally inherited and that tends to live in harmony with the surrounding culture. Upon my return to Germany I enthusiastically aimed to integrate this newly discovered evangelical conception of faith into my Catholicism, to the surprise of my parents who were perplexed as their son started to wear a "What Would Jesus Do?" bracelet.

Having always had a strong curiosity in all things international and not sensing any particular call to the priesthood or monastic life, studying International Relations (IR) seemed like a natural choice, especially as I had dreamed about pursuing a career in diplomacy. Studying in Aberystwyth—the founding place of modern IR—provided me with a fascinating intellectual introduction into the history, as well as into classical, normative, and contemporary theories of IR. Undergoing the Aberystwyth experience made me attentive to the social construction of global politics as well as to the connectedness between the "empirical" world and our moral and analytical "theories" about them. For some reason, the Catholic in me was never too worried about the philosophical consequences which a post-positivist deconstruction of reality has for the question of Christian truth, as personified by Jesus Christ.

What puzzled me was the extent to which IR simply neglected religious ideas and actors. It was only when I moved to Oxford in 2005 to pursue an MPhil in International Relations that a broader theoretical literature on religion and IR had begun to emerge. Reading more about the Catholic Church during the Cold War left me irritated, however, about the dominance of neoconservative stories that put the emphasis almost exclusively on the church's anti-communism. In my MPhil dissertation,[2] I showed that the Holy See's international positions under Pope John Paul II did not only include anti-communism but also critical interventions on issues of development and disarmament as well as a broader critique of certain aspects of Western liberal capitalism. In papal social encyclicals

2. Stummvoll, "John Paul II, the Cold War, and the Catholic Tradition."

I identified the normative sources which help us understand the unique breadth and autonomy of Catholic engagement with global politics.

I have always been fascinated by the relationships between theory and practice. As a student I seized every chance I could to complement my studies with internships. As I was gaining practical insights in the field of foreign policy as a trainee in the Cabinet of the President of the EU Commission, José Manuel Barroso, and at the EU Delegation to the Holy See in Rome, I realized that the relationship between Catholic social doctrine and Holy See diplomacy was more complicated than I had assumed. This is especially the case if we want to understand not only the core threads of Holy See diplomacy but also concrete decisions and positions.

I was grateful when the only PhD application I submitted was accepted by the European University Institute (EUI). In November 2012, I defended my PhD dissertation in the Department of Political and Social Sciences which serves as the basis for this book.[3] Following my PhD, I spent a year as Visiting Assistant Professor at DePaul University's Department of Catholic Studies and its Center for World Catholicism and Intercultural Theology, followed by another year as postdoctoral fellow at the *Instituto de Ciencia Política* of the *Pontificia Universidad Católica de Chile*. My time in Chicago and in Santiago provided me with stimulating environments for rewriting my dissertation into this book. Both at DePaul and at "La Católica" I benefitted immensely from teaching courses on Catholic social doctrine in which my students read, debated, and wrote about all major papal social encyclicals from *Rerum Novarum* to the current day.

Throughout my university years, my exposure to a variety of Catholic experiences as well as to liberal secular environments made me increasingly skeptical about both the practical possibility and the normative necessity of making Catholicism conform to Western liberal secular culture. Engaging with the collected works of Joseph Ratzinger helped me to better appreciate the nature and demands of traditional church teaching as an important ethical source that unifies the Catholic Church across space and time. This book may thus disappoint liberal Catholics who look for a forceful critique of the Holy See's role in global politics. At the same time, however, I continue to be highly suspicious of conservative

3. Stummvoll, "A Living Tradition."

narratives that frown upon the Holy See's active promotion of justice and peace issues.

Rather, my aim in this book is to draw a more holistic and dynamic conception of Catholic social doctrine as it underpins the international agenda of the Holy See. My book will hopefully help its readers to create some bridges between theology and IR, between religion and politics, between liberal and conservative Catholics, between North American and European Catholics, as well as between religious and secular worldviews with a view to enhance mutual understanding and dialogue. Such dialogue is urgently necessary in a time where the Catholic Church, Western democracies, and academia are all suffering from the isolating and stifling effects of tribalism in its various manifestations.

Not only the Holy See, but all Catholic Christians and, in fact, all people of good will, have a responsibility to hold together what liberal and conservative Catholics so often want to divide. Living out Catholic social doctrine in global politics is a challenging yet not impossible endeavor. Certainly, the Holy See has a privileged responsibility to protect, guide, and develop this living tradition according to the signs of the time, especially in relation to states and other powerful international actors. But if Catholic social doctrine is to truly unfold its powerful potential on behalf of the war-torn, the repressed, the unborn, and the poor, it has to be lived out and incarnated by every single Christian in our everyday lives.

Acknowledgments

The European atmosphere at the EUI, the Tuscan hills, the surrounding Catholic-Italian culture, the geographical proximity to Rome, and the help of my supervisor provided a congenial atmosphere for my doctoral research. Friedrich Kratochwil possesses an unrivaled ability to immediately identify and accurately describe the analytical problems of dissertation drafts. At times his criticism left me close to tears as I humbly had to go back to the drawing board. Without his help my project would never have come to fruition. My external supervisor Scott Thomas has guided and inspired me since I first informally contacted him from Oxford. Our ongoing dialogue on all things academic, spiritual, and political is a true gift. I am grateful he accepted to become my son's godfather. The comments of the additional members of my PhD jury—Mariano Barbato and Olivier Roy—have been most welcome. Thanks to the support of Olivier Roy and together with Pasquale Annicchino, Maria Birnbaum, Georges Fahmi, Kristina Stoeckl, and Timothy Peace, I am grateful to have contributed to the foundation of the Religion and Politics Working Group which transformed the EUI into a very exciting place for the study of religion and politics.

Spending four years solely on research would not have been possible without generous financial support. I want to express my gratitude about the financial support I received from my father, the Economic and Social Research Council (UK), the University of Oxford's Department of Politics and International Relations, St. Antony's College, the Austrian *Bundesministerium für Wissenschaft und Forschung*, the European University Institute, its Department of Social and Political Science, the Paderewski Grant of the European Centre in Natolin, and DePaul University's Center for World Catholicism and Intercultural Theology. The Millennium Nucleus for the Study of Stateness and Democracy in South America, hosted by the *Instituto de Ciencia Política* of the *Pontificia Universidad Católica de Chile* in Santiago, funded my post-doctoral year in Santiago.

During my extensive archival research trips, I enjoyed the hospitality of both Michael Cocoman and Kai Whittaker (London), Kevin and Jane Gingras, as well as Josh and Rebecca Good (Washington), Sam Denton (Austin), Suzette Little (Ann Arbor), Kelly Lovato (Simi Valley), Guillaume Touchard (Paris), Tobias Rupprecht (Berlin), and Laura and Francesco Puccio (Rome). The additional research assistance provided by Nicole Hassan, Eric Heine, and my father, Franz Stummvoll, has been priceless. Special thanks go to Heino Claussen. In 5th grade, he was my first English teacher. 24 years later, he proofread the final manuscript of this book.

While working on this research project, I had the privilege of living in very different settings around the globe. They were nevertheless similar in that they allowed me to live and work in caring communities rather than in academic solitude. In Settignano I appreciated Milvia's love, cooking, washing, ironing, and introduction into all things Italian. I am grateful to Mauro-Giuseppe Lepori, OCist, and Meinrad Tomann, OCist, for letting me eat, pray, and live with a remarkable community of young monks around the world in the *Casa Generalizia* of the Cistercian Order on the Aventino in Rome. Finally, I want to thank my wife's Chilean family for having accepted me with open arms.

The person who inspired me the most, my grandfather, passed away as I was working on this project. I miss him deeply and his love and example continues to inspire me. To you, *Opapa*, I dedicate this book. To move from the past to the present, meeting my future wife on a cold February night in EUI's infamous Bar Fiasco was the best and most unexpected thing that happened to me while working on this book. Thank you, Carolina, for your love, patience, and support. To you, Lucas Karl, and Emilie Luz I dedicate my future.

Abbreviations

AA	German Diplomatic Archives (*Politisches Archiv des Auswärtigen Amts*), Berlin
AD	French Diplomatic Archives (*Archives Diplomatiques*), La Courneuve, Paris
BStU	Archives of the Federal Commissioner for the Records of the State Security Service of the former German Democratic Republic, Berlin
CIDSE	*Coopération Internationale pour le Développement et la Solidarité*
FCO	Foreign and Commonwealth Office
FWCW	Fourth World Conference on Women
FRUS	Foreign Relations of the United States
GF	Gerald R. Ford Presidential Library, Ann Arbor, Michigan
GNP	Gross National Product
HIPC	Heavily Indebted Poor Countries
ICC	International Control Commission
ICPD	International Conference on Population and Development
IFI	International Financial Institution
IFPP	International Federation of Planned Parenthood
IMF	International Monetary Fund
IR	International Relations

JC	Jimmy Carter Presidential Library, Atlanta, Georgia
LBJ	Lyndon B. Johnson Presidential Library, Austin, Texas
NGO	Non-governmental organization
NSC	National Security Council
NLF	National Liberation Front (Vietcong)
PCJP	Pontifical Council for Justice and Peace, Vatican City
PrepCom	Preparatory Committee
PRG	Provisional Revolutionary Government of the Republic of South Vietnam
PRSP	Poverty Reduction Strategy Paper
RN	Richard Nixon Presidential Library, Yorba Linda, California
RR	Ronald Reagan Presidential Library, Simi Valley, California
SAP	Structural Adjustment Program
SEATO	South East Asia Treaty Organization
TNA	The National Archives of the United Kingdom, Kew, London
USCCB	United States Conference of Catholic Bishops
XGS	Annual export of goods and services

1

Introduction

Introduction

The Holy See is both a religious and a political actor in the international system. As Bishop of Rome and successor of the Apostle Peter, the pope is the spiritual and organizational head of the Catholic Church, the largest religious community of the world. Its baptized members count approximately 1.2 billion or 17.5 percent of the world's population. Thanks to its international legal personality, the Holy See simultaneously can act like a state by maintaining diplomatic relations with other states and being an active part of international organizations. Catholic social doctrine provides a living tradition of thought and practice to the Holy See that stipulates normative guidelines on how Catholic Christians and all people of good will ought to engage with global topics such as war and peace, socialism, capitalism, sexuality, or family values.

Do popes and their diplomats only preach these norms or do they actually live, promote, and incarnate them in the sphere of global politics? Drawing upon the case studies of the Vietnam War, John Paul II and Poland, the United Nations' (UN) conferences on population control and women in the nineties, and the global anti-debt campaign in the year 2000, I will argue that international relations are a difficult but not impossible realm for authentically living out Catholic social doctrine. International politics, by its very nature, remains a realm of compromise and suboptimal, temporary solutions. To reconcile political constraints and moral principles, the Holy See tends to live out Catholic social doctrine prudently and pragmatically, paying close attention to particular circumstances and possible repercussions for the safety of local Catholic constituencies, its global reputation, and the unity of the Catholic Church.

Joseph Stalin once mocked the Holy See's lack of military power by asking "The pope! How many divisions has *he* got?"[1] His invisible divisions, however, have shaped world affairs for over two millennia. In Roman times, the Bishop of Rome emerged from the catacombs. In the Middle Ages, he had become the spiritual leader of Christendom. In modern times, his authority has been inextricably intertwined with religious wars, European colonialism, and the global missionary movement that helped spread Catholicism to the Americas, Asia, and Africa. Until the nineteenth century, the papacy even ruled over the large territory of the Papal States, located on the Italian peninsula. It had its own army and frequently participated in the formation of diplomatic alliances and wars. After it had lost control over the Papal States in 1870 to Italian nationalists, the papacy was forced to recede to the tiny Vatican territory inside the city of Rome.[2] As a consequence, popes had to recast their role in global politics with a fresh stress on moral authority and a new reliance on words and symbols rather than military and economic strength.[3]

The Holy See did not only play an important role in global politics in the distant past but it has and will continue to do so in the recent past, the present, and the future. Yet despite its importance in global politics, the Holy See remains understudied within the academic disciplines of political science and International Relations.[4] Apart from some journal articles and book chapters,[5] only a handful of monographs have been published on Vatican diplomacy in English over the last five decades. Notwithstanding some helpful insights, they are either outdated,[6] have

1. On being asked by Winston Churchill in 1935 to encourage Catholicism in Russia by way of conciliating the pope. Quoted in Jay, *Oxford Dictionary*, 438.

2. Technically, the Vatican only denotes the geographical territory inside Rome where the Vatican City State is located. It is the Holy See, rather than the Vatican, that engages in diplomatic relations as a sovereign entity. In common parlance, both concepts are often used interchangeably though.

3. See Duffy, *Saints & Sinners*.

4. Following conventional practice, I use the term "International Relations" to denote the academic study of the practice of international relations.

5. Barbato, "State"; Chong and Troy, "Universal Sacred Mission"; Murphy, "Vatican Politics"; Neale, "Bodies of Christ"; Ryall, "How Many Divisions"; Ryall, "Cross and the Bear"; Ryall, "Catholic Church"; Shelledy, "Vatican's Role"; Vallier, "Roman Catholic Church."

6. Graham, *Vatican Diplomacy*, provides a classic introduction into the historical,

a narrow institutional-legal focus,[7] fail to consult archival sources,[8] or neglect to offer a broader theoretical account that explains the process through which religious norms and traditions influence, shape, and constrain religious actors' practices in global politics.[9] This book aspires to fill these lacunas by exploring the normative tradition underpinning Holy See diplomacy, and the political and ethical dilemmas that arise from translating and faithfully living out this tradition into the realities and complexities of global politics.

The lack of attention given to the Vatican's role in global politics reflects a deeper secular disinterest which the social sciences in general and political science in particular have displayed toward religious issues.[10] Traditionally, the popular assumption has been that modernity progressively leads to the decline of religion in the world. Religion, from this perspective, then simply is a cover for more important geopolitical conflicts between states or socioeconomic struggles between classes. Hence, the argument goes, we should study "real issues" instead of giving undue attention to religious norms or actors. Since the end of the Cold War and the terror attacks of 9/11, religion has increasingly become a more popular object of inquiry.[11] The dominant mode of this budding literature is a focus on religion's impact on politics. The politics that takes

---

legal, and theological sources of Vatican diplomacy of the Holy See with a special focus on the historical origins of modern papal diplomacy, its key organs, and the nature of Holy See sovereignty.

7. Cardinale, *Holy See and the International Order*, is a widely-cited source for scholars trying to make sense of the institutional intricacies of papal diplomacy and its protocol. See also Araujo and Lucal, *Papal Diplomacy*. Their two volumes examine the relationship between the Holy See and the League of Nations and the United Nations until the end of the pontificate of Paul VI.

8. Hanson, *Catholic Church*, was the first monograph that connected analysis of Vatican diplomacy with theoretical IR discussions about power, culture, and ideology. However, his broad case studies on Western Europe, the United States, the Soviet Union, and the Third World, as well as his failure to consult primary archives, weakens the strength of his analysis which fails to provide an in-depth examination of the tensions and dilemmas of papal diplomacy.

9. Kent and Pollard, *Papal Diplomacy*, is an edited volume though, that provides rich descriptions of the Vatican's relationship with various great and middle-size powers of the nineteenth and twentieth centuries.

10. On the traditional paucity of religious issues in political science and IR see Thomas, *Global Resurgence of Religion*.

11. For a good review article see Philpott, "Has the Study of Global Politics."

place inside politically influential religious communities has not been receiving nearly as much, if any, attention.

How do religious actors make their deliberations and decisions that underpin their engagement with international politics? What factors help us to understand why a religious actor like the Holy See acts the way it does in global politics? Scholars such as Scott Appleby, Ron Hassner, or Daniel Philpott provide some helpful insights and arguments for answering that sort of questions. Their work on the ambivalence of the sacred,[12] on sacred places,[13] and the political ambivalence of religion[14] explains why religious actors generally tend toward violent or peaceful dispositions. What their studies overlook, however, are the difficulties and challenges religious communities—especially moderate, non-violent, and non-fundamentalist ones—face when they faithfully want to live out their very own religious norms in conditions of violent conflict, diplomatic tension, or political crisis.

While social scientists often overlook the importance of religious norms and the ways in which religious leaders have interpreted and implemented them in world affairs, religious elites often overstate their importance. Such moves result in broad statements such as "the Catholic Church promotes peace and social justice" or "Evangelicals foster democratic ideas and practices." Such generalizations, even as they may contain some truth, equally prevent analysis of the political challenges that are inherent in attempts to promote peace, social justice, or democracy in concrete historical circumstances and in the face of competing political interests.

Theoretically, religious traditions are living traditions that provide a source of inspiration and advice, shape the perception of global politics, constitute actors' identities and interests, and serve as constraints for what legitimately can be said or done. To fully unfold their meaning, however, religious traditions need to be interpreted and lived out by real people in real places. In the chaotic and inconclusive world of global politics, faithfully living out a religious tradition is, politically, considerably more difficult than preaching its content from a pulpit. Making sense of the logic of religious action in global politics and of the ensuing dilemmas thus requires not only careful theoretical and conceptual analysis, but

12. Appleby, *Ambivalence of the Sacred*.

13. Hassner, *War on Sacred Grounds*.

14. Philpott, "Explaining the Political Ambivalence of Religion."

also consideration of theological norms and historical context. For this reason, I will offer a fresh view of papal diplomacy which takes on a key issue: how religious traditions function in global politics and how even religious actors are not immune to the painful yet unavoidable dilemma of whether to raise their voices for moral considerations or to remain silent for prudential reasons.

Religious Traditions in International Relations

The relationship between religious ideas and religious actors' politically salient practices remains largely unexamined. Alfred Stepan belittles the importance of religious ideas by arguing that they are so ambivalent—"multivocal"—that they can be used to justify any political project, from authoritarianism to democracy, from anti-Semitism to human rights.[15] Fred Halliday insinuates that religious ideas are an ideological menu-of-choice that religious elites invent, manipulate, and control to disguise their own pre-defined political projects.[16] Daniel Philpott, Timothy Shah, and Monica Duffy Toft, on the other hand, recognize the importance of political theology by arguing that "a religious actor's political stance is traceable, at least in part" to their underlying "set of ideas." Their assertion that "political theology translates basic theological claims, beliefs and doctrines into political ideals and programs" falls short, however, of analyzing how these normative programs actually are interpreted, debated, and applied in concrete circumstances. In *God's Century*, they seek to provide the "strongest general explanation of why religious actors act as they do."[17] By this they mean the "kind of politics" they pursue, such as supporting or resisting democracy, terrorism, civil war, or peacemaking. By definition, their approach is unable to shed more light on the choices and dilemmas religious groups face when promoting peace or democracy in circumstances of ongoing warfare such as during the Vietnam War. Scott Appleby's work on the "ambivalence of the sacred" has popularized the argument that religion can either be a force for peace or for conflict in the world. While this was a timely and important insight, his argument underplays the practical and political dilemmas involved in discerning what it actually means for a religious actor to promote peace in concrete

15. Stepan, "World's Religious System."

16. Halliday, "Culture and International Relations."

17. Toft et al., *God's Century*, 27.

and challenging circumstances. Taking the ambivalence of the sacred seriously requires a more concerted effort to study how religious norms are interpreted, applied, and used in practice.

Alasdair MacIntyre's definition of a living tradition, I will argue in the next chapter, offers a helpful springboard for understanding the nature of religious traditions and the relationship between traditions and decisions. Living traditions are historically extended, socially embodied arguments about the "good life." They are dynamic and evolving bodies of thought that do not only convey norms and ideas, but are intrinsically connected to real-life practices. Traditions are historically evolved bundles of norms that serve important functions which make them a principled basis for practice. They provide inspiration and advice, constitute identity and interests, and constrain what legitimately can be said or done. When the focus is to understand concrete decisions, positions, and policies, however, the causal impact of tradition becomes more difficult to recognize. Decisions may be shaped, guided, provoked, or constrained by tradition, but are never determined by it. Religious leaders are not bloodless puppets of their traditions but have the authority and the responsibility to interpret and implement them. Hence, there is always a gap between tradition and decision which can only be bridged by interpretation and application. Religious leaders play a crucial role in this process.

Remaining at a general level of argumentation disables us to get a vague idea of how religious traditions get translated into concrete practice. Politically and socially relevant religious traditions such as Catholic social doctrine are vast bodies of thought that cover a wide variety of different issue areas, objectives, and concerns. They do not automatically translate themselves into policies but depend on religious people to translate them into concrete situations. Clashes in priorities and competing value considerations can lead to challenging dilemmas. For example, should religious leaders speak out on behalf of specific normative goals such as the imperative of peace, or should they mute their criticism of existing power structures for prudential reasons in order to protect local believers? The process of living out religious norms in global politics needs to be carefully analyzed rather than viewed as straightforward or dismissed as irrelevant.

Themes and Case Studies

This book is structured around four key themes of Catholic social doctrine: war and peace, communism, sexual ethics and family values, and capitalism. Converting communism has been on the Holy See's agenda since the mid-nineteenth century. At first, communism was simply a rival idea about the world. Following the 1917 Russian Revolution, the civil wars in Mexico and Spain, and the imposition of Stalinist regimes in Eastern Europe in the late 1940s, communism became a real threat for the church. Promoting peace is a core demand of Catholic social doctrine and a central theme of contemporary papal diplomacy. As wars are viewed as a breakdown of order rather than a natural part of international politics, the Holy See has a strong interest in bringing violent conflicts to peaceful and just ends. While the church has reconciled itself with democracy and human rights over the course of the twentieth century,[18] liberalism's focus on freedom and autonomy is frequently at odds with deeper Catholic notions of moral truth. The Holy See's positions on same-sex marriage, birth control, divorce, or abortion exemplify this tension between Catholicism and liberalism. Criticizing capitalism has been on the agenda since Pope Leo XIII's 1891 encyclical *Rerum Novarum*. Following the end of the Cold War, this theme became a key concern for Pope John Paul II who warned against the dangers of unbridled capitalism.

Norms are only one side of the story. The other side is the practice of interpreting and applying norms during specific circumstances. Taking the living nature of religious traditions seriously requires scholars of religion and politics to study not only the texts of religious traditions but to also pay close attention to the interaction of religious ideas, religious agency, and historical context. To do so, this book focuses on exemplary case studies for each theme under consideration: the Vietnam War (1965–75), the Polish crisis (1978–89), the 1994 UN International Conference on Population and Development (ICPD) in Cairo, and the 1995 UN Fourth World Conference on Women (FWCW) in Beijing, as well as the Jubilee 2000 anti-debt campaign.

The Vietnam War was the most significant "hot" war of the Cold War era throughout which both an ardent desire for peace and a strong fear of a communist victory shaped papal diplomacy. Due to the significant presence of Catholics in Vietnam, the importance and length of this conflict makes it a slightly more suitable case study than the nuclear

18. Philpott, "Catholic Wave."

weapons issue which, however, remains an interesting case study for future research. John Paul's role in Poland in the early 1980s and his relationship with the Solidarity movement was the most crucial episode of the Holy See's challenge to communism. John Paul II and his diplomats had to walk a fine line between challenging the legitimacy of communism while maintaining dialogue with the Polish government. The Vatican's reaction to liberation theology in South America would have been another possible choice but the Polish case arguably exceeds its significance. The Holy See seized the 1994 ICPD in Cairo and the 1995 FWCW in Beijing as opportunities to lament Western liberal secular permissiveness and advance the Catholic viewpoint on population policy, contraception, abortion, and women. Before and during the year 2000, the Holy See helped lobby for debt relief for the world's poorest countries as part of welcoming the new millennium. The Jubilee 2000 anti-debt campaign then was a very significant episode that also brought to light revealing convergences between secular and religious criticism of capitalism in the post-Cold War era.

The time span under consideration also limits my scope. The case studies do not precede the Second Vatican Council (1961–1965). While the council's purpose, meaning, and implications remain subject to ongoing theological and ecclesial debate, there can be no doubt that the Second Vatican Council is the most important reference point for what it means to act as a good Catholic in the contemporary world. In order to move beyond the political and conceptual constraints of the Cold War era, this book will also examine the decade following the end of the Cold War. The 1990s showed that the Holy See did not join the triumphant liberal Western choir that proclaimed the "end of history."[19] Unbridled capitalism and liberal secular relativism quickly replaced communism as the Holy See's main "Other" in global politics. To understand the reasons behind this shift without adding unnecessary complications, Holy See diplomacy in the aftermath of the terror attacks of 9/11, the war on terror, and the rise of violent Islamism will remain outside the scope of this book.

As the next section highlights, another limitation is the current impossibility to consult the Holy See's own diplomatic files and archives for the time span of this study. It goes without saying that my analysis will remain incomplete until the Holy See finally opens up its archives for the

19. Fukuyama, *The End of History.*

relevant time period. As this may well take several decades, it would be disingenuous to reward the Holy See's overly restrictive archival policy by providing it with immunity from historical and academic scrutiny in the meantime. The problem of sources is nevertheless a good reminder that even the most careful studies only advance "an argument . . . rather than an infallible disquisition or edit on the past."[20]

The Problem of Sources: Reading Tea Leaves?

A major disadvantage of research into recent or contemporary Vatican politics is the current closure of the Vatican Secret Archives for documents produced after the death of Pope Pius XI in 1939. The Vatican archives provide a rich source of documents from the Roman Curia and papal embassies (i.e., nunciatures) from around the world. "Secret" does not mean that the archive is mysterious but rather denotes its personal and confidential character. It is the private archive of the Roman Pontiff, over which only he himself exercises the supreme jurisdiction.[21] Contrary to Western diplomatic archives, the Vatican's archive does not operate on a customary thirty-year rule. Instead, popes have used their jurisdiction by granting archival access for entire pontificates at irregular intervals. In 2002, Pope John Paul II liberalized access for the pontificate of Pope Pius XI who ruled from 1922 to 1939. The only two current exceptions that go beyond his pontificate are selected documents related to the Second Vatican Council and the Second World War.[22]

Given the impossibility of using the Vatican Secret Archives, the process of researching Holy See diplomacy has been likened to "reading tea-leaves."[23] The obvious problem is misinterpreting the policies of the Holy See. Clearly, there is a danger that research is guided by personal speculation or political commitments rather than adherence to rigorous academic standards. Popular beliefs about the secrecy and mystery of the Vatican, as well as bad scholarship, exacerbate the impression that Vatican research consists of mere personal ruminations or that only insiders

20. Smith, *History and International Relations*, 184.

21. See official website: http://www.archiviosegretovaticano.va.

22. See Alberigo and Melloni, *Storia Del Concilio Vaticano II*, and Holy See, *Actes Et Documents*. The Vatican is expected to grant full access to documents of the pontificate of Pope Pius XII (1939–58) in the near future.

23. Shelledy, "Legions not always visible," 48.

such as Vatican officials or journalists can legitimately write about the Vatican. Nevertheless, examples of excellent research demonstrate that the problem of sources can be mitigated in a satisfactory way, especially if scholars consult a diversity of sources in various languages.

Publicly available Vatican sources provide the official view. The Vatican's official website provides an excellent online archive that allows scholars to consult all recent papal encyclicals, speeches, and documents. With the exception of major encyclicals, Second Vatican Council documents, and World Peace Day messages, minor documents may only be available in the original Italian.[24] Then there is the category of so-called *officioso* (i.e., semi-official) sources. The Holy See's daily newspaper *L'Osservatore Romano* is commonly acknowledged as official without being confirmed as such. Indeed, the usage of this channel can be a subtle way for the Holy See to let others know its standpoint or to probe new arguments, while simultaneously offering the possibility to distance itself from specific articles. Memoirs, books, interviews, or speeches by protagonists both inside and outside the Vatican provide further firsthand observations, as do autobiographies of statesmen, diplomats, and politicians who dealt with the Holy See on particular issues. The same holds true for personal interviews with Vatican leaders or foreign diplomats who dealt with papal diplomats.

Very interesting and often overlooked primary sources can be found in the diplomatic archives of other states that maintain diplomatic relations with the Holy See. As Peter Kent explains:

> Not only do these archives contain reports of negotiations and formal discussions between the accredited diplomats and the pope and representatives of the Vatican Secretariat of State, but they also include details of informal and unofficial conversations between these diplomats, Vatican officials, and diplomats of other nationalities accredited to the pope. Many of these conversations contain speculation about the course and direction of current Vatican policy. The diplomats also inform their home governments about important speeches, sermons, and pronouncements made by church leaders, frequently enclosing translations of these public documents.[25]

Usually, these documents are available to the public thirty years after they are drafted.

24. In this case, I personally translated the original texts into English.

25. Kent, *Lonely Cold War*, 7.

The preparation, conduct, and analysis of archival research can be a time-consuming and expensive process, especially if several archives in different countries need to be consulted. For the case studies on Vietnam and Poland, I consulted archival material from the British National Archives, the US National Archives in Washington, several US presidential libraries, the diplomatic archives of the French Foreign Ministry in Paris, the political archives of the German Foreign Ministry, and the archives of the federal commissioner for the records of the state security service of the former German Democratic Republic. Whenever possible, I submitted declassification requests. The excellent quality of the material provides access to a plethora of unpublished confidential, or even top-secret, reports and memorandums. As Western ambassadors to the Holy See frequently share relevant material with their ministries, a sensitive document sometimes is still classified in one country while it is already declassified in another country.

For my two post-Cold War case studies, the daily volumes of the *L'Osservatore Romano* provided the most important background information. Moreover, the documentation center of the Pontifical Council for Justice and Peace (PCJP) is a very helpful resource. Research at the center provides access to a wealth of relevant newspaper clippings, draft speeches, and conference proceedings that offer the best available source material on the post-Cold War era until foreign diplomatic archives and the Vatican Secret Archives will eventually open up for the period under consideration.

Overview

This book is divided into two main parts, followed by a conclusion. The theoretical and conceptual part consists of chapters 2 and 3. The second chapter provides a general conceptual and methodological framework for understanding how religious traditions shape the decisions and practices of religious actors in global politics. Starting with Alasdair MacIntyre's definition of a "living tradition," I will provide an analytically useful and robust concept of tradition that can account for change over time, internal debate, and the relationship between tradition and practice. Drawing upon the IR literature on norms, I will argue that religious traditions provide meaning, significance, and context for action which elicit practices that, in turn, shape and reshape the underlying tradition.

Chapter 3 will provide a more applied discussion of how Catholic social doctrine shapes Holy See diplomacy. I will show that this social teaching fulfills MacIntyre's criteria of a living tradition and provide a short outline of its key characteristics, history, and core themes. After providing an institutional introduction into Holy See diplomacy, I will also discuss some general mediating factors that influence the interpretation and application of Catholic social doctrine.

Chapters 4 through 7 form the second, the empirical, part of the book. Each chapter will first outline the complex origins of Catholic social teaching on the underlying key issue both prior and during the events of each case study. I will then analyze the Holy See's interpretation and implementation of these specific teachings during each case.

Chapter 4 examines how the Holy See interpreted and applied Catholic teaching on peace during the Vietnam War, from the intensification of US intervention in 1965 to the fall of Saigon in 1975. The Holy See struggled to promote peace in a consistent and principled manner. Fear about the political and pastoral consequences encouraged Pope Paul VI and his diplomats to live out Catholic teaching on peace in a manner that offered the highest possible degree of safeguards for South Vietnamese Catholics. Pope Paul VI had considerable sympathy for the United States and never questioned its presence in South Vietnam. Unlike the Catholic Left or the 1968 student movement, the Holy See never called for an unconditional withdrawal of US troops from Vietnam. Only as the horrors of the war unfolded more visibly did the Holy See become more critical of US bombing efforts and secretly encourage the White House to lead a more defensive campaign.

In chapter 5, I am going to analyze how the Holy See lived out Catholic teaching on communism toward Poland from the election of Pope John Paul II in 1978 to his third pastoral trip to Poland in 1987. Contrary to the triumphalist neoconservative thesis that portrays Pope John Paul II as a powerful spiritual ally of the Western world, my analysis rather suggests that the Holy See pursued a prudent approach. The pope did present communism as a serious philosophical, anthropological, and moral mistake to be converted by Christianity rather than a threat to be contained by geopolitical means or Western values. In the period of martial law (1981–83), the Holy See refused to publicly bless the economic sanctions imposed by the White House and instead opted for dialogue and a second papal journey to Poland. The Holy See implemented Catholic teaching on communism in a cautious manner. The key objective was to promote gradual social change rather than legitimate a destabilizing, and potentially violent, political revolution.

Chapter 6 moves the narrative of the book into the post-Cold War period by looking at the Holy See's diplomatic initiatives during the 1994 ICPD in Cairo and the 1995 FWCW in Beijing. Drawing upon debates and diplomatic negotiations on abortion, contraception, and gender, I will show how and why the Holy See lamented Western liberalism's perceived emphasis on freedom at the expense of truth and morality. The Holy See's delegations to the ICPD and FWCW fought hard to oppose unacceptable draft paragraphs, particularly with regard to the abortion issue. Once papal diplomats realized there was nothing more to gain through tough negotiations, however, the Holy See pragmatically agreed to join the international consensus at both conferences in a partial manner yet not without simultaneously submitting lengthy reservations. The Cairo and Beijing cases show that even on a supposedly non-negotiable topic such as abortion, Holy See diplomats creatively used their margin of discretion to signal continuous commitment to international law and the UN system.

Chapter 7 looks at the Holy See's involvement with the topic of international debt relief in the run-up to the Jubilee Year 2000. The Holy See engaged in a sustained critique of the international debt spiral and its enormous human costs, making debt relief an integral part of the church's spiritual preparations for the 2000th anniversary of the birth of Jesus Christ. The international debt crisis allowed the Holy See to remind the world that economics should not be immune from moral scrutiny and that economic growth does not automatically translate into justice for all. The Holy See lived out Catholic teaching on capitalism in a non-revolutionary way. This style differed from more radical anti-globalization movements by opting for close institutional dialogue with, rather than criticism of, the International Monetary Fund (IMF) and the World Bank.

The conclusion draws out some larger implications. The first section will discuss the case studies' theoretical implications for understanding how tradition affects politically salient religious practices in global politics. The second and final section will identify the major practical implications for Holy See diplomacy.

2

Religious Traditions in International Relations

Religious communities look to the past for guidance and inspiration. Muslims consult the Koran, Jews the Hebrew Bible, and Christians the Old and the New Testament. In addition, religious communities also draw upon a plethora of supplementary religious literature which has accumulated throughout the centuries and that provides more specific guidelines on how the primary religious texts are to be understood and applied to real-world issues. In this chapter, after discussing the problematic concept of religion and the reason for considering traditions in the first place, I will provide a theoretical framework for understanding the relationship between tradition and practice. It will use Alasdair MacIntyre's concept of a "living tradition" as an axiomatic starting point and draw upon the existing IR literature on norms to examine how religious traditions are lived out in global politics.

The Tricky Concept of Religion

To most ordinary people and academic scholars, the meaning of religion is commonsensical. It is about faith in a higher being, being part of a community of believers, or awe of the sacred. Most IR approaches to religion draw upon such substantive definitions of religion which focus on what religion *is*. A different approach to the concept of religion prefers a functionalist definition of what religion *does*, for example providing a source of identity, meaning, and sense of belonging to a specific community. Functionalist definitions expand the definition of religion "to include ideologies and practices—such as Marxism, nationalism, and market ideology."[1] Jeroen Gunning and Richard Jackson illustrate that if

> one brackets beliefs and focuses on functionality and behaviour, religious structures and practices lose their distinctiveness, as parallels can be readily found in the secular world: priests have their counterparts in charismatic community or national leaders; mosques perform functions overlapping with those offered by community halls; rituals, foundational texts and their gatekeepers (priests, prophets, party leaders) can be found in both religious and secular communities (cf. Marxist or nationalist).[2]

In fact, delineating the sacred from the secular or religion from politics is inherently difficult. Elizabeth Shakman Hurd has shown that these relationships are "not fixed but rather socially and historically constructed."[3] Rather, there are various historically contingent types of secularism. Each type defines the relationship between religion and politics differently. French laicism, for instance, as it developed from the French Revolution onwards, purports to expel religion from the public sphere with a view to protect the state from undue religious interference. Judeo-Christian secularism, on the other hand, as it evolved during and after the American Revolution, aims to ground secular democracy in religious values and tries to protect religious groups from state repression.[4]

Any delineation of the fuzzy boundaries between religion and politics is a political act by itself. Religion is not an objective, neutral descriptive term, but a politically charged and essentially contested concept. The very origins of the contemporary meaning of the term reveal that the concept of religion was invented in the early modern period. From a Christian perspective, it is noteworthy that religion barely appears in the Bible and not at all in the Nicene Creed. As William Cavanaugh reveals, the concept's origins derive from the Latin word *religio* which denotes a powerful requirement to perform some action. Until the Middle Ages, religion was a minor concept which was mainly used to distinguish secular priests who were ordained and worked for dioceses from religious

1. Cavanaugh, *Myth of Religious Violence*, 58.
2. Gunning and Jackson, "What's So 'Religious,'" 374.
3. Hurd, *The Politics of Secularism*, 1.
4. Roy, *Secularism Confronts Islam*.

priests who belonged to religious orders such as the Benedictines or the Dominicans.

The modern Western notion of religion as a set of privately held beliefs and doctrines that are separate and distinct from politics, economics, and culture is mostly a product of the sixteenth century—a time when the authority of the church declined and the sovereign modern state emerged. The modern concept of religion did not only reflect changing configurations of authority and power but was implicated in constituting a new era through the works of political philosophers such as Thomas Hobbes or John Locke. Through Western imperialism, the modern concept of religion was later exported to the rest of the world with a view to cast local religions such as Hinduism as deficient and to push religious practices away into the private sphere.[5] Scott Thomas views the invention of religion as a pillar of the "political mythology of liberalism." This myth presents the state as an actor that saves us from the violence caused by a mixing of religion and politics. In fact, however, the origins of the modern state were heavily implicated in the violence associated with the wars of religion of the sixteenth and seventeenth centuries. These conflicts actually helped to bring about the modern understanding of religion.[6]

Given the problematic nature of the concept of religion, there is a need for a pragmatic approach which acknowledges that religion is a politicized concept with a variety of possible meanings. While some scholars such as Ron Hassner dodge "altogether the responsibility of grappling with the definition of 'religion,'"[7] William Cavanaugh suggests treating religion as a social construct instead. "Religion does exist, but as a constructed category. Religion is not simply an object; it is a lens, one that often distorts. International relations scholars need to stop looking through that lens and start looking at the lens."[8]

In this spirit, the subsequent analysis of religious traditions recognizes the politically charged and socially constructed nature of religion. It does not do so in order to perpetuate entrenched definitions that relegate religion into the sphere of privately held beliefs that can easily be separated from the political, economic, or social spheres. Rather, the methodological focus is underpinned by a belief that religious communities are

5. Cavanaugh, *Myth of Religious Violence*, 57–122.

6. Thomas, *Global Resurgence of Religion*, 21–26.

7. Hassner, *War on Sacred Grounds*.

8. Cavanaugh, "What Is Religion?," 56–57.

particularly self-conscious about the importance of tradition. This trait makes them exemplary cases for reflecting on the relationship between tradition and practice.

Why Tradition?

A tradition-focused approach to religious actors differs from rational-choice approaches. The latter assume that religious actors opportunistically calculate which positions, policies, and decisions best suit their interests. Rational-choice approaches generally posit explanations such as interest, money, or competition to account for religious practices. Anthony Gill, for example, explained the Latin American Catholic Church's varied responses to authoritarian regimes in the 1960s and 1970s with reference to Protestant competition.[9] Assuming that religious actors aim to maximize membership and financial resources, the Catholic Church in Latin America, Gill argues, preferred an alliance with authoritarian states in exchange for privileged legal and financial status. Threatened by Protestant competition, especially among poor people who support democratization, the Catholic Church moved toward a support of democracy. The Holy See's embrace of human rights and a changing post-Vatican II conception of justice do not feature prominently in Gill's analysis, Daniel Philpott criticizes. Rational-choice conceptions of religious preferences rest thin and "in this way avoid deep analysis of doctrines, theology, ritual and practices, or internal structure."[10] A tradition-focused approach to religious practice in global politics, I argue, can provide this "deeper" analysis which Philpott calls for.

Religious communities extend across space and time. In this sense religious traditions are not only *living* traditions, they have indeed been *lived* for centuries, if not millennia. Being part of a religious community comes with a sense of being part of a larger story which unites adherents of a particular faith across different generations and across states. The concept of tradition denotes this historical extension that connects the past, present, and the future. Among religious people there is a strong tendency to consult the past for advice. While "presentism"—moving

9. Gill, *Rendering Unto Caesar*.

10. Philpott, "Has the Study of Global Politics," 193.

from present concerns to past origins—is anathema to historians, it is quite characteristic of the behavior of adherents to a tradition.[11]

Religious communities also attach a lot of importance to foundational texts like the Bible. But tradition does not simply refer to any past. A great deal of past thought and practice does not make it into the present but fades away. We speak about tradition when the past is an authoritative part of the present by providing a specific normative way of seeing, engaging with, and talking about the world. Hence, traditions involve an oral or written transmission process that links the past with the present.[12]

Religious traditions then resemble what Terry Nardin calls "ethical traditions in international affairs."[13] They provide normative evaluations and guidelines for action. These norms do not only bear upon private morality but also touch upon public issues such as conflict, the economy, and the legitimacy of alternative worldviews. Religious traditions aspire to be more than pedagogical devices or pure doctrine because they want to be lived and practiced in concrete circumstances. In this sense, to extend an IR theory argument made by Christian Reus-Smit and Duncan Snidal, they are "practical discourses" that are concerned with the question of "how should we act?"[14]

A tradition-focused approach to the study of religion and politics requires adequate responses to common criticisms. Skeptics maintain that religious traditions are either mere rhetoric, too static, or hopelessly broad to serve as explanatory factors.

To begin with, it has been insinuated that norms are mere fig leaves that serve to justify deeper political or economic interests. Fred Halliday, for example, maintains that to "explain behaviour in terms of cultural values is to engage in circular argument." Halliday notes that cultural values are "(a) manipulated by interest groups for their own purposes, and (b) defined and often invented for precisely this end." His critique casts religious traditions as a seemingly endless "menu-of-choice" rather than a possible factor for understanding practice. The manipulation of religious traditions for political purposes is always a possibility—especially when political leaders misuse religious ideas for their own aims. Halliday's claim that cultural norms are "often" invented and "created by contemporary political and social actors for their own purposes" reminds us

11. Krygier, "Law as Tradition," 249–50.

12. Ibid., 250–51.

13. Nardin, "Ethical Traditions," 1.

14. Reus-Smit and Snidal, "Between Utopia and Reality," 4.

of the ever-present possibility of hypocrisy. Such behavior occurs when religious actors claim to act in accordance with tradition when, in fact, they do not.[15]

Critics throw out the baby with the bathwater, however, when they *a priori* rule out the role of tradition. The question of whether and, if yes, how religious traditions shape practice should be answered by historical analysis rather than by methodological or ideological assumption. By showing how the Holy See's views on peace, communism, abortion, contraception, and capitalism are rooted in a historically preexisting tradition of thought and practice, my case studies challenge the notion that traditions are merely invented for the pursuit of predefined objectives.

Religious traditions also often get accused of their static nature. They can neither account for change over time nor for debate inside traditions. This criticism makes an important point since change within religious traditions is too frequent and too important to overlook.[16] In the nineteenth century, for example, the Catholic Church condemned religious freedom whereas it became its champion in the late twentieth century. Moreover, interpretive struggles over the demands of one's religious tradition frequently take place within large and vibrant religious communities. However, the critique that traditions are too static does not challenge tradition *per se*, but only essentialist conceptions that suggest tradition is both unchanged and unchangeable. The Gallic fifth century theologian, Vincent de Lérins, for example, defined tradition as something that "has always been believed, everywhere by everyone."[17] MacIntyre's concept of a "living tradition," I will show later, provides a different and more dynamic conception of tradition that does account for debate and change over time.

A healthy skepticism toward the explanatory power of the concept of tradition can be viewed as a friendly warning rather than a hostile critique. It invites further epistemological and methodological reflection on the nature of causal relations in the social world. Skeptics may concede that tradition may play some role while doubting the extent to which religious traditions determine practice. While secularist critics like to downplay the causal role of religious traditions, religious actors have a tendency to exaggerate their causal impact. This happens frequently

15. Halliday, "Culture and International Relations," 57–59.

16. Noonan, *Church That Can and Cannot Change*.

17. Nichols, *Shape of Catholic Theology*, 165.

when religious elites explain practices solely in relation to guiding principles such as human dignity or the promotion of peace. Such reasoning suggests that politically relevant practices derive entirely from moral and theological considerations. This line of argumentation depoliticizes religious traditions as it obscures and downplays the theopolitical challenges involved in living out and applying religious traditions to concrete issues.

Living Tradition

The political philosopher Alasdair MacIntyre interprets religion as a type of social tradition that is constituted by a set of practices. By practice he understands "any coherent and complex form of socially established cooperative human activity through which goods internal to that form of activity are realized in the course of trying to achieve those standards of excellence which are appropriate to, and partially definitive of, that form of activity."[18] MacIntyre argues that "our lives as a whole are held together by a narrative unity" that is central to a person's identity and that forms the precondition for responsibility for past action. MacIntyre's philosophy presupposes that human lives are oriented toward a goal which transcends the individual. This goal is not predetermined but is the result of a "communal quest" for the good life.[19] Debates about what it means to pursue a good life take place inside traditions. A living tradition then "is an historically extended, socially embodied argument, and an argument precisely in part about the goods which constitute that tradition."[20]

I will unpack the key elements of this definition. A tradition is historically extended in the sense that it links past, present, and future. "Every tradition is composed of elements drawn from the real or an imagined past. This is central to what it means for something to be a tradition."[21] However, we only speak about a "living" tradition when the past is an "authoritative significant part of the present" by providing a specific normative way of seeing, engaging with, and talking about the world.[22] In the case of Catholic social doctrine, this transmission process is highly formalized and institutionalized. It leaves traces in the form of

18. MacIntyre, *After Virtue*, 87.

19. Porter, "Tradition," 41–42.

20. MacIntyre, *After Virtue*, 22.

21. Krygier, "Law as Tradition," 240.

22. Ibid., 245–50.

church institutions, church councils, encyclicals, and a plethora of further documents.

A tradition is socially embodied in the sense that past norms, values, and beliefs are not free-floating, but embodied by a particular community for which the tradition serves as a principled basis for thought and practice. This linkage between tradition and social practice is the result of the kind of knowledge that traditions transmit. Religious traditions do not simply pass on technical or factual information but standards for appropriate behavior. If religious traditions are simply understood in terms of dogmatic ideas, a crucial connection between tradition and practice is overlooked. Fred Halliday's critique of cultural values as a tool for the powerful, for example, neglects how participation in a tradition "involves sharing a way of speaking about the world which, like language though more precisely and restrictively than natural language, shapes, forms and in part envelops the thought of those who speak it and think through it."[23]

Traditions are dynamic and evolving bodies of thought and practice. They are "traditions of argument, not uniform and unchanging doctrines."[24] Conflict within traditions can be just as tense as conflict between traditions. The history of Christianity, for example, is full of interpretive and political struggles about "true" beliefs. The "most important social conflicts," Scott Thomas stresses, "take place *within* traditions as well as *between* them. These conflicts are about the various incommensurable goods that members of a particular tradition pursue, and *a viable tradition is one that holds conflicting social, political, and metaphysical claims in a creative way*."[25] Hence, debate is vital to the life of a living tradition. When a tradition becomes a fixed and static washing list of demands, MacIntyre dismissively dubs it a "Burkean" tradition which is "always dying or dead."[26]

Healthy religious traditions are not fundamentalist bodies of thought and practice that posit crystal-clear answers to all possible religious, social, or political questions. As Scott Appleby suggests, such an assumption is a big temptation for religious fundamentalists who tend to "have little patience and no time for the ambiguities of the vast,

23. Krygier, "Law as Tradition," 244.

24. Nardin, "Ethical Traditions," 2.

25. Thomas, *Global Resurgence*, 88.

26. MacIntyre, *After Virtue*, 222. Edmund Burke (1730–1797) was an Irish-British political theorist, philosopher, and politician who is widely regarded as the philosophical founder of modern conservatism.

multivalent religious tradition" and "grow impatient with mere traditionalists, who insist on disciplining themselves to the tradition as an organic, mysterious, irreducible, life-giving whole."[27]

How Tradition Affects Practice

Religious traditions are not simply explanatory tools for better understanding the world. In an increasingly secular world, they offer powerful and often countercultural moral perspectives. If taken seriously, they may result in both different worldviews and different political practices. To apply Marysia Zalewski's typology of different meanings of theorizing, religious traditions are not merely "tools" for understanding the world but offer a moral "critique" for changing the world and even constitute an "everyday practice."[28] Religious traditions identify pressing moral problems such as global hunger or widespread abortion practices and advance corresponding solutions such as promoting global solidarity or protecting unborn life. Religious traditions also exemplify how scholars should think of theory not only as a noun but as a verb. Zalewski's argument that "theorising is a way of life, a form of life, something we all do, every day, all the time" resonates with committed religious people and their leaders who aspire to holistically embody and practice their underlying traditions.[29]

Once we acknowledge the claim that the way we think, talk, and theorize does not simply reflect the world but helps to shape, re/produce, and construct it, a constructivist argument is being advanced. Constructivism, as understood by IR scholars, is a broad school of thought which is underpinned by a belief that norms and ideas matter just as much, if not more, than material factors. Norms and ideas condition the identities, interests, and practices of actors. They affect what actors see as the realm of possibility, they provide reasons and justifications for action, and they can place constraints on actors' conduct.[30] Constructivists question the rationalist view that actors simply pursue predefined interests. Interests are not given but constructed. Interest formation consequently needs to be explained as their articulation requires justification, convincing rea-

27. Appleby, "Rethinking Fundamentalism," 231.

28. Zalewski, "All These Theories," 341.

29. Ibid., 346.

30. Reus-Smit, "Constructivism," 216–19.

sons, consideration of consequences, specification of affected values, and the assessment of relative costs.[31] Applying the broader constructivist IR literature on norms to the study of religious traditions suggests various pathways through which religious traditions induce practice.

For starters, religious traditions provide a source of inspiration and advice. Most religious traditions have a long history. In the case of Catholic social doctrine, popes inherit numerous documents, speeches, and messages that previous popes dedicated to political and social issues. These traditional documents then provide encouragement, warnings, and moral instructions about how Catholic leaders and lay people ought to engage with the world. Inspirational figures such as mystics, renowned teachers, leaders, or saints provide members of a religious community with further concrete examples of how to emulate, practice, and faithfully live out the underlying tradition.

Religious traditions also result in different ways of seeing global politics. The political world does not present itself in a clear and unequivocal way. "There can be no 'objective' observation, nor any 'brute experience,'" Steve Smith argues from a constructivist perspective. "Observation and perception are always affected by prior theoretical and conceptual commitments."[32] Catholic social doctrine provides such beliefs, principles, and assumptions through which popes perceive and interpret global politics. This process of reading global politics through a religious tradition is particularly noticeable in the make-up and methodology of papal social encyclicals.[33] These texts often commemorate a past papal social encyclical by praising its enduring relevance, restressing its key points, and reapplying these arguments to an analysis of present political circumstances.[34] In such a way, religious traditions, like any other theory of IR, help define what gets included and what gets excluded in the subject matter of global politics. While conventional theories overlook abortion

31. Kratochwil, "On the Notion of 'Interest.'"

32. Smith, "Positivism and Beyond," 20.

33. Encyclicals are among the most far-reaching and significant papal publications. They take the forms of open letters addressed to Catholics and often even non-Catholics and usually explain, critique, or comment on problems of the day. They take their names from the first words of their initial sentence of the Latin text.

34. *Laborem Exercens* (1981) marks the ninetieth anniversary of Leo XIII's *Rerum Novarum* (1891), and *Centesimus Annus* (1991) marks its one hundredth anniversary. *Sollicitudo Rei Socialis* (1987) marks the twentieth anniversary of Paul VI's *Populorum Progressio* (1967).

or would regard it as a private issue, for example, Catholic social doctrine defines it as a major public policy issue.

Moreover, religious traditions constitute the identity and preferences of religious actors. Rational-choice approaches focus on interests and power, but fail to raise deeper questions of the normative purposes behind interests and power. In this sense, religious traditions are an important source of identity. Before an actor can calculate what is in his best interest, he needs to know who he is. Catholic social doctrine helps to constitute the identity and preferences of the Holy See. There has never been any doubt, for example, that the Holy See was for peace during the Vietnam War, critical of communism during the Polish crisis in the early 1980s, pro-life at the 1994 ICPD in Cairo and the 1995 FWCW in Beijing, and skeptical toward unbridled capitalism during the Jubilee 2000 anti-debt campaign. How these general predispositions were translated into specific decisions and positions are entirely different questions that will be at the core of the empirical analysis of the case studies.

Finally, religious traditions constrain action. While religious traditions empower religious leaders, they also circumscribe the legitimate scope of their actions and discourses. There is an underlying expectation emanating from a given religious community that their leaders defend and promote the core of the tradition. While religious leaders always have some leeway to encourage new thinking on certain fronts, they have to do so within the constraints of existing arguments and propositions. Individual popes may not sense these constraints to the extent that they are fully socialized into the Catholic tradition. Yet as Michael Walsh notices, a pope "cannot challenge earlier teaching without calling his own authority into question."[35] These constraints are a major reason why significant changes in religious thinking often only emerge in gradual, piecemeal fashion and will have to be justified by principles and reasons integral to the tradition.

If we view religious traditions as living traditions, we must not treat them as static. Normative foundations such as religious traditions do not remain unchanged. On the contrary, the interpretation and application of tradition leads to practices which, in turn, will shape the future understanding of that very tradition. In *A Church that Can and Cannot Change: The Development of Catholic Moral Teaching*, for example, John T. Noonan reveals how the Catholic Church's teaching on slavery,

35. Walsh, "Introduction," xiv.

religious freedom, usury, and divorce changed significantly throughout time due to complex interplay of political struggles, theological debate, and changing cultural and historical circumstances.[36]

Therefore, religious traditions are decidedly not fixed Archimedean points of view; they are living traditions rather than static bodies of norms. Lived religious traditions have changed in the past and will continue to do so in and through present and future practices. As this book's case studies will implicitly illustrate, there has been a tightening of Catholic teaching on the legitimacy of war during the Vietnam War, a move away from the demonization of communism as the Cold War progressed, as well as trends toward a more conservative defense of sexual ethics and family values and a more critical evaluation of the human costs of unbridled capitalism in the post-Cold War period. In sum, tradition does not only affect practice, but practice inevitably also affects the ongoing evolution of both form and content of tradition. This feedback mechanism raises many interesting and important questions. They go, however, well beyond the scope of this book whose primary interest is to understand how tradition gets lived out in practice rather than how practice changes tradition over time.

Evidently, religious elites play a critical role in interpreting, applying, and living out religious traditions. They are not simply bloodless puppets of their traditions. Agency matters in living out religious traditions one way rather than another. Traditions do not speak for themselves. They need to be lived, interpreted, and applied. The next section will therefore take a closer look at both Catholic social doctrine and the Holy See, its main institutional bearer in global politics.

36. Noonan, *Church that Can and Cannot Change.*

3

Catholic Social Doctrine and Holy See Diplomacy

In this chapter I will move forward to a more applied analysis of the relationship between Catholic social doctrine and Holy See diplomacy. In the first section I will present Catholic social doctrine as a prime example of a living tradition by presenting its nature, modern origins, and core themes. In the second section I will then discuss the institution and actors that make up Holy See diplomacy and that play a leading role in living out these traditional norms in global politics. In the third section I will identify various factors that tend to influence how these actors interpret and apply Catholic social doctrine. Finally, I will show how the presence of both pull and push factors results in a recurring dilemma as to whether the Holy See should speak out for prophetic reasons or remain silent for prudential ones.

Catholic Social Doctrine

While there is a tendency to use the terms Catholic social doctrine, Catholic social thought and Catholic social teaching interchangeably, the first term puts a special emphasis on the magisterium's authoritative interpretation. The concepts of Catholic social thought or Catholic social teaching imply a broader tradition of thought that includes a stronger emphasis on intra-Catholic debate. This book's preference for Catholic social doctrine reflects the Holy See's own preference for that term, but should not be misconstrued as an ontological reduction of the broader tradition of Catholic social thought to official papal teachings only. In this sense, the study of Catholic social doctrine can be seen as

> a study of official pronouncements of the magisterium that function like a series of snapshots taken at given moments in history. These snapshots offer normative articulations of an always broader and more variegated tradition. These snapshots, however helpful and necessary, can never do justice to the much richer ecclesial conversation out of which they emerged. These official teachings will tend to be conservative, often eschewing the controversial and even prophetic stand of the few in favor of positions that have some hope of achieving a broader consensus in the Church.[1]

Among liberal Catholics, there is a tendency to reduce Catholic social doctrine to teachings on peace, war, and economic justice. More conservative issues such as traditional family values, the protection of unborn life, or sexual ethics are often relegated into the sphere of moral theology. Among conservative Catholics, especially in the United States, there is an opposite tendency. Any theological reduction of the scope of Catholic social doctrine is an inherently theopolitical move for it privileges certain issue-areas at the expense of others. In this book, I will follow the Holy See's alternative approach that accepts Catholic social doctrine as a coherent and consistent whole that transcends the divide between liberals and conservatives.

Its historical evolution suggests that Catholic social doctrine is not set in stone. Rather, it grows and develops among changing social, geopolitical, and moral circumstances. In its modern articulation, Catholic social doctrine traces back to the late nineteenth century, more specifically to Pope Leo XIII's 1891 encyclical *Rerum Novarum*.[2] In this encyclical, the pope examined the problems workers were facing and offered a vision of social reform that deliberately opposed the revolutionary remedies suggested by communism. Both *Rerum Novarum* and the second major social papal encyclical, Pope Pius XI's *Quadragesimo Anno* (1931), exclusively dealt with issues of economic justice, the social question, the

1. Gaillardetz, "Ecclesiological Foundations," 87. Unfortunately, he makes this statement in relation to Catholic social teaching. The point, however, remains the same.

2. It would be wrong to think, however, that the church had no social teaching before 1891. On the intellectual predecessors of modern Catholic social doctrine, see Schuck, "Early Modern Roman Catholic Social Thought."

question of how to define a just wage, and the problems of socialism as well as unbridled capitalism. With the encyclicals *Mit brennender Sorge* (1937) and *Divini Redemptoris* (1937), Pope Pius XI expressed grave concern about the abuse and violence of the Nazi government in Germany and condemned the "atheistic communism" of the Soviet Union.

Following the horrors of the Second World War and in the midst of the Cold War, Pope John XXIII expanded the scope of Catholic social doctrine by systematically dealing with issues of war, peace, and nuclear weapons in his 1963 encyclical *Pacem in Terris*. With *Gaudium et Spes* (1965) the participants of the Second Vatican Council created the broadest single authoritative expression of Catholic social doctrine. The text combined a discussion of family life, marriage, culture, economic relations, the political system, and international affairs. However, as Ian Linden argues, *Gaudium et Spes* "never pretended to be more than a work in progress."[3] By developing core themes or adding new dimensions, future popes played a crucial role in further developing and refining both the content and scope of Catholic social doctrine.

The encyclical *Humanae Vitae* (1968), by Pope Paul VI, played a crucial role in shattering liberal Catholic hopes about a change in Catholic teaching on birth control, as it cemented the Holy See's stance on contraception at that time. The controversial encyclical also brought birth control into the remit of Catholic social doctrine as it should not be viewed as an encyclical that only aims to regulate private or moral behavior.[4] The next key move in the broadening of the tradition's subject matter was made by Pope Paul VI when he identified the question of authentic international development as a new and crucial concern in his 1967 encyclical *Populorum Progressio*. The social question of the nineteenth century had become the global question of the twentieth century.

In *Laborem Exercens* (1981), commemorating the ninetieth anniversary of *Rerum Novarum*, Pope John Paul II reflected about human work, differentiating its "objective" dimension of providing income from its "subjective" dimension of finding self-fulfillment. *Sollicitudo Rei Socialis* (1987) expressed concern about the stagnation of the Third World and blamed Cold War superpower confrontation for being a key cause of stagnation for the global South. *Centesimus Annus* (1991), published at the hundredth anniversary of *Rerum Novarum*, reflected on the fall of

3. Linden, *Global Catholicism*, 87.

4. Benedict XVI, *Caritas in Veritate*, para. 15.

communism and criticized unlimited capitalism rather than uncritically rejoicing in the triumph of Western liberal democracy. With *Evangelium Vitae* (1995), Pope John Paul II brought the protection of unborn life, the abolition of the death penalty, and the traditional definition of marriage under the remit of Catholic social doctrine. In the politically charged context of the UN conferences in Cairo and Beijing, the pope presented these issues as a key priority for the church's relations with the world of politics and culture.

In sum, modern Catholic social doctrine looks back to a dynamic history. Its scope evolved from a narrow preoccupation with a just wage and the relations between labor and capital, to a broader tradition which contains all issues that, from a Catholic Christian point of view, have moral implications, including economics, politics, culture, family values, and even sexuality. To encapsulate this gradual broadening of the scope of Catholic social doctrine, its subject matter should be understood as the totality of socially relevant issues identified and discussed by papal social teachings.

Clearly, Catholic social doctrine fulfills the criteria of MacIntyre's concept of a living tradition as a historically extended, socially embodied argument. It forms an organic system developed over the course of time, even if it was not initially conceived as such. Given changing external circumstances, ongoing debates, and continued reflection, it also encapsulates change. As the *Compendium of the Social Doctrine of the Church* elaborates:

> the Church's social doctrine shows a capacity for continuous renewal. Standing firm in its principles does not make it a rigid teaching system . . . The Church's social doctrine is presented as a "work site" where the work is always in progress, where perennial truth penetrates and permeates new circumstances, indicating paths of justice and peace.[5]

Catholic social doctrine is also socially embodied because it purports to guide behavior for the Catholic community rather than simply providing intellectual speculation about the world.[6] While the pope is the primary bearer and shaper of Catholic social doctrine, its addressees include individual Catholics, the institutional church, and humanity at large.[7] Catholic social thought is also an ongoing argument that has

5. Pontifical Council for Justice and Peace, *Compendium*, paras. 85–86.

6. Ibid., para. 73.

7. Ibid., para. 84.

taken place within the Catholic Church both across space and time. In the nineteenth century, Pope Pius IX—who proclaimed the doctrine of papal infallibility—reportedly claimed: "I am the tradition."[8] A century later, the official *Compendium of the Social Doctrine of the Church* clarifies that "the social doctrine belongs to the Church because the Church is the subject that formulates it, disseminates it and teaches it. It is not a prerogative of a certain component of the ecclesial body but of the entire community." However, the *Compendium* also maintains that the magisterium has the right to authoritatively interpret Catholic social doctrine, to form it into a unified whole, and to determine its future development.[9]

In matters pertaining to global politics, a couple of themes have been at the heart of Catholic social doctrine since the Second Vatican Council. The first major feature is the primacy of the human person. In every single person, the church sees the living image of God. From this act of divine creation, the Catholic tradition derives an inalienable human dignity and a holistic notion of the human person. This view on human nature neither supports a boundless individualism nor regards the person "simply as an element, a molecule within the social organism" where the good of the individual is completely subordinated to the good of the society.[10] The defining traits are not human intellect, consciousness, or freedom, but the "unrepeatable and inviolable uniqueness" of every single person.[11] The dignity of human life applies to all equally. After the Catholic tradition rejected human rights until the nineteenth century, Catholic social doctrine now sees the human rights movement as one of the most significant attempts of responding effectively to the demands of human dignity. Contrary to more liberal strands and in opposition to pro-choice and pro-euthanasia movements, the Catholic Church contends that human life extends "from conception to natural death."

Furthermore, Catholic social doctrine underlines the centrality of morality in international affairs. The tradition posits the existence of a universal moral order that defines and limits the scope of legitimate domestic and international politics. Political authority, both domestically and internationally, "must always be exercised within the limits of the moral order and directed toward the common good."[12] The common good is

8. Duffy, *Saints & Sinners*, 231.

9. Pontifical Council for Justice and Peace, *Compendium*, para. 79.

10. John Paul II, *Centesimus Annus*, para. 13.

11. Pontifical Council for Justice and Peace, *Compendium*, para. 131.

12. Paul VI, *Gaudium et Spes*, para. 74.

proposed as a key moral principle for judging social affairs, interactions, or organizations. It is defined as "the sum total of social conditions which allow people, either as groups or as individuals, to reach their fulfilment fully and more easily."[13] The common good is the *raison d'être* of the state whose duty it is to harmonize different particular interests with the requirements of justice.[14] Another key principle is the universal destination of goods, which demands that each person must have access to a level of material well-being necessary for his or her full development because "the goods of this earth are originally meant for all."[15] Subsidiarity forbids assigning "to a greater and higher association what lesser and subordinate organizations can do,"[16] whereas participation encourages the possibility of citizens to take free, active, and responsible part in the direction of public affairs and election of political leaders.[17]

Another core theme is support for international community. This community is to consist of both states and individuals and entails respect for political and cultural diversity. The foundation and cornerstone of this international community is the divinely willed unity of the human family which is derived from biblical accounts of creation and the covenants God made with Noah and Abraham. The aim of the international community of states is directed at the provision of the common good of the entire human family. It can be enhanced via two pathways: law and morality. Legally, the Catholic tradition supports international law that is seen as the guarantor of the international order. The Holy See is also a firm supporter of the UN system.[18] International law grants sovereignty to each member state, promotes stability in international relations, fosters negotiation and dialogue, and limits the recourse to war.[19] The legal order, however, must always remain in conformity with the moral order. The same moral values that apply to human beings apply to relations between states: truth, justice, active solidarity, and freedom.[20]

13. Ibid., para. 26.

14. Catholic Church, *Catechism*, para. 1908.

15. John Paul II, *Sollicitudo Rei Socialis*, para. 42.

16. Pius XI, *Quadragesimo Anno*, para. 79.

17. Catholic Church, *Catechism*, para. 1913–1917.

18. For a good overview on the Holy See's traditional support for the UN, see Chong and Troy, "Universal Sacred Mission."

19. Pontifical Council for Justice and Peace, *Compendium*, para. 436–39.

20. John XXIII, *Pacem in Terris*, para. 80.

Promoting peace is another core theme of Catholic social doctrine. According to its Catholic conception, peace is more than "merely the absence of war" or "a balance of power between enemies" as realism considers it. Nor "is it brought about by dictatorship."[21] It is essentially an "irrepressible aspiration" of mankind and an ethical duty. The Catholic Church rejects the idea that violent struggle is inescapable as realism holds it, or desirable as some Marxist strands of thought argue.[22] War and violence are "a scourge" and never an appropriate way to resolve social conflict and problems that arise between nations.[23] While peace always remains fragile and threatened, humanity must believe that peace is possible, that it is desirable, that it is necessary. Profound peace is indivisible and requires justice within and among states. Catholic social doctrine refuses to accept fatalist or determinist arguments that minimize the potential of human agency. "A Christian does not believe that history is dictated by fate. By the grace of God, man can change the trajectory of the world's history."[24] Yet, despite its idealism, Catholic social doctrine remains sober in its expectations. The "Church is well aware that it is difficult to cure man of the temptation of war, of egoism, of hatred. She has sometimes been called utopian. She is not so naive as to think that one will succeed on earth in exorcising all violence."[25]

This overview of the nature, sources, and key themes of Catholic social doctrine shows that it qualifies as a living tradition in a MacIntyrean sense. Its modern articulation, as summarized by *the Compendium of the Social Doctrine of the Church*, draws upon social encyclicals and minor documents such as papal messages for the annual World Day of Peace on January 1, or papal addresses to the diplomatic corps accredited to the Holy See. This makes Catholic social doctrine both a normative source as well as a product of politically, economically, and socially salient papal statements.

21. Paul VI, *Gaudium et Spes*, para. 78.

22. John Paul II, "Message of His Holiness Pope John Paul II for the Celebration of the Day of Peace, 1 January 1979," n.p.

23. Pontifical Council for Justice and Peace, *Compendium*, para. 497.

24. John Paul II, "Discorso di Giovanni Paolo II al Corpo Diplomatico Accreditato presso la Santa Sede, January 14, 1984," para. 8.

25. John Paul II, "Address of Pope John Paul II to the Diplomatic Corps accredited to the Holy See, January 12, 1985," para. 8.

Holy See Diplomacy

The Vatican engages in diplomatic relations as Holy See and not as Vatican City State.[26] With its international legal personality, the Holy See counts as sovereign actor in international relations. Its claim to sovereignty does not rest on effective control over the Vatican City State but on a *sui generis* claim of spiritual sovereignty.[27] The Holy See maintains official diplomatic relations with over 170 states[28] and more than forty international organizations. In the UN, it enjoys the status of a permanent observer and reserves the right to become a full member. Papal ambassadors abroad are called nuncios. They start their careers as priests and are usually ordained archbishops once appointed nuncios. They are the personal representatives of the pope and represent the Holy See both *vis-à-vis* other governments and the respective national Catholic Churches. According to the 1961 Vienna Convention on Diplomatic Relations, states may grant precedence to the representatives of the Holy See.[29] Up to the current day, the apostolic nuncio automatically is dean of the diplomatic corps in many countries, especially in Catholic ones. In diplomatic circles, papal diplomats enjoy a reputation for their excellent skills acquired during their training at the Pontifical Diplomatic Academy in Rome. At the local and national church level, however, the nuncios' reputations are not always so positive. They sometimes get accused of interfering in local church affairs, especially when they are held responsible for the appointment of controversial bishops.[30]

The Roman Curia includes a series of departments—so-called "dicasteries"—that fulfill a similar role as state ministries. They help the pope manage both his internal work for the church and his external relations with the outside world. These offices are linked to the Holy See, not to the administration of the Vatican City State, which has its own offices. There are different types of departments with various roles, powers, and

26. The Vatican City State is only a member of some technical international institutions which pertain to its technical functions, for instance, the International Telecommunications Union or the Universal Postal Union.

27. Köck, "Sonstige Völkerrechtssubjekte," 184.

28. Notable countries with which the Holy See does not have diplomatic relations include Afghanistan, the People's Republic of China, North Korea, and Saudi Arabia.

29. United Nations, "Vienna Convention," Article 16(3).

30. Rossi, *Der Vatikan*, 65–74.

responsibilities, such as the Secretariat of State, Congregations, Tribunals, Pontifical Councils, or the Synod of Bishops.[31]

The most important dicastery is the Secretariat of State that is located in immediate proximity to the pope in the Apostolic Palace in the Vatican. The Secretariat of State is headed by a Secretary of State who traditionally has the rank of cardinal. He often is dubbed "Vice-Pope" and is effectively the Holy See's most important representative, immediately behind the pope. The Secretariat's work is divided into two sections. The Section for General Affairs is responsible for handling matters regarding the everyday service of the Supreme Pontiff. It oversees the Holy See's relations to local churches and is responsible for overseeing the work of other dicasteries of the Roman Curia. Moreover, it is in charge of relations with foreign embassies accredited to the Holy See. It is headed by an archbishop, the Substitute for General Affairs, also known in Italian as *sostituto*. The Section for Relations with States has the duty of attending to matters which involve civil governments. It is responsible for the Holy See's diplomatic relations with states and its presence in international organizations and conferences.[32] It is also headed by an archbishop—the Secretary for Relations with States—colloquially known as the Vatican's foreign minister.

People frequently wonder whether the Holy See is a political or a religious actor. In fact, what is distinctive about the Holy See's agency is not that it is uniquely religious or merely political, but the extent to which it simultaneously can draw upon both religious and political discourses, tools, and roles. The Holy See shares many characteristics with other states, especially those relating to its bilateral and multilateral diplomatic relations. Indeed, the Holy See's privileged position under international law makes it a rather atypical religious actor. However, its interventions into global politics frequently draw upon theological discourses, values, and norms. Its agency is thus inspired by aims that are not reducible to modern articulations of national or Western interests. In addition, the Holy See's power rests not only on legal sovereignty but also on religious and moral authority. It is the papal claim to speak as Vicar of Christ—on behalf of a higher truth—that underpins the Holy See's agency in global politics and makes it distinct from conventional states.

31. The exact number, responsibilities, and categorizations of the dicasteries are currently in flux due to Pope Francis's ongoing reform of the Roman Curia.

32. Holy See, "The Secretariat of State," n.p.

Why do other international actors in global politics such as states, the European Union (EU), or non-governmental organizations (NGOs) bother dealing with the Holy See in the first place? Diplomatic relations are not cheap and states follow Vatican affairs at considerable costs for their taxpayers. The answer rests in the belief that the Holy See matters and that it is better to maintain relations with it rather than ignore it.

One of the oldest arguments in favor of diplomatic relations with the Holy See is the conviction that the Vatican is a privileged listening post. After the Second World War and the expansion of Nazi Germany significantly reduced the diplomatic presence of the Allies, the Vatican became an important strategic post for the Allies' observation of European affairs and for the coordination of humanitarian work.[33] During the Cold War the Holy See was also an important listening post for Central and Eastern European affairs. A related argument is the belief that the Vatican has one of the most overlooked yet extensive informal intelligence networks that, through local bishops and priests, reaches down to every Catholic parish in the world. "The Holy See," argues the former UK ambassador to the Holy See, Francis Campbell, "has a highly respected diplomatic corps with sharp eyes and ears which gets far closer to the ground than any ordinary diplomatic corps, through its network of bishops in each region and clergy in each locality."[34]

Supporters and critics agree that the Vatican is one of the world's key opinion-formers. Papal words on issues like communism, abortion, or war matter in influencing public debate and the beliefs of individuals, particularly of the 1.2 billion Catholics spread across the world. The Holy See is in the privileged position to shape public opinion and reportedly hosts the second largest press corps in Europe outside of Brussels. The transnational and centralized character of the Catholic Church makes the Vatican a unique target for public diplomacy. "It is very hard and next to impossible to make them do what they do not want to do," Ambassador Campbell concedes. But "it is possible to influence prioritization of current events and new accents." The Holy See has many "domestic triggers" available to influence public opinion in other states. An accentuation of the Vatican's position on an important political issue, argues Campbell, often has more impact on domestic opinion in another country than

33. Chadwick, *Britain and the Vatican*; Tittmann and Tittmann, *Inside the Vatican of Pius XII*.

34. Campbell, "The UK, the Holy See, and Diplomacy," n.p.

direct political intervention by a foreign government.[35] Diplomatic relations with the Holy See therefore do not only matter for bilateral reasons, but also have implications for a state's relationship with other countries.

As a consequence, the Holy See is a potential partner or troublemaker for other international actors. "Your weighing of the Holy See and of the value of diplomatic relations with the Vatican in many ways depends on your vision of politics," argues the former Irish ambassador to the Holy See, Philip McDonagh. "If politics is just about pursuing crude material interests and balancing power as Metternich laid down, then diplomatic relations with the Holy See may not really pay off. However, if you believe politics is about the deliberation of what is right and wrong, you want to have dialogue." Each state has a different reason for such dialogue with the Holy See and that reason can change over time. For Muslim governments, interreligious dialogue and peace in the Middle East are key issues.[36] For Washington, the Vatican's shared anti-communist sentiments was a compelling reason to intensify contacts with the Holy See during the Cold War, resulting in the nomination of a US ambassador to the Holy See in the 1980s.[37]

Mediating Factors

The tradition of Catholic social doctrine sums up the Holy See's underlying normative basis by providing reasons for action, positing general principles, and deriving more specific prescriptions or proscriptions. Like any living tradition, it provides inspiration, colors the Holy See's perception of global affairs, shapes its preferences, and limits what legitimately can be said or done. However, a living tradition does not serve as an efficient cause for action. It only unfolds its full impact by virtue of being interpreted and applied in the world. This process is subject to mediating factors that provide a general set of considerations. These help to understand how a religious tradition is embodied and lived out by real people in real places. While these factors will differ across religious

35. Personal interview with Francis Campbell, UK ambassador to the Holy See, Rome, October 5, 2006.

36. Personal interview with Philip McDonagh, Irish ambassador to the Holy See, Rome, October 2, 2006.

37. Essig and Moore, "U.S.-Holy See Diplomacy."

actors, the following section will discuss the most important factors as they pertain to Holy See diplomacy.

Most importantly, the Holy See places a premium on the physical safety and religious liberty of Catholics worldwide. This commitment to protect the freedom of the church includes the freedom to worship, the appointment of bishops, the construction of churches and seminaries, and the very survival of Catholics who live under authoritarian or violent conditions. Religious freedom is frequently threatened under authoritarian regimes or during interstate or civil wars. Unlike decentralized Protestant or evangelical communities, the Catholic Church is particularly vulnerable if it cannot appoint bishops. According to Catholic doctrine, bishops are not only the visible signs of the unity of the church but are essential to guarantee its survival. Only bishops can consecrate priests, and only priests can administer the sacraments of the Eucharist and confession. If there are no bishops, the sacramental life of the Catholic Church is severely threatened. To highlight these organizational imperatives, John A. Coleman has coined the term *raison d'église* to denote the church's "bottom-line, non-negotiable interests and institutional purposes."[38] This stress on the safety and liberty of Catholics suggests that the Vatican will feel a strong urge to safeguard the well-being of Catholics, especially when no other domestic or international actor protects them.

The Holy See's international legal neutrality prevents it from formally taking sides in armed conflicts. Article 24 of the 1929 Lateran Accords between the Holy See and Italy stipulates that the Holy See

> will remain outside of any temporal rivalries between other States and the international congresses called to settle such matters, unless the contending parties make a mutual appeal to its mission of peace . . . Consequently, Vatican City will always and in every case be considered neutral and inviolable territory.[39]

Legal neutrality requires the Holy See to remain neutral in the case of armed conflict and impartial *vis-à-vis* the belligerents of wars. It does not oblige the Vatican to stay in a position of "ideological neutrality." International law recognizes that a

> neutral state is not obliged to remain indifferent to the belligerents' ideological positions; it has the full right to sympathize or identify with one of them. Indeed, international law does not

38. Coleman, "Raison d'Église," 252.

39. Vatican, "Treaty Between the Holy State and Italy," Article 24.

> prohibit the neutral state . . . from displaying verbal sympathies or condemnation towards the belligerents.[40]

In this spirit, Article 24 of the Lateran agreement between Italy and the Holy See mentions the Holy See's right to "exercise its spiritual and moral influence."[41] In sum, in conditions of armed conflict, the Holy See is highly likely to remain legally neutral while reserving the right to openly or secretly pass moral judgment.

Traditionally, the Holy See is fiercely interested in presenting itself as a moral rather than political actor, both domestically and internationally. This self-imposed de-politicization has both political and ethical reasons. On the one hand, it serves the political purpose of presenting the Holy See as a non-aligned moral broker detached from geopolitical realities, ideological blocs, or party politics. On the other hand, the wish to play a moral rather than political role in society has ethical roots in the natural law tradition which Thomas Aquinas defined as "nothing other than the light of intellect infused within us by God. Thanks to this, we know what must be done and what must be avoided." According to Catholic theology, this law is "natural" because it is written into the heart and conscience of every human being and is promulgated by reason proper to human nature.[42] This commitment to natural law not only provides a deeper intellectual foundation of Catholic social doctrine but constrains the Holy See to delineating the moral boundaries within which politics legitimately may take place. It does not allow the Holy See to intervene with technical solutions or specific policy plans on which reasonable people may legitimately disagree.

As the liberal, secular West no longer uncritically accepts natural law arguments, the Catholic Church is confronted with a new challenge: its self-perceived moral opposition to controversial topics such as abortion or same-sex marriage is commonly dismissed as undue political intervention. While the church supports the institutional separation of state and church, it does not view the spheres of religion and politics as totally separate. Rather, the Catholic Church claims the right, "at all times and in all places," to have "true freedom to preach the faith, to teach her social doctrine . . . and also to pass moral judgement on those matters which regard public order when the fundamental rights of a person or

40. Karsh, *Neutrality and Small States*, 23–24.

41. Vatican, "Treaty Between the Holy State and Italy," Article 24.

42. Pontifical Council for Justice and Peace, *Compendium*, paras. 69–70.

the salvation of souls require it."[43] Hence, in normal conditions we should expect the Holy See to restrict itself to highlighting and defending the moral boundaries of the political sphere as understood and defined by natural law and Catholic social doctrine.

Furthermore, the Holy See has a strong impulse to maintain and defend doctrinal purity. The Holy See is historically averse to schism and internal division. It guards over the development of Catholic doctrine to ensure it "remains the indispensable unifying centre of Catholicism."[44] Concern for doctrinal purity and church discipline has become acute in the decades following the Second Vatican Council. Liberal Catholics began pushing the limits of Catholic doctrine and social thought especially on cultural hot-button topics such as contraception, abortion, or divorce. Traditionalist circles, on the other hand, led by the French Archbishop Marcel Lefebvre,[45] became alienated from Rome. They believed that certain innovations initiated by the Second Vatican Council, such as religious freedom or the usage of vernacular language during mass, undermined the eternally valid truth of the Catholic tradition.

Papal personality also matters. The individual background of popes can influence the style and priorities of Holy See diplomacy. This was particularly noticeable during the pontificate of John Paul II whose biographical background helps to explain both his interest in, and his impact on, the affairs of his Polish home country. Moreover, papal personality tends to have a strong impact on the variation of the priorities and the style of papal diplomacy across different pontificates. The humble background and extroverted personality of Pope John XXIII predisposed the Holy See toward putting a new stress on dialogue with socialist countries as opposed to the aristocratic and introverted personality of his predecessor Pope Pius XII, who had taken a very outspoken position *vis-à-vis* communism. As a former university professor, for example, Pope Benedict XVI's passion was teaching the Catholic faith and promoting faith in a secularized world. The Latin American background of his successor Pope Francis, on the other hand, helps to understand his different priorities

43. Paul VI, *Gaudium et Spes*, para. 76.

44. Linden, *Global Catholicism*, 282.

45. Archbishop Lefebvre (1905–91) was Archbishop of Dakar (1959–62), Bishop of Tulle (1962), and Superior of the Holy Ghost Fathers (1962–68). Disappointed by the Second Vatican Council, he founded the Society of Saint Pius X. Following his illegal ordination of four bishops in 1988, he caused a schism. Discussions about a possible full reconciliation with the Catholic Church continue to this day.

related to fighting poverty and social exclusion. While papal personality is unlikely to lead to doctrinal changes, we can expect the Holy See to adopt a new style and priorities during successive pontificates.

Finally, the general organizational culture of the Roman Curia also mediates the way the Holy See moves from tradition to practice. There is also a certain Vatican worldview, a specific way of doing things.[46] Vatican observer John L. Allen points out that Holy See officials value authority, loyalty, or patience:

> Taking something on authority is not the sacrifice of one's own conscience, but a decision to shape one's conscience in accord with the tradition, on the theory that doing so will lead to greater clarity and insight . . . It's a way of saying 'I'm not an isolated atom but a member of this community of inquiry, and I trust its wisdom.'"[47]

The role of tradition encourages the Vatican's tendency "to think in centuries"[48] as well as cross-culturally. The transnational nature of the Catholic Church, in turn, also requires the Roman Curia to reflect upon the global consequences of a decision.

Key Dilemma

The interplay between the living tradition of Catholic social doctrine and these mediating factors helps to understand why the Holy See frequently faces a recurring key dilemma in global politics. Should the Holy See speak out for prophetic moral reasons, or remain silent for prudential considerations? In the absence of military or economic means, the Holy See's words and gestures are its most important tools to make a difference in global politics. By speaking out, the Holy See can signal its disapproval with a view to delegitimize other practices, actors, or developments. A direct, forceful, public critique is the strongest means for the Holy See to exercise its moral authority in global politics. By remaining silent, the Holy See signals that it wants to avoid causing more harm than good or that it may feel constrained for some alternative ethical reason. Even though the Holy See has strong and good reasons to speak out on behalf of truth and morality, there is no underlying automatic mechanism that

46. Allen, *All the Pope's Men*, 94–140.

47. Ibid., 96.

48. Ibid., 133.

would cause the Holy See to do so. There may, in fact, be powerful reasons for the Holy See to remain more or less silent. These reasons stem both from Catholic social doctrine and from the previously discussed mediating factors.

It would be misleading to regard Catholic social doctrine as a purely prophetic tradition that only puts pressure on the Holy See to raise its voice. This is because this tradition recognizes prudence as a "cardinal virtue" that helps to apply moral principles to concrete cases.[49] In Catholic social doctrine, prudence is not equated with Machiavellian "shrewdness, with utilitarian calculations, with diffidence or with timidity or indecision," but underlines the importance of acting "with realism and a sense of responsibility for the consequences of one's action."[50] Prudence serves as a brake on the intensity of the Holy See's statements in global politics whenever its leaders believe that raising the moral voice may do more harm than good.

The Holy See's legal neutrality could restrict the scope or intensity of its moral criticism, especially on security issues of war and peace. Moreover, the Holy See's responsibility for safeguarding Catholic communities and the sacramental life of the church may result in accommodation rather than confrontation in order to better protect persecuted Christians. Its commitment to natural law may also prevent the Holy See from offering specific political or technical solutions that are outside its moral competence. The Holy See's wish to maintain unity helps us understand why the Holy See would want to discipline or silence outspoken critics who arrive at radically different conclusions of what it means to be a good Catholic in global politics. Finally, papal personality and the organizational culture of the Roman Curia, with its preference for prudence, may result in a preference for a cautious, diplomatic way of expressing discontent.

To conclude, the Holy See authoritatively embodies the living tradition of Catholic social doctrine and carries the responsibility to interpret and apply these normative guidelines in its foreign policy. As this process is complicated and includes the negotiation of a variety of conflicting normative interests, this chapter has identified some of the most important mediating factors. The tension between speaking out and remaining silent plagues other religious actors as well. There would be no dilemmas

49. Catholic Church, *Catechism*, para. 1806.

50. Pontifical Council for Justice and Peace, *Compendium of the Social Doctrine of the Church*, para. 548.

if policy choices were predetermined. Religious elites are usually not keen to publicly discuss their own dilemmas. Scholars, faithful people, and the general public therefore have a responsibility to study those predicaments.

4

Promoting Peace in Vietnam

Introduction

The Vietnam War put the Holy See into a terribly difficult situation. The bloodshed and brutality of the conflict called for a strong moral response. More than 10 percent of the entire Vietnamese population—approximately four million soldiers and civilians—were killed or wounded in addition to the deaths of 85,000 US soldiers that served in Vietnam.[1] At the same time, the Holy See also had to protect its local interests given the strong Catholic presence in Vietnam. Approximately 1.6 million Vietnamese adhered to the Catholic faith which missionaries had brought to Vietnam in the sixteenth century. Following the 1954 division of Vietnam along the 17th parallel, a mass exodus of Catholics from the North into the South, encouraged by CIA propaganda, had "altered the religious balance of Vietnam . . . In the North, the number of Catholics declined from 1,133,000 to 457,000, while the number in the South increased from 461,000 to 1,137,000."[2] South Vietnamese Catholics became a "fiercely anti-Communist constituency."[3] In 1955, one of them—Ngo Dinh Diem—became South Vietnam's first president. Following his victory on a nationalist and anti-communist platform during a rigged election, Diem ruled until his assassination in 1963.[4]

1. Karnow, *Vietnam*, 11.
2. Jacobs, *America's Miracle Man*, 131.
3. Karnow, *Vietnam*, 238.
4. Jacobs, *America's Miracle Man*.

The premium which the Holy See placed on safeguarding the safety and liberty of Vietnamese Catholics and a strong fear of a North Vietnamese communist victory resulted in a cautious papal peace diplomacy that did not tap into more critical interpretations of Catholic social doctrine. From the US-led escalation of the conflict in 1965 until the fall of Saigon in 1975, the Holy See showed considerable sympathies for US and South Vietnamese interests, consistently refraining from calling for an unconditional withdrawal of US troops. At the same time, however, the Holy See consistently resisted US diplomatic pressure to publicly bless America's cause. Only as the human costs of the war became more visible did the Holy See begin to arrive at a more critical position of the US bombing campaign against North Vietnam. Even then, the Holy See's affinity with US objectives meant that such criticism was mostly expressed behind closed doors. The papal peace formula—bilateral concessions, a limitation of the war, and the promotion of a just rather than unconditional peace—favored the strategic interests of the United States and South Vietnam. The Holy See only disassociated itself from Washington and Saigon as it dawned upon papal diplomats that the Vietnam War was a lost cause.

Catholic Teaching on Peace

The Catholic tradition of peace forms an integral and central part of Catholic social doctrine. This body of teaching on issues of war and peace traces itself back to the very founder of the Catholic Church, Jesus Christ, whom his followers worshiped as the messianic Prince of Peace.[5] The development of the Catholic peace tradition is, however, too complex to draw a straight causal line from Jesus Christ to the contemporary Catholic conception of peace. Historically, this peace tradition has oscillated between principled pacifism and a pragmatic defense of the just war tradition.

Pacifism was strong in the early church. Jesus did not meet popular messianic expectations of violently resisting the Roman occupiers. Instead, the Beatitudes assert: "Blessed are the peacemakers, for they shall be called sons of God" (Matt 5:39, NAB). Jesus replaced the *lex talionis* (an eye for an eye) with his new code—"do not resist the evildoer" (Rom 12:21, NAB). While Jesus defined the concept of peace primarily

5. Matt 5:9, NAB.

in terms of inner conversion, Saint Paul stressed that it could not be defined in an acquiescent or passive way, thereby legitimating communal peace-making activities by linking the promotion of peace to the active pursuit of the good.[6] Yet these scriptural citations would not determine pacifism as the official position of the church. With the conversion of the Roman emperor Constantine, the persecuted church of the martyrs eventually became the privileged church of the state. In this context, in his book *City of God*, Saint Augustine developed an embryonic theory of a just war which held that violence was justifiable under certain conditions.[7] Throughout the centuries, this dominant just war theory, Ronald G. Musto demonstrates, would repeatedly be challenged by a lingering, more pacifist peace tradition as articulated and lived by penitential movements, radical religious orders such as the Franciscans, or Christian humanists such as Erasmus.[8]

A key reference point for the contemporary Catholic concept of peace is the Second Vatican Council's document *Gaudium et Spes* (1965). It maintains that peace is "not merely the absence of war. Nor can it be reduced solely to the maintenance of a balance of power between enemies. Nor is it brought about by dictatorship. Instead, it is rightly and appropriately called an 'enterprise of justice.'"[9] War has to be avoided as contemporary warfare with its weapons of mass destruction leads to a "savagery far surpassing that of the past." Yet as "long as the danger of war remains and there is no competent and sufficiently powerful authority at the international level, governments cannot be denied the right to legitimate defense once every means of peaceful settlement has been exhausted."[10] This was an important disclaimer. The council fathers temporarily ruled out an unconditional defense of pacifism—at least until a supranational authority would be established. In the meantime, peace must be promoted through verifiable disarmament and moral education to counter hostility, contempt, and distrust.[11]

In line with the just war tradition, *Gaudium et Spes* draws a distinction between legitimate self-defense and immoral "subjugation of other

6. Musto, *Catholic Peace Tradition*, 15–30.

7. Augustine, *City of God*.

8. Musto, *The Catholic Peace Tradition*.

9. Paul VI, *Gaudium et Spes*, para. 78.

10. Ibid., para. 79.

11. Ibid., para. 81.

nations." It also distinguishes between *ius ad bellum* and *ius in bello*. The "mere fact that war has unhappily begun" does not "mean that all is fair between the warring parties." The document praises international humanitarian agreements that "are aimed at making military activity and its consequences less inhuman." These must be honored. In a reference to weapons of mass destruction, the council fathers ruled that "any act of war aimed indiscriminately at the destruction of entire cities of extensive areas along with their population is a crime against God and man himself. It merits unequivocal and unhesitating condemnation." The council did not forbid the possession of such weapons for the purpose of deterrence, but warned that the "arms race . . . is not a safe way to preserve a steady peace."[12]

The Second Vatican Council encouraged both the church and the world to reconsider war not as a normal feature of international affairs, but as a serious disruption of order and a threat to human life. By laying down general principles, *Gaudium et Spes* provides only a broader framework for evaluating whether there are just reasons for going to war and whether the conduct in war also adheres to moral principles. Catholic teaching on peace thus remains abstract. Its "translation into policy positions involve[s] complex political judgments as well as difficult theological problems."[13] This lack of specificity means that Pope Paul VI and his diplomats had a considerable margin of discretion in living out the Catholic teaching on war and peace to the Vietnam War.

Paul VI and the Vietnam War

Pope Paul's own position on how to bring peace to Vietnam picked up several key themes of Catholic social doctrine's teaching on peace. Crucially, however, he shied away from publicly evaluating whether or not US intervention in the Vietnam War was just or not. Neither did he assess which side was to blame for the conflict. Nor did he ever condone pacifism as a legitimate reaction to the conflict. Instead, the pope reflected about the demands of peace in a general manner only, stressing the need to actively build peace and to abhor violence. *Mense Maio*, Paul's second encyclical, was published on April 29, 1965, two months after the beginning of US bombings in North Vietnam. The Holy Father warned about

12. Ibid., paras. 80–81.

13. O'Brien, "American Catholic Opposition," 123.

the worsening tensions and voiced his "anxious concern . . . that these tensions may degenerate into a bloody war." He called for "discussions and negotiations on every possible occasion."[14]

The day before the publication of this encyclical, Pope Paul received British Prime Minister Harold Wilson for a private audience. Wilson noted the pope's "anxiety" about Vietnam and was "impressed by his very worried state of mind about real peace and the feeling he gave of almost frustration at not being able to do more about it." The Holy Father "kept asking whether there was anything he could do but stressed that, as Pope, he could not make a political intervention." The prime minister encouraged the pope to accept an invitation extended by UN Secretary General U Thant to address the UN. Even if the pope spoke "in general terms," Wilson replied, "he might put the various nations under strong moral pressure."[15]

The White House was not concerned about general papal statements. The Johnson administration worried that the pope might explicitly mention Vietnam or criticize specific aspects of US policy. Intelligence suggested that there was "increasing pressure both from Afro-Asian sources and from the French for the pope to allude to the Vietnam problem" in his then-forthcoming UN speech.[16] His aides briefed President Johnson "to impress the pope with our passion for peace in Vietnam, and everywhere else. There have been faint indications that not all Vatican circles are persuaded on this point."[17]

When Pope Paul finally addressed the UN on October 4, 1965, the feast day of Saint Francis of Assisi, he supported the UN's mandate to foster peace and international cooperation on the basis of the principle of the sovereign equality of states. In the most memorable passage of his

14. Paul VI, *Mense Maio*, para. 7.

15. Memorandum, "Confidential Record of the Prime Minister's talk at the Vatican with the Pope—Wednesday, April 28, 1965 at 6.30pm.," Box "PREM 13–1910 1966–1967 Vatican," The National Archives of the United Kingdom (TNA). The Buddhist UN Secretary General U Thant from Burma invited Pope Paul VI in response to a disarmament appeal that the pope had launched during his visit to India in December 1964.

16. Letter, Thomas Patrick Melady to McGeorge Bundy, September 13, 1965, "Visit of Pope Paul VI to the U.N.," Box "EX CO 305 2/18/67 Box 78," Folder "CO 310 Vatican City," Lyndon B. Johnson Presidential Library (LBJ).

17. "Memorandum for the President by McGeorge Bundy," October 3, 1965, Box "National Security File, Country File, Box 231 The Vatican," Folder "Memos Vol. I 10/64 to 12/67," LBJ.

speech, the pope cried out: "No more war, war never again. It is peace, peace which must guide the destinies of peoples and of all mankind."[18] This papal call for peace was loud; but the implications for the Vietnam War remained unclear. This vagueness allowed the pope to act as an impartial moral actor but also limited the forcefulness of his intervention. Soviet propaganda, for its part reacted favorably to the pope's speech while noting that he made "no concrete proposals" with regard to the Vietnam War.[19]

Pope Paul VI believed his task was to form the conscience of global leaders and the broader public rather than making specific policy recommendations. The papal launch of World Peace Day, to be celebrated on January 1 of each year, exemplifies this pastoral approach. Nevertheless, the most pressing moral issues on the international stage were rather specific questions: Who was the aggressor and who was the victim? Which military means were proportional and which were excessive? What kind of compromises should be made during negotiations? What would a just peace actually look like? In his public discourses, the pope avoided these questions. To get a more complete picture on the Holy See's peace diplomacy during the Vietnam War, we have to go beyond the study of public pronouncements and examine the record of papal diplomacy as it unfolded behind the scenes.

Promoting Peace in Vietnam

Americanization of the Vietnam War

Following the defeat of the French by Ho Chi Minh in the 1954 battle of Dien Bien Phu, almost a million "boat people" fled from the communist North to the southern part of the country. The majority of them were Catholics. Having been deliberately frightened by the CIA to flee down South,[20] they became the key pillar of southern anti-communism. From 1954 to 1960, South Vietnam was under the authoritarian rule of Ngo Dinh Diem, a devout Catholic, nationalist, and staunch anti-communist.

18. Paul VI, "Address of the Holy Father Pope Paul VI to the United Nations Organization," para. 5.

19. Letter, British Embassy in Moscow to the Foreign Office, October 8, 1965, "Soviet propaganda adopted a favourable view on the Pope's visit to the U.N.," Box "FO 371–183257," TNA.

20. Gunn, *Spiritual Weapons*, 167.

Diem was well connected with Cardinal Francis Spellman of New York and enjoyed the support of the US government. Buddhist resentment against Diem's dictatorial rule, his favoritism toward Catholics, and his violent clampdown of popular protest led to his assassination in 1963.[21] In August 1964, the Johnson administration distorted reports of North Vietnamese attacks on a US destroyer, thus obtaining congressional approval for the use of military force without a formal declaration of war. The "Tonkin Resolution" led to a massive build-up of US military force. The "Americanization" of the civil war between North and South Vietnam had begun.[22]

In February 1965, shortly before the arrival of the first US combat troops, the Holy See informed the United States that the pope was "deeply worried over developments in Southeast Asia." He feared that the "gravity and delicacy of the situation" would "lead to general war."[23] President Johnson replied by identifying "persistent and ferocious aggression of Communists directed from North Vietnam" as the "root cause of the trouble in Southeast Asia." He assuaged the pope "that the actions of the US Government are being carefully controlled" and "will be measured and temperate." The president was determined to impress upon the pope that he would "do all in his power to avoid any wider war."[24] However, not realizing that North Vietnamese leaders were preferring annihilation over capitulation, President Johnson's Vietnam policy would ultimately escalate rather than limit the war.[25]

President Johnson justified this escalation by citing the need to contain communist advances and to secure the independence of South Vietnam. He offered a "billion-dollar" Southeast Asian development plan to Ho Chi Minh in exchange for peace.[26] In a message forwarded to the White House two days after the speech, the pope refrained from "offering him advice" but underlined his "continuing concern regarding the situa-

21. Ibid., 155–96.

22. Karnow, *Vietnam*, 402.

23. Telegram, US Embassy Rome to Department of State, February 10, 1965, Box "National Security File, Head of State Correspondence File, Box 11," Folder "Vatican, Pope Paul, et al., Correspondence December 8, 1963 [2 of 2]," LBJ.

24. Ibid.

25. Karnow, *Vietnam*, 402. Karnow quotes an analogy President Johnson made in front of his press secretary, Bill Moyers: "I feel like a hitchhiker caught in a hailstorm on a Texas highway. I can't run. I can't hide. And I can't make it stop."

26. Johnson, "Address at Johns Hopkins University."

tion in Southeast Asia." The pope's aims were "to avoid war, to reestablish peace, and to promote the well-being of the people of South Asia."[27] An unsigned Vatican memorandum submitted to the US embassy in Rome listed more specific interests:

> 1. Foreseeing a possible agreement concerning Vietnam, there is some reason to fear for the fate of the Catholic population, not only because of the well-known radically hostile attitude of the communists, but also because of a possible opposition on the part of the Buddhists. 2. The Catholics of South Vietnam numbered, in 1964, about a million and a half and at the same time there were 1,310 diocesan priests. In North Vietnam there remained about half a million Catholics and four hundred diocesan priests. The Catholic population comprises an important sector of the intellectual elite, having received superior education. The diminution or exclusion of their civil rights would implicate a gross injustice and a great loss to the entire country, which would be deprived of some of its choicest elements in the highest fields of education and leadership, who, with qualified representatives of other beliefs, constitute an essential bulwark against subversion. 3. Vietnamese Catholics have always proved themselves to be loyal citizens, eager to serve their country. They constitute an irreplaceable element of stability and of civic wisdom, important for the national welfare. They are fully disposed to entertain friendly relations with the Buddhist population and to collaborate with them for the common good and for the prosperity and peace of their fatherland. 4. In view of the above, it is most urgently necessary that the Catholics of Vietnam be not sacrificed in any way whatsoever during the foreseen negotiations, but rather fruitfully employed for the pacification and restabilization of the nation. The very official representatives of the United States of America in Vietnam have testified on many occasions to their importance in the life of the nation, their loyalty, their potentialities for the future of Vietnam.[28]

In this secret memorandum, the Holy See called for a just rather than unconditional peace. Interestingly, it couched this demand in Cold War

27. Telegram, US Embassy Rome to Department of State, April 9, 1965, Box "National Security File—Special Head of State Correspondence File, Box 58," Folder "Vatican—Presidential Correspondence [5 of 5]," LBJ.

28. Telegram, US Embassy Rome to Department of State, April 19, 1965, Box "National Security File, Country File, Box 231," Folder "The Vatican—Cables, Vol. I, 10/64 to 12/67," LBJ. The unnamed Vatican official who handed over the memo stressed that the memorandum "had been seen and personally approved by the Pope."

rhetoric rather than in moral terms. South Vietnamese Catholics are presented as an "essential bulwark against subversion," i.e., against communist North Vietnam. Clearly, a peace that would undermine religious freedom and bolster the power of Hanoi was not a just peace in the eyes of the Vatican.

From Christmas Day 1965 until the end of January 1966, the United States suspended its bombing campaign.[29] The pope immediately suggested arbitration by neutral nations under the auspices of the UN.[30] President Johnson diplomatically called this suggestion an "interesting idea" but preferred to bring Vietnam on the table of the UN Security Council—an initiative that was doomed to lead nowhere. The president justified the bombing resumption by Hanoi's intransigence and promised to send the pope evidence of North Vietnamese military activity during the bombing suspension.[31] In sum, the White House was interested in obtaining papal support to legitimize its strategy rather than listening to papal policy advice.

Publicly, the pope continued sitting on the fence with regard to allocating responsibility for the war. Privately, however, he began to blame Hanoi for the escalation of the conflict. On May 3, 1966 the White House sent its ambassador to South Vietnam, Henry Cabot Lodge, Jr., to the Vatican to personally explain US policy to the Holy Father. Lodge argued that the "North Vietnamese believe they will win not due to American military weakness, but because Hanoi believes the US government lacks the will to win. Hanoi interprets appeals for peace as a sign of weakness, largely due to the Oriental mentality with a Communist overlay." Lodge lobbied the pope not to send any further peace appeals to North Vietnam since "such appeals could actually lengthen the war." While the Holy Father did not respond to this criticism, Lodge noted the pope "seemed impressed and understanding that the real problem was a lack of Hanoi's desire for peace rather than a lack of channels of communication."[32] In-

29. Karnow, *Vietnam*, 496–97.

30. Paul VI, "Discorso di Paolo VI all'Unione Cattolica."

31. Message, President Johnson to Pope Paul VI, January 30, 1966, Box "NSF, Head of State Correspondence, Box 11," Folder "Vatican, Vol. 1, Pope Paul, et al, Correspondence 12/8/63," LBJ. The President did not mention the parallel ground activity of US troops during the bombing suspension. See Karnow, *Vietnam*, 496–97.

32. Cable, "Text of Cable from Ambassador Lodge (Rome, 2696)," May 3, 1966, Box "National Security File, Country File, Box 231," Folder "Vatican—Memos Vol. I 10/64 to 12/67," LBJ.

deed, four days later, during an audience for the US ambassador to Italy, G. Frederick Reinhardt, the pope "observed that all the evidence led to the conclusion that for the time being there was no interest in peace on the part of North Vietnam."[33]

To put it in a nutshell, the Holy See framed the conflict as a just war in all but name in its secret diplomatic conversations. Publically, however, the pope never expressed such a position, limiting himself to abstract contemplations about the possibility of peace. This was a cautious middle ground that differed from both conservative US Catholic support for US involvement in Vietnam but also from liberal Catholic moral critique against it. Like most Catholic bishops in the United States,[34] Paul trusted President Johnson's intentions of waging a limited war and displayed considerable sympathy for the positions of the White House. Contrary to the US bishops, however, the pope did not publicly endorse the US military's presence in South Vietnam even as he privately believed such presence was necessary. On its part, the Johnson administration only paid lip service to the pope's appeals for bombing suspension and international mediation without changing the course of its Vietnam policy.

Bombing Campaign

During the Vietnam War, the United States heavily relied on the use of air power to preserve the integrity of a non-communist South Vietnam, to prevent Soviet or Chinese intervention, to weaken North Vietnamese military capabilities, and to signal US commitment to South Vietnam. The first bombing campaign, Operation Rolling Thunder, lasted from March 1965 to November 1968.[35] Approximately 800 tons of bombs a day were dropped during the campaign. Rolling Thunder was a strategic failure as it forced Hanoi neither into submission nor to the negotiation table. On the contrary, North Vietnam became ever more resolved to resist the US government and Saigon.

The Second Vatican Council's teaching on the morality of war, as expressed in *Gaudium et Spes*, was vague on the topic of bombing. It

33. Telegram, US Embassy Rome to Department of State, May 7, 1966, Box "National Security File, Country File, Italy, Box 197," Folder "Italy—Cables Vol. IV, 12/65 to 12/66," LBJ.

34. Morgan, "Change of Course," 125.

35. Clodfelter, *Limits of Air Power*, 39–72; Karnow, *Vietnam*, 468.

condemned any indiscriminate act aimed "at the destruction of entire cities of extensive areas along with their population,"[36] yet remained silent on the conditions under which bombing military targets may be morally permissible. Initially, the Holy See did not consider large-scale bombing to be an immoral means of waging war *per se*, but only bombing which indiscriminately killed civilians. While the pope always applauded bombing suspensions and wanted the United States to avoid targeting civilians and populated areas, he fell short of calling for an unconditional unilateral bombing halt. The strong trust which the Holy See continued to display toward the US government, based on a shared opposition to a communist victory, blinded it toward the scope of the humanitarian costs of the bombing campaigns. It was only in the latter years of the conflict that the Holy See would adopt a more principled opposition to large-scale bombing.

On June 29, 1966, the United States started bombing strategic petroleum, oil, and lubricant storage areas near the Hanoi-Haiphong area despite criticism from European allies, including the United Kingdom. Reportedly, 10,000 people a day fled from the capital area.[37] On July 9, 1966, Ambassador Goldberg returned to the Vatican to explain the rationale behind the expansion of air strikes.[38] Hanoi's intransigence and its "categoric" rejection of peace, the US envoy insisted, necessitated bombing. The pope found it "unexplainable" that Hanoi refused to negotiate. He was puzzled as to why global public opinion did not better isolate Hanoi. The Holy Father approvingly noted that the US tried to avoid populated areas in bombing but "deplored the efforts of the communists to give the impression that they are the aggrieved and are the victims of aggression." When Goldberg explained the need to bomb political targets to counter infiltration, the pope replied "terrible, terrible." According to Goldberg, this comment referred to Hanoi's aggression rather than North Vietnamese civilian casualties. Pope Paul was pleased to note the US government's "limited objectives" in Vietnam yet "recommended" the White House "to avoid useless destruction of property and life.[39]

36. Paul VI, *Gaudium et Spes*, para. 80.

37. Van Staaveren, *Gradual Failure*, 279–93.

38. Telegram, "For President and Secretary from Ambassador Goldberg," July 8, 1966, Box "National Security File, Country File, Box 197, Italy," Folder "Italy—Cables Vol. IV, 12/65 to 12/66," LBJ.

39. Ibid.

Paul VI trusted the intentions of the Johnson administration. He left US diplomats with the impression that the Holy See supported America's Vietnam policy. By showing sympathies for the US position rather than expressing concern about civilian costs, the Holy See's moral critique of US bombing remained weak. It was only a series of critical articles in *The New York Times* by journalist Harrison Salisbury in late 1966 that brought the bombing issue to the forefront of international attention. Salisbury challenged the Johnson administration's portrayal of their air offensive as a "surgical" campaign limited to military targets. He disclosed how, in fact, the US bombing campaign hit cities and towns and killed many civilians.[40] On December 29, 1966, the *L'Osservatore Romano* reacted to the Salisbury articles. Rather than condemning the United States, the papal newspaper stressed that "moral pressure should be exercised on both sides." The British legation to the Holy See cabled back to London that the "general upshot of the article would seem to be more critical of those, such as some French Catholics, who have concentrated their criticism on United States action."[41]

A meeting between Ambassador Lodge and Pope Paul VI on January 16, 1967, demonstrated the extent to which the Vatican's belief in Washington's moral cause continued to result in limited criticism of US bombing. Before Lodge even began talking, the pope made "an obviously deeply-felt statement about how badly our case was being presented in the world." While he was convinced that America had "a strong case" and "was morally right" he recommended that its cause "must be better stated." Concretely, he suggested both a bombing suspension and multilateral action under the framework of SEATO[42]—once again without eliciting a positive response. Ambassador Lodge argued that the loss of Vietnam would mean that "all of the Catholics would be put to the sword and the results for Catholics in the countries on the edge of East Asia would be very precarious." The Holy Father "agreed vigorously" to this suggestion.[43]

40. Karnow, *Vietnam*, 503–4.

41. Letter, British Legation to the Holy See to the Foreign Office, January 2, 1967, Box "FCO 15–594 Exchanges with Vatican on Vietnam peace initiatives," TNA.

42. SEATO was the South East Asia Treaty Organization. This weak organization existed from 1955 to 1977 to block communism. Member states included Australia, France, New Zealand, Pakistan, the Philippines, Thailand, the United Kingdom, and the United States.

43. Telegram, "Eyes Only for the Secretary from Ambassador Lodge," January 17, 1967, Box "National Security File, Country File, Box 197," Folder "Italy—Italy Cables Vol. IV 12/65 to 12/66," LBJ.

The papal emphasis on public relations advice, his geopolitical ruminations, and his wish that the United States "wins morally and psychologically,"[44] reflect the extent to which the Holy See lived out Catholic teaching on peace in a pro-American manner by early 1967. It stands in sharp contrast to the pope's neutral peace posture that he maintained in public. Paradoxically, the Holy See appeared to be more concerned about the damage done to US credibility than about the civilian costs of the war. Until the Holy See releases its own archival documents it is difficult to evaluate whether this stress really reflected the Vatican's priorities, whether Ambassador Lodge misinterpreted the Holy Father's statements, or whether the rhetoric was simply a tactical move to impress the president. Notably, the pope endorsed the US argument about the strategic necessity of the bombing campaign by signaling an "understanding" nod. The pope's comments also highlighted the Holy See's continued belief in the domino theory. Lodge got an immediate papal endorsement by invoking this strategic nightmare scenario which, rather surrealistically, was said to threaten 370 million people, including Australia and New Zealand. The Holy Father's suggestion of mediation through SEATO reflects the Holy See's broader preference for multilateralism and international negotiations. But, as with almost all of the Vatican's specific policy suggestions, the Johnson administration simply ignored papal advice as it did not suit its international interests.

After his audience with the pope, Lodge conversed with Monsignor Paul Marcinkus.[45] The Holy Father understood that there could be no unilateral cessation of bombing, Marcinkus argued. He explained that the reason why the pope cannot publicly say "Americans are right" resides in the fear that this would lead to loss of "all contact with Eastern Europeans." Lodge, in contrast, stressed the "situation of millions of other Catholics, some of them close friends of mine, who were saddened when it appeared that the communists and the Americans in Vietnam were being equated." While Marcinkus responded that Paul VI "often spoke to visiting American and other delegations to express approval of the United States," Lodge deplored that he had seen "no public word of approval out

44. Ibid.

45. Paul Casimir Marcinkus (1922–2006) was a translator and aide of Pope Paul VI. In 1969, he became archbishop. He served as president of the "Vatican Bank" (*Istituto per le Opere di Religione*) from 1971 to 1989, and was implicated in the 1982 scandal involving the collapse of the Banco Ambrosiano.

of Rome . . . such word would mean a great deal."[46] Hence, while the Holy See refrained from putting more public pressure on the United States, it also resisted the administration's wish of providing moral legitimacy.

During an audience for Vice President Hubert Humphrey, Paul VI expressed his concern over bombing once again in strategic rather than moral terms. The pope argued that the campaign "was eroding America's moral position," particularly in Europe. He conceded that North Vietnam was unwilling "to talk peace." Nevertheless, the bombing campaign cost the United States "more in world opinion and moral leadership than it was worth militarily." He had a "heavy heart" that "the only news was about American killing and bombing" and deplored that "America appears to be the aggressor." While Paul VI "knew that was not true," it nevertheless appeared so "to the person looking at television, listening to the radio and reading the newspapers that big, strong America is being brutal and cruel." "Why doesn't the government in Saigon be the spokesman for South Vietnam? Why does America have to be the spokesman? . . . This kind of situation leaves the big United States looking like a bully against little North Vietnam," the pope lamented. He advised that "it would be better for even the military announcements to be made by the South Vietnamese spokesmen, and surely all of the social improvement announcements should come from South Vietnam—at least for the European audience."[47]

While Pope Paul VI couched his critique in indirect terms, he did not oppose America's presence in South Vietnam. In fact, he implicitly equated it with its post-World War II security role in Europe. "Don't give up. Don't tire of your tasks," the pope encouraged Humphrey. Asked whether "there was anything he could do to be helpful," Humphrey wished the pope to identify Hanoi as "blocking peace" and "causing the continuation of this painful struggle." The pope volunteered to do so—but only in line with the Holy See's general commitment to exercising moral rather than political leadership. Humphrey left the meeting with the belief that the pope cherished an "obvious friendship for Americans and the United States."[48]

46. Telegram, "Eyes Only for the Secretary from Ambassador Lodge," January 17, 1967, Box "National Security File, Country File, Box 197," Folder "Italy—Italy Cables Vol. IV 12/65 to 12/66," LBJ.

47. Miller, *Foreign Relations of the United States, 1964–1968*, Document 308.

48. Ibid.

In the context of increasing international media scrutiny, ongoing debates within the American Catholic Church, and continued US bombing, the Holy See finally arrived at a more critical position at the end of 1967. On December 23, President Johnson made an impromptu visit to the Vatican, immediately following a surprise visit to US troops in South Vietnam.[49] The pope stated his view more bluntly this time: "You went to South Vietnam to protect and defend a small country and now you are engaged in a great war." He let the president know that he had to declare his "position to the world as friends of peace and foes of war." Despite Johnson's "good intentions," the pope made it clear that he "must differentiate" his position and that he simply could "never agree to war." He noted that he had "received messages from great personages of the world to plead with you to stop the bombing. The Church cannot give its approval to bombing as a means of defending liberty." "Perhaps," the pope suggested to the president,

> the methods you are now using will not arrive at your expected goal. North Vietnam will not cease its activities—especially when it has great powers supporting it. I do not believe the war will end but I do believe that its character can change, becoming a defensive rather than an offensive war.[50]

The British Foreign Secretary admonished the Holy See's foreign minister Archbishop Agostino Casaroli that "it was important not to criticise the United States government in public. The American government needed friends and public criticism put the President in a difficult position." Casaroli contended that the Vatican could "not agree that present American bombing policy was wholly acceptable from a moral point of view." While "it might be morally acceptable to try to prevent the infiltration of supplies from North to South, it was not morally right to use air bombardment as a means of breaking the spirit of the North Vietnamese which now seemed to be the objective of the United States Military Command." The pope recognized the US government's obligation to defend South Vietnam but did "not agree that bombing should be used to break the spirit of the North Vietnamese people."[51]

49. Davis, "When LBJ Took a Flying Leap at Peace."

50. Miller, *Foreign Relations of the United States, 1964–1968*, Document 310.

51. "Record of conversation between the Foreign Secretary and the Vatican Foreign Minister after lunch at the British Minister's residence in the Vatican City on 31 December 1967," Box FCO "15–594 Exchanges with Vatican on Vietnam peace initiatives," TNA.

Casaroli further explained that the "Vatican did not doubt that there was a basic community of view between themselves and the United States Government in that they both sought a just peace. They did not doubt that the United States Government were sincerely seeking peace. But the Holy See was a spiritual power and while taking note of the military situation the Vatican were bound to see some things in a different light from the United States Government." Yet Casaroli was under no illusion and realized "that it was unreasonable to expect the Americans to stop bombing North Vietnam . . . unless there was some certainty of a corresponding move by the North Vietnamese."[52]

After President Johnson withdrew from the US presidential race in March 1968, he announced an immediate reduction of the bombing campaign followed by a complete bombing halt which would become effective on November 1.[53] Operation Rolling Thunder had ended without achieving any of its main objectives. About 52,000 North Vietnamese civilians lost their lives.[54] While Pope Paul VI expressed his "profound rejoicing" at the bombing halt,[55] Lawrence J. Andrews exaggerates the pope's power and misrepresents the Holy See's position by arguing that "the president surrendered to the pope."[56] First, the decision by President Johnson to stop the bombing campaign came in response to the devastating surprise attack by the Vietcong in the January and February 1968 Tet Offensive that led to the attack of more than 100 cities and towns, including Saigon. It "shattered" the conviction that US bombing could prevent such attacks,[57] caused President Johnson's approval rates to plummet, and allowed Robert Kennedy to present himself as a credible alternative on an anti-war platform, thus facilitating President Johnson's downfall.[58] Second, the Holy See did not push for a unilateral US bombing halt but linked its demand for a cessation of US bombing raids with a simultaneous call for the other side to stop its ground attacks in South Vietnam. The

52. Letter, British Minister to the Holy See to the Foreign Office, December 29, 1967, Box "FCO 15–594 Exchanges with Vatican on Vietnam peace initiatives," TNA.

53. Karnow, *Vietnam*, 580.

54. Clodfelter, *Limits of Air Power*, 136.

55. Letter, Apostolic Delegate Raimondi to President Johnson, November 1, 1968, Box "National Security File, Special Head of State Correspondence, Box 58," Folder "Vatican—Presidential Correspondence (I)," LBJ.

56. McAndrews, "Lonesome Dove," 253.

57. Clodfelter, *Limits of Air Power*, 112.

58. Karnow, *Vietnam*, 528–81.

Holy See welcomed the bombing stop. But overall, by refusing to lobby more forcefully for unilateral bombing halts and by showing significant sympathy for the United States until late 1967, the Vatican's reaction to Operation Rolling Thunder remained more cautious than prophetic.

In 1972, Johnson's successor, President Nixon, resumed bombing operations against North Vietnam. Operation Linebacker I ran from May to October 1972 with the aim of undermining North Vietnam's capacity to transport supplies in its attempt to invade South Vietnam. Due to Operation Linebacker I, 20 to 40 percent of Hanoi's population had to evacuate the city and 120,000 North Vietnamese soldiers were killed.[59] The pope renewed his general plea for an end of the war but did not specifically criticize the renewal of the US bombing campaign. Rather, the Holy Father once again asked for an end of the war in ever more emotional terms: "We echo the cries of so many innocent victims, we speak on behalf of a population exhausted by the carnage and the ruins, we raise the cry of civilized humanity and of the believer in justice and love . . . to plead with those who can and must discuss and decide: Enough!"[60]

Operation Linebacker II was conducted from December 18–29, 1972. Also known as the "Christmas Bombing," the campaign dropped around 40,000 tons of bombs on the heavily populated area of Hanoi and Haiphong.[61] Whereas Operation Linebacker I aimed to thwart North Vietnamese military offensives, Operation Linebacker II had the psychological aim of breaking the will of North Vietnam. The operation aimed to terrorize the North Vietnamese population by deploying mighty and frightening B-52 bombers.[62] This time, the Holy Father was even more heartbroken. The bombing not only took place during the holy season of Christmas, but would also cause approximately 1,600 civilian casualties.[63]

Following Nixon's announcement of a suspension of the bombing on Christmas Day, the pope reacted with "deep satisfaction and consolation." He let President Nixon know that "even prescinding from every consideration of a moral nature, the continuation of the bombing of cities and population centers of the North is neither required nor advantageous" to safeguard the integrity of South Vietnam.[64] The Holy See shared

59. Clodfelter, *Limits of Air Power*, 167, 169.

60. Paul VI, *Angelus Domini*, n.p.

61. Karnow, *Vietnam*, 667.

62. Clodfelter, *Limits of Air Power*, 182–84.

63. Ibid., 195.

64. Telegram, US Embassy Rome to Department of State, December 24, 1972,

the goals of protecting the independence and safety of South Vietnam as well as the US government's underlying anti-communist fears. On the other hand, it abhorred the violence and the human suffering of the conflict and could not accept the morality of the large-scale bombing of North Vietnam.[65]

In summary, the Holy See's position on the US bombing campaign evolved throughout the Vietnam War. Contrary to pacifist Christian anti-war activists, the Holy See did not condemn the bombing in general terms. Initially, it saw bombing as a legitimate military response to North Vietnamese raids even if it refrained from publicly legitimizing it. When the human costs of the bombing had become more widely recognized in late 1967, the Holy See began to arrive at a more principled opposition to heavy-scale bombing. Even then, however, the Vatican believed that a unilateral bombing halt was neither feasible nor prudent. By the time the Nixon administration restarted the bombing campaign in 1972, the Holy See had become more outspoken. The pope was now more forthcoming with public criticism even as he continued to be sympathetic toward the underlying cause of the United States. The Holy See's fear of a communist victory, its diplomatic affinity with the White House, and its concern for the well-being of South Vietnamese Catholics resulted in a cautious rather than forceful critique of the US bombing campaign against North Vietnam.

The Holy See's Peace Formula

The belligerent parties and the international media carefully monitored whose peace initiatives the Holy See legitimized and whose proposals it criticized. The translation of the broader framework of Catholic teaching on war and peace into a concrete peace formula is a morally complicated and politically sensitive process. The Holy See never interpreted Catholic teaching on war and peace in a way that lent itself to a principled pacifist call for unconditional peace. Rather, the Holy See's tripartite peace formula—a call for bilateral concessions, a more "limited" war, and a "just" peace—remained close to US interests and the American vision of an "honorable" peace.

"Verbal Msg from Pope to President Nixon," Box "NSC Files, Presidential Correspondence, Box 765," Folder "Vatican Pope Corres.," Richard Nixon Presidential Library (RN).

65. Ibid.

When Soviet President Nikolai Podgorny[66] visited the Vatican on January 30, 1967, to discuss the Vietnam War, the pope outlined the first major component of the Holy See's peace formula—a preference for a "bilateral" solution. The pope mentioned his concern for the "the fate of the Catholics of the two regions of Vietnam," saying that he was "more than willing to do whatever he can do for peace, to favour it, and to support the efforts of others in their attempts to secure peace." Nevertheless, "the formula for finding a solution to the conflict cannot be 'unilateral' but must be 'bilateral'. It is necessary to obtain simultaneously both the cessation of the bombardments and the suspension of military infiltration of South Vietnam from the North." The Holy Father hoped that Russia would "use its good offices to favor the conditions for negotiations" by obtaining the necessary "suspension of military infiltration" from North Vietnam.[67]

Motivated by Podgorny's visit,[68] Pope Paul VI dispatched letters to President Johnson, Ho Chi Minh, and South Vietnam's President Thieu. The Holy Father hoped that the truce for the Vietnamese lunar year (Tet) would pave the way for negotiations.[69] President Johnson informed the pope that he was "prepared to talk at any time and place, in any forum, with the object of bringing peace to Vietnam." However, he trusted that the Holy See "would not expect us to reduce military action unless the other side is willing to do likewise."[70] Ho Chi Minh asked the pope to put moral pressure on the United States. The "US imperialists have sent to South Vietnam half a million US and satellite troops and used more than 600,000 puppet troops to wage a war against our people. They have committed monstrous crimes," he wrote to the pope, insisting on an end to aggression, a complete bombing halt, withdrawal from South Vietnam of all US troops, recognition of the South Vietnamese National Liberation

66. Nikolai Podgorny was Chairman of the Presidium of the Supreme Soviet of the Soviet Union from 1965 to 1977.

67. Telegram, US Embassy Rome to Department of State, February 3, 1967, "Podgorny's conversation with Pope Paul concerning Vietnam," Box "National Security File, Country File, Box 231," Folder "The Vatican—Cables, Vol. I, 10/64 to 12/67," LBJ.

68. Telegram, US Embassy Rome to Department of State, February 8, 1967, Box "National Security File, Country File, Box 231," Folder "The Vatican—Cables, Vol. I, 10/64 to 12/67," LBJ.

69. Ibid.

70. Ibid.

Front (NLF),[71] and self-determination for the Vietnamese people.[72] The pope thanked President Johnson for the "noble gesture" of the Tet bombing suspension[73] but was "discouraged" by the "negative tone" of Ho Chi Minh's response.[74] In fact, the Holy See never picked up anti-colonial nationalism as a key theme of papal discourses on the Vietnam War. This clearly would have helped Saigon's cause.

In mid-1967, the Holy See went public with its preference for a "bilateral" solution to the conflict. To "reach a lasting peace," the pope told a group of Vietnamese pilgrims,

> it is not sufficient to suspend acts of war: the underlying reasons for the conflict . . . must be eliminated. The bombardments on the territory of North Vietnam must then cease, and the infiltrations of arms and raw material into the south must stop at the same time; there must also be an end to all those acts of terrorism.[75]

The Daily Telegraph's correspondent in Washington noted that the "Pope's appeal is seen here as coming close to the basic American condition of 'reciprocity' in arranging a cease-fire, as distinct from one-sided action in ending the bombing of North Vietnam."[76]

The second major component of the Holy See's peace vision was its call for a "limited" war. "Is there some way the U.S. could give an impression of a change in the character of this war to gain world favor?" the pope asked the president during their meeting in the Vatican on December 23, 1967. He was "hurt and saddened that the U.S. moral position is

71. The National Liberation Front, also known as Vietcong, was a communist party based in South Vietnam that aimed to overthrow the government to seek reunification with the North. It had a guerrilla force, regular army units, and its own diplomatic corps.

72. Memorandum, "Ho Chi Minh Sends Reply to Pope's Message. Hanoi VNA International Service in English," February 14, 1967, Box "National Security File, Country File, Box 231 Vatican," Folder "Memos Vol. I, 10/64 to 12/67," LBJ.

73. Memorandum, Message from the Pope delivered by the Apostolic Delegate to the White House, "Subject: Vietnam," Box "National Security File, Special Head of State Correspondence, Box 58, Vatican," Folder "Presidential Correspondence [3 of 5]," LBJ.

74. Telegram, US Embassy Rome to Department of State, February 14, 1967, Box "National Security File, Country File, Box 197, Italy," Folder "Cable Vol. V 2/67 to 12/68," LBJ.

75. Paul VI, "Discours du Pape Paul VI à un Pèlerinage du Vietnam."

76. *The Daily Telegraph*, May 25, 1967. Copy in Box "FCO 380/189," TNA.

injured by world opinion." Making "it a more defensive war instead of an offensive war," Paul VI stressed, "will strengthen your moral position in the world. You are now being accused of being unjust. You can make the same propaganda yourself by changing the war." In effect, the pope supported Johnson's strategy of "Vietnamization" with the new motto being "Peace in South Vietnam and by South Vietnamese." The idea was to encourage talks between the South Vietnamese government and the NLF, also known as Vietcong, so that both North Vietnam and Washington could stop their military activities. The president had a specific request for the pope. "It would be very useful," he asked, "if the pope through his sources in South Vietnam could persuade Thieu and others to talk to the NLF informally. Anything the Holy Father can do to encourage this will be very beneficial. This would be one effective way of disengaging the NLF from Hanoi—and South Vietnam from us." The pope agreed to "do whatever is possible."[77]

Hanoi indicated a willingness to talk with the US government, but there was disagreement about where to meet. The White House "played his papal card" by suggesting that the pope should offer the Vatican as a neutral place for negotiations.[78] The apostolic delegate in Washington, Archbishop Luigi Raimondi, responded positively, stating that "the Holy Father is . . . ready to offer hospitality for the proposed meeting, assuring his abstention from the talks and guaranteeing absolute neutrality." The Holy See wanted to know when to make the offer, whether to keep it confidential or make it public, and whether it could also invite the South Vietnamese government.[79] White House official Joseph A. Califano, Jr., replied that "the sooner the pope makes an announcement of his statement the better . . . we think it's important that the pope make a public invitation without any prior notice" in order to put pressure on the North Vietnamese.[80]

This blunt attempt to use the Holy See for political purposes was not well received in the Vatican. The apostolic delegate informed Califano that, "for grave, serious reasons," the Holy See had decided to issue

77. I found no evidence that the Holy See acted up on this issue.

78. Califano, "President and the Pope," 238.

79. Memorandum, "Subject: Vietnam," April 27, 1968, Box "National Security File, Special Head of State Correspondence, Box 58, Vatican," Folder "Presidential Correspondence (I)," LBJ.

80. Califano, "President and the Pope," 239. The Johnson administration claimed that an invitation to the NLF would be "unnecessary" since the NLF was not invited and Saigon was being kept "informed anyway."

"the invitation privately through diplomatic channels. The Holy Father thought the parties might be able to meet secretly without anyone knowing about the meeting and that this would relieve external pressure on them." The White House accepted the offer but only for purely tactical reasons. As Califano remembers, the president hoped "that this kind of pressure would bring the North Vietnamese to the table somewhere, even if not at the Vatican. The North Vietnamese knew that Johnson would not let the offer from the pope remain secret if they turned it down, and that would cost them dearly in the psychological and public relations battle they were waging for world opinion." As a response to the Holy See's offer, Hanoi ultimately agreed to start negotiations in Paris, not in Rome.[81]

The third component of the Holy See's peace vision was its underlying wish for a just peace. This interest converged with the wish of both the Johnson and the Nixon administrations for an "honorable" peace that would not condemn South Vietnam. President Johnson, when informing the pope of the 1967 bombing halt, stressed the "concern of many good people in South Vietnam, including many Roman Catholics, who may fear that the bombing cessation and the participation of the NLF representatives in the Paris peace talks mean that we intend to abandon them, force a coalition government upon them, or even treat the NLF as an independent entity." The president reassured the pope that this was not the purpose of the US government which rather aimed for an "honorable and stable peace in Southeast Asia."[82] According to Casaroli, the pope "shared the President's concern lest an end to hostilities lead to 'losing the peace.'" As the Holy See's foreign minister, Casaroli thought it would be tragic "if the US and its allies, having made such efforts to resist a communist takeover in South Vietnam, should let these efforts go for naught."[83]

When the Nixon administration took over the White House in January 1969 it continued good relations with the Vatican. On March 2, 1969, President Nixon already paid his first official visit to Pope Paul VI. The president pledged that he "was doing everything" to end the war

81. Ibid.

82. Letter, President Johnson to Pope Paul VI, October 31, 1968, Box "National Security File, Head of State Correspondence, Box 11, Vatican," Folder "Pope Paul VI [1 of 2]," LBJ.

83. Telegram, "Subject: Conversation with Archbishop Casaroli," US Embassy Rome to Department of State, 9 December 1968, Box "National Security File, Country File, Box 197, Italy," Folder "Cables Volume V (1 of 4)," LBJ.

"through negotiations and to achieve a just peace." The pope hoped that "during the course of negotiations the President would bear in mind the large Christian and largely Catholic communities in South Viet-Nam." They come "from the middle and upper classes and should there be an undesirable settlement, they could be killed." Nixon reassured the pope that the United States "could not precipitously abandon South Vietnam or make a peace that would condemn these people to death."[84]

A memorandum that the pope handed to President Nixon repeated the Vatican's desire for a "solution that will correspond to justice, and to the people's legitimate aspirations for freedom and independence." It applauded the continued bombing halt and deplored that the territory of South Vietnam continued to be a "theatre of widely-ranging military operations, and continual acts of terrorism and sabotage, of which the unarmed civilians are the victims." Despite the "present period of arid polemics" at the Paris peace conference, the pope expressed his "constant trust in the wisdom of all parties" to re-engage in constructive dialogue. He also conveyed "certain anxieties and worries of the South Vietnamese" and asked the US for "a particular solicitude" for their freedom and independence. In sum, it was the Vatican's position that in "the settlement of the conflict, recognition and respect should be given to the rights of the Christians, and that guarantees be secured of full religious liberty for the Catholic Church in Vietnam."[85]

Papal support for Nixon's vision of an "honorable" peace predisposed the Holy See and conservative US Catholics as targets for Nixon's campaign to win further domestic moral support for the war. In his famous 1969 "silent majority" speech, President Nixon blamed public antiwar demonstrations on a "vocal minority" that was opposed by a "silent majority." Nixon asked the latter for united support "to end the war in a way that we could win the peace."[86] Before the speech, White House official Peter Flanigan met with the apostolic delegate in Washington to brief him "on the upcoming speech" and to ask for the "moral support of the Holy Father." Personally, the apostolic delegate, Archbishop Raimondi, supported this request as "the only acceptable position."[87]

84. Memorandum of Conversation, Meeting of President Nixon and Pope Paul VI, March 2, 1969, Box "NSC Country Files – Europe, Box 732, Vatican," Folder "Vol. II (June 1970 – 31 Dec 71) (2 of 2)," RN.

85. Ibid.

86. Karnow, *Vietnam*, 614–16.

87. Memorandum, Peter Flanigan to Dr. Kissinger, November 3, 1969, Box "NSC Country Files—Europe, Box 732, Vatican," Folder "Vol. I thru May 1970," RN.

Despite this support by the papal delegate, the Holy See refused to accommodate this request. Having received instructions from Rome, Archbishop Raimondi assured Flanigan that the "Holy Father and the Vatican were in complete sympathy with the President's position and aims" and shared the commitment to the "defense of the fundamental rights of South Vietnamese and the right of self-determination." However, the pope was unable to provide a favorable statement "due to concern over the effect of such a statement on the US religious who were in favour of an immediate withdrawal." The archbishop made it clear that he had not much sympathy for them and dismissed their critique as coming from academics living in the "unreal world of ideas." Flanigan was upset and deplored that "it appeared that the Holy Father was giving a veto over his statements to the kind of people who were demonstrating today in Washington." He could not understand why the pope apparently shared its goals but was "unwilling to share the difficulty and the risk of reaching them." Put on the defense, Archbishop Raimondi admitted that while this meant "putting the situation too strongly . . . it could be viewed in that light."[88]

In sum, under Pope Paul VI, the Holy See continued to live out Catholic teaching on peace during the Vietnam War very cautiously. Its preference for a bilateral solution, as opposed to an immediate withdrawal, pleased the White House and went against the interests of both North Vietnam and the liberal US anti-war movement. The US government and the Holy See were united in their desire to reach a "just" and "honorable" peace. For both Johnson and Nixon, this meant to protect the freedom of South Vietnam as well as US credibility. The Holy See, for its part, was primarily concerned with South Vietnamese Catholics. The importance which it attached to their well-being and security shaped the kind of peace that the Holy See called for through diplomatic channels. It also helps us understand why the Holy See did not call for an unconditional US withdrawal from Vietnam. Still, the Holy See refused to support President Nixon's "silent majority" campaign and continued to push for a more limited and defensive war. Pope Paul VI saw himself as a personal friend of the US but not as its political ally.

88. Memorandum, Peter Flanigan to President Nixon, November 15, 1969, Box "NSC Country Files—Europe, Box 732, Vatican," Folder "Vol. I thru May 1970," RN.

Losing the Peace

The Paris Peace Accords of 1973 laid down a sixty-day period for the total withdrawal of US forces, enabled a prisoners' exchange, and stipulated a cease-fire allowing both North and South Vietnamese troops to remain at their respective positions. Yet a surge of US military aid just before the cease-fire meant that South Vietnam could significantly roll back communist troops. The North began to upgrade supply paths on the Ho Chi Minh trails and planned for a counterinvasion that would successfully take place in 1975. Neither Saigon nor Hanoi were truly committed to peace but instead used the cease-fire for military preparations. South Vietnam outnumbered the North in terms of artillery, tanks, aircraft, and combat troops. But it heavily depended on US economic aid to keep its military functioning, especially as the oil price was rising. This strategic dependency became a liability for South Vietnam in the aftermath of the 1974 Watergate scandal when US domestic support for South Vietnam began to evaporate.[89] In this endgame of the Vietnam War, the Holy See's policy was discreetly guided by two conflicting major considerations: supporting continued US commitment to South Vietnam while opening up dialogue with North Vietnam to hedge against the possibility of "losing" the peace.

Two months after the Paris Peace Accords, South Vietnam's President Nguyen Van Thieu visited the Holy Father on April 9, 1973 to talk about "national reconciliation and prisoners." President Thieu told the pope that the "problem of so-called political prisoners is an enormous communist lie." The Vatican could help by exercising "proper influence, directing an appeal" to the Soviet Union and China "to cease military and economic aid" to North Vietnam. The protocol reserved for President Thieu's visit suggested that the Vatican was keen to increase its distance from the President. An advance notice published on April 8, 1973 in the *L'Osservatore Romano* justified the audience for Thieu as part of the pope's general discussion with world leaders on the theme of war and peace. It drew a parallel to a meeting the pope had two weeks previously with Xuan Thuy, chief of the North Vietnamese delegation to the Paris talks. After the visit, the Vatican's semi-official newspaper published no picture of the pope and President Thieu. It simply expressed the pope's pleasure at the cease-fire accord and stressed the need for healing moral and physical wounds.

89. Karnow, *Vietnam*, 669–84.

Local diplomatic observers, the US ambassador to Italy noticed, "have decried Vatican handling of [the] Thieu visit as at best egregious and at worst hypocritical." Even though "Vatican officials are prone to express privately warmness and rather general understanding for Mr. Thieu's government," the article reflected a "chilling of atmosphere" on the eve of a visit by a Catholic leader of a "country traditionally close to the Holy See." Monsignor Gaspari, the Holy See's deputy foreign minister, informed the US embassy in Rome that both leaders had a "frank, warm and friendly exchange" and that the pope made a "forceful appeal for prompt release of political prisoners held by all sides." While he believed that Thieu had a "strong, decisive personality," Monsignor Gaspari worried that the situation in South Vietnam "may be stronger than Thieu's—or perhaps anyone's—ability to control."[90] Given the movement of North Vietnamese troops into the South, the attack on ICC[91] helicopters, and continued fighting in Cambodia, Monsignor Gaspari believed that "Hanoi has clearly demonstrated its intention to disrespect [the] cease-fire agreement." He explained the "justification" of the Thieu visit in the *L'Osservatore Romano* as a reaction against the public interpretation of the audience as "some sort of triumphal progress to receive papal blessing." Robert Illing from the US embassy thought this was a lame explanation. From his point of view, the Vatican was taking its distance from Thieu—a suggestion to which Monsignor Gaspari "smiled knowingly."[92]

A week before the pope's meeting with President Thieu, the Vietcong's chief negotiator in Paris, Nguyen Van Hieu, visited Rome at the invitation of an Italian-Vietnamese committee. During the visit the delegation expressed a desire to meet up with the Holy Father. The Italian ambassador to the Holy See forwarded this request to the Vatican. Surprised

90. Telegram, US Embassy Rome to Department of State, April 11, 1973, "President Thieu at Vatican," Box "National Security Advisor, NSC Vietnam Information Group: Intelligence and other reports, 1967–1975, Subject File Taxation, 1969–1971, Box 12," Folder "Thieu, President Nguyen Van, 1972–1973 (3)," Gerald R. Ford Presidential Library (GF).

91. The International Control Commission was an international force that operated from 1954 to 1973 to oversee the implementation of the 1954 Geneva Accords. Following the 1973 Paris Peace Accords, it was renamed the International Commission of Control and Supervision.

92. Telegram, US Embassy Rome to Department of State, April 13, 1973, "President Thieu's Papal Audience," Box "National Security Advisor, NSC Vietnam Information Group: Intelligence and other reports, 1967–1975, Subject File Taxation, 1969–1971, Box 12," Folder "Thieu, President Nguyen Van, 1972–1973 (3)," GF.

and unprepared, the Holy See instead offered a meeting with Monsignor Casaroli which the delegation refused.[93] The Holy See nevertheless signaled an interest in talking with the Vietcong. The pope finally granted an audience to Nguyen Van Hieu on May 12, 1973.[94] The Vietcong delegation shared the pope's wish for a complete pacification of Vietnam. Predictably, however, the delegation only criticized alleged violations of Saigon rather than acknowledging any communist violation. Nguyen Van Hieu and his delegation complained about the partiality of the South Vietnamese clergy and insisted on a separation of the South Vietnamese church from the Thieu regime as a precondition for the church to act as a "neutralist" actor. Archbishop Casaroli countered that more than half of South Vietnamese Catholics are refugees from the North "for whom it would be difficult to befriend themselves with a communist regime."[95]

Washington was not pleased about the Holy See's outreach to Hanoi. President Nixon's deputy national security advisor, Brent Scowcroft, informed Lodge about the administration's concern that the Vatican was "taking an even-handed approach to all parties in the area . . . which places Hanoi and its subordinate allies, including the PRG,[96] on the same footing as those defending" South Vietnam. "Any kind of recognition extended to the PRG weakens the international and political position of the Government of South Vietnam, which is the sole safeguard of religious and other human freedoms in the area."[97]

To reach out to the isolated Catholic Church in North Vietnam, the Holy See authorized a semi-official mission of the president of the German Caritas, Monsignor Georg Hüssler. The North Vietnamese

93. Cable, French Embassy to the Holy See, "Visite à Rome d'une Délégation du Gouvernement Révolutionnaire Provisoire du Sud-Vietnam, April 10, 1973," Box "Asie-Océanie, Conflit Vietnam, 1965–1975, No. 27," Folder "Relations avec les Pays. Front Nationale de Libération et Gouvernement Révolutionnaire Provisoire: Relations avec les pays d'Europe occidentale," Sub-folder "Vatican février 1971—mai 1973," French Diplomatic Archives (AD).

94. Letter, German Embassy to the Holy See to Foreign Ministry, May 21, 1973, "Besuch einer Delegation des Vietkong beim Papst," Box "Zwischenarchiv 101446, Vatikan, Band 26, Jan 1, 1973—Dec 31, 1974," German Diplomatic Archives (AA).

95. Ibid.

96. Provisional Revolutionary Government of the Republic of South Vietnam.

97. Memorandum, Helmut Sonnenfeldt to General Scowcroft, "Your meeting with Ambassador Henry Cabot Lodge, September 6, 11:00 a.m.," September 6, 1973, Box "NSC Files, Name Files, Box 823," Folder "Lodge, Henry Cabot, VII, 20 Apr 70, [1969–1970], [1 of 2]," RN.

government had issued the invitation with a view to investigate the possibility of receiving more humanitarian aid. Monsignor Hüssler visited the country from October 15–20, 1973, inspecting development projects and promising technical assistance for local hospitals. The situation of the local church was dire. On the one hand, there was no active persecution of Christians and all ten dioceses were occupied by local bishops. On the other hand, the communist government had severely restrained the living space of the church, restricting its activities to the liturgical sphere. Many churches remained destroyed by the war. Monsignor Hüssler was allowed to meet the Archbishop of Hanoi, to whom he gave a letter of spiritual support signed by Pope Paul VI. Realizing that the letter was handwritten by the Holy Father, the Archbishop was moved to tears.[98]

The Holy See wished to further intensify contact with the church in North Vietnam. In July 1974, Archbishop Benelli told the German ambassador to the Holy See that Hüssler's visit had born "rich fruits." Contacts between the Holy See and the North Vietnamese bishops began to increase. Pope Paul VI received a reply from the Archbishop of Hanoi through the normal post. The archbishop thanked the pope for the Holy See's persistent efforts to reestablish dialogue. The government in Hanoi signaled a willingness to allow the local church to adopt the new post-council liturgical texts which had not been known so far. Archbishop Benelli was pleased that Hanoi projected a new inclination to end the isolation of the Catholic Church in North Vietnam which, over time, might permit a gradual normalization of relations.[99]

Reaching out to Hanoi was a prudent reaction to the diminishing prospects of the just peace that the Holy See initially had worked for. By early February 1975, Casaroli confided to Robert Illing that "the Vatican now had to give serious consideration to [the] possibility of changing its whole approach to Vietnam, especially if the cause really appears to be lost." Alarmed, Illing warned his government that the Vatican may now "take actions which unwittingly work to undermine" the stability of South Vietnam, especially in the "realm of morale." Casaroli thought that

98. Cable, German Embassy to the Holy See to Foreign Ministry, "Kontakte des Heiligen Stuhls zu Nord-Vietnam. Hier: Reise von Prälat Hüssler im Auftrage des Päpstlichen Staatssekretariats," October 31, 1973, Box "Zwischenarchiv 101446. Vatikan, Band 26, Jan 1, 1973—Dec 31, 1974," AA.

99. Cable, German Embassy to the Holy See to Foreign Ministry, July 26, 1974, "Kontakte des Heiligen Stuhls zu Nord-Vietnam," Box "Zwischenarchiv 101446, Vatikan, Band 26, Jan 1, 1973—Dec 31, 1974," AA.

the "balance may be irretrievably shifting against democratic forces" in favor of a communist takeover of Vietnam.[100]

The US embassy in Saigon stated that Casaroli's ideas were "greatly overdrawn," probably due to the "pessimism" of Henri Lemaitre, apostolic nuncio in Saigon, and the "zeal" of the South Vietnamese ambassador to the Holy See, Nguyen Van Hieu. In response to Casaroli's question about whether or not the US government thought South Vietnam could defend itself against communist adversaries, the embassy in Saigon recommended a "clear and unequivocal yes."[101] The Department of State instructed Illing to assure Casaroli that the US "remains totally committed to continuing required assistance for Viet-Nam" and that South Vietnam would "hold against attacks" once the US Congress approved an additional $300 million US dollars in military help.[102] Archbishop Casaroli admitted that his "pessimistic viewpoint" was "derived mainly from various [South Vietnamese] sources, including Ambassador Hieu." He understood that "Saigon's technique may be to exaggerate the seriousness of [the] situation in order to assure Catholic support in difficult moments." The US government, for its part, trusted that the "Catholic Church, as opinion-maker in the South" would do "nothing which could undermine" the population's determination to resist the North.[103]

Yet Paul VI was disappointed about declining US commitment to South Vietnam. The US ambassador to Italy briefed President Gerald Ford who had assumed the presidency following Nixon's resignation in August 1974 that the pope is "concerned about Cambodia, Vietnam—that our prestige may sink. I called your words to his attention. He said maybe the people were tired; he said it was inconceivable after losing

100. Telegram, US Embassy Rome to Department of State, February 6, 1975, "Vatican ponders its future course in Vietnam," Box "National Security Advisor Presidential Country Files for Europe and Canada, Country File: Italy (1), Box 8," Folder "Italy—State Department Telegrams To SecState—Exdis (1)," GF.

101. Telegram, US Embassy in Saigon to Department of State, "Vatican views on Vietnam," February 12, 1975, Box "National Security Adviser, Presidential Country Files for East Asia and the Pacific, Country Files: Vietnam—State Department Telegram, Box 21," Folder "Vietnam—State Department Telegrams. To SecState Exdis(1)," GF.

102. Ibid.

103. Telegram, US Embassy Rome to Department of State, February 18, 1975, "Vatican views on Vietnam," Box "National Security Advisor Presidential Country Files for Europe and Canada, Country File: Italy (1), Box 8," Folder "Italy—State Department Telegrams To SecState—Exdis (1)," GF. RVN is the abbreviation of Republic of Vietnam, (i.e., South Vietnam).

50,000 lives and billions of dollars that we couldn't put a few more paltry dollars in."[104] Contrary to the wishes of the Ford administration and the Holy See, the US Congress never approved President Ford's request for additional funding for South Vietnam. With a crumbling economy and without US military aid, it was only a question of time until North Vietnam would win the conflict. On April 30, 1975, the US embassy in Saigon was abandoned and communist troops invaded the city.[105]

Conclusion

Catholic teaching on peace provided an important yet inconclusive motif that connected the Holy See's numerous reactions, statements, and diplomatic initiatives regarding the Vietnam War. In fact, Pope Paul VI ceaselessly searched for opportunities for peace for over a decade through his public exhortations, letters, diplomatic conversations, and calls for bombing halts. The pragmatic and cautious logic which he pursued fell short, however, of living out Catholic teaching on peace more radically and prophetically.

The non-negotiable bottom line was to protect local Catholic interests by preventing a communist victory. Many liberal Catholics, especially in the US and Western Europe, believed the Vietnam War did not fulfill the criteria for a just war and promoted a pacifist approach.[106] The bishops of South Vietnam, on the other end of the Catholic spectrum, argued that pacifism would be a gross misinterpretation of the spirit of the Second Vatican Council. Bishop Phan Ngoc Chi, a major spokesperson for Catholics who had fled from the North, opined that the only way of dealing with communists was "to destroy them." Bishop Chi dismissed the pope's call for peace as "simply a voice in the desert." For him, there "was no Catholic view, only a nationalist view."[107]

Fear of a communist victory encouraged the Holy See to strongly commit itself to the territorial integrity and political freedom of a noncommunist South Vietnam. Even though the pope criticized the

104. Gerald R. Ford Presidential Library, "Memorandum of Conversation between the President and Ambassador John Volpe."

105. Karnow, *Vietnam*, 683.

106. O'Brien, "American Catholic Opposition."

107. Telegram, US Embassy Saigon to Department of State, April 20, 1968, Box "National Security Advisor—NSC Vietnam Information Group: Intelligence and other reports, 1967–1975, Box 1," Folder "Catholics, 1967–73 (1)," GF.

escalation of the war in 1965, he did not question US intervention. Rather, Holy See diplomacy displayed an enduring conviction that the US government's underlying cause in South Vietnam was necessary and just. Anti-communism blinded the pope and his close advisors to the deeper anti-colonial dimensions of the Vietnam War. Also, conscientious objectors had to look in vain for explicit Vatican support to legitimize their personal decision not to participate in the war. The Holy See's preference for a "bilateral" solution as well as its emphasis on a "just" peace further reflected this underlying worry about a communist takeover. Anti-communism, support for Nixon's strategic vision of an "honorable" peace, and an interest in a free, independent, and non-communist South Vietnam kept the United States and the Holy See closely together until the endgame of the Vietnam War, even in the absence of full-fledged diplomatic relations.

Yet there are important aspects of its peace diplomacy that anti-communism cannot account for. Even though it took more than two years, the Holy See arrived at a principled critique of the US bombing campaign. Access to internal Vatican deliberations would be necessary to better explain the reasons for this delay. Available evidence suggests that the Holy See was too naïve in trusting President Johnson's assurances of limited airstrikes. It is also likely that the Vatican actually did not have the information to understand the humanitarian costs of US bombing of North Vietnam. Global public opinion did not find out about the gravity of the issue until the publication of the Salisbury articles in *The New York Times* in December 1966. Moreover, contrary to the military strategy of the US and in line with Catholic teaching on peace, Paul VI called for a more limited and defensive war. He supported US defense of South Vietnam, but criticized that US escalation had transformed the nature of the conflict into an "offensive" war. Despite sustained high-level lobbying, the Holy See consistently refused to publicly bless the military efforts by the US and South Vietnamese governments.

As global leader of the Catholic Church the pope has a heavy responsibility to protect its freedom around the world. The secret 1965 memorandum that the Vatican submitted to the US government unmistakably stressed that "the Catholics of Vietnam be not sacrificed in any way."[108] This is another major theme that ran through the entire history

108. Telegram, US Embassy Rome to Department of State, April 19, 1965, "National Security File, Country File, Box 231," Folder "The Vatican—Cables, Vol. I, 10/64 to 12/67," LBJ. The unnamed Vatican official who handed over the memorandum made

of the Holy See's involvement with the Vietnam War. It ensured that the Holy See would insist on a just peace that would not endanger local Catholic interests. A unification of Vietnam under communist rule could not possibly be just in the Vatican's view since it would threaten the well-being and religious freedom of South Vietnamese Catholics. By asking for a "bilateral" peace, the Holy See did what was in its limited power to make sure that Hanoi could not misuse concessions for military advantages.

In theory, the Holy See ought to care about its flock equally. In practice, available evidence suggests the Holy See privileged the well-being of South Vietnamese Catholics over the well-being of those Catholics who were left in North Vietnam. More consideration for the well-being and safety of North Vietnamese Catholics may have led to a stronger critique of US bombing operations. Almost all diplomatic references to the situation of Vietnamese Catholics referred to the South rather than the North. This privileged concern was due to a combination of factors such as the isolation of the North Vietnamese church from Rome, diplomatic relations with the South Vietnamese government, the strong anti-communist sentiments prevailing in the South Vietnamese church, and the Holy See's wish to save what still could be saved in terms of the church's institutional freedom.

Yet Vatican concern for South Vietnam was not infinite. In fact, Saigon officials were disappointed because they thought the Vatican was too critical of South Vietnam. Former South Vietnamese foreign minister Nguyen Phu Duc, for example, bitterly complained that Pope Paul VI did not visit South Vietnam during his lengthy 1970 papal Asian trip.[109] He explained the distance which the Vatican now kept with regard to South Vietnam as part of the "regrettable effects of the Americanization of the war."[110] Also, the Holy See treated South Vietnamese President Thieu with surprising distance when he visited the Vatican in 1973. By that time the pope prioritized maintaining a public posture as an impartial force for peace over giving personal support to President Thieu. Following the 1973 Paris Peace Accords, the Holy See made overtures to representatives of North Vietnam and the Vietcong against the interest of the White

---

it clear that the memorandum "had been seen and personally approved by the Pope."

109. The pope's pilgrimage to West Asia, Oceania, and Australia took place between November 25 and December 5, 1970, and took him to Iran, Pakistan, the Philippines, West Samoa, Australia, Indonesia, Hong Kong, and Ceylon (Sri Lanka).

110. Duc, *Viet Nam Peace Negotiations*, 160.

House. Yet Pope Paul VI did not forget North Vietnamese Catholics. Rapprochement with communist authorities at the end of the conflict was a necessary step toward reestablishing communication with them.

Wars are by nature violent and difficult to end. Defining a coherent position is a challenging endeavor for religious actors even if, and when, in the case of the Holy See, they have an in-built normative preference for peace. In the case of principled pacifist communities such as the Quakers or the Mennonites, there would be much less, if any, discretionary margin as their normative tradition would delegitimize the quest of finding justifications for war. In the Catholic case, on the other hand, only a war fought for unjust reasons and a war fought with unjust methods is ruled out. Even in those cases, this chapter has shown, religious leaders have to confront complex and delicate moral and political questions about how to apply just war theory to concrete conflicts.

5

Converting Communism in Poland

Introduction

Poland was the most important Catholic country ruled by a socialist regime during the Cold War. For centuries, the Polish nation and the Catholic Church had been inextricably intertwined. The imposition of socialism after the end of the Second World War caused serious problems for the Polish church which nevertheless managed to retain an autonomous space in which Poles could express their discontent about life under socialism. The election of the Polish Cardinal Karol Józef Wojtyła as Pope John Paul II on October 16, 1978 took communist leaders in Warsaw and Moscow by utter surprise. Conventional wisdom stresses that Pope John Paul II helped to overthrow communism in secret alliance with the workers' movement Solidarity and the Reagan administration. The pope is cast as a moral ally of President Reagan's Cold War struggle. In sum, this conservative triumphalist thesis focuses on the incompatibility of communism and Catholicism with a view to present Western liberal democracy as a morally and politically superior system.[1]

Asserting an irreconcilable enmity between Catholicism and communism to understand Holy See diplomacy, however, is inaccurate and

1. Bernstein, "Holy Alliance"; Bernstein and Politi, *His Holiness*; Burleigh, *Sacred Causes*; Gaddis, *Cold War*; Nicholson, *United States and the Holy See*; O'Sullivan, *President, the Pope, and the Prime Minister*; Tindal-Robertson, *Fatima, Russia and Pope John Paul II*; Weigel, *Final Revolution*.

incomplete in the Polish case. First, such an assumption overlooks how Catholic teaching on communism has evolved throughout time. Broadly speaking, it has shifted from relative neglect in the mid-nineteenth century to condemnation in the mid-twentieth to dialogue in the later decades. Second, such an explanation is too reductionist. It mistakenly assumes that a philosophical critique of communism results in clear policy prescriptions. While Catholicism's stance on communism has compelled popes to offer far-reaching theoretical criticisms, it does not provide a clear foreign policy strategy for how to do so. Contrary to proponents of the triumphalist thesis, I argue that the Holy See interpreted and applied Catholic social doctrine on communism in a prudent manner that differed significantly from the Reagan administration's Poland policy in style, rhetoric, and content. At no point did the Holy See engage in escalatory rhetoric against communism as, for example, President Reagan did by referring to the Soviet Union as an "evil empire."[2] Nor did the Holy See have a vested interest in defending the free West. The main interest of the Holy See was to help convert communism by presenting it as a serious anthropological, economic, social, and political mistake. The Holy See promoted moral change but wished such change to take place in a context of political order rather than violent revolution.

While the pope's pastoral journeys to Poland, his public speeches, and his emphasis on human rights—including support for independent trade unions and religious freedom—inspired and united Poles across the country, the Holy Father and his diplomats largely left the management of day-to-day relations with the government to Polish church leaders and refused to become the Reagan administration's moral cheerleader or Solidarity's uncritical ally. The leaders of the Polish church—Cardinal Stefan Wyszyński followed by his successor Cardinal Józef Glemp—frequently used this margin of discretion to call for social peace rather than endorsing calls for more radical change that came from both younger clergy and some Solidarity members. The vision of peace and social reform that the Holy See promoted in Poland under Pope John Paul II helped de-escalate domestic tension, legitimized social opposition to the regime, but did not support more revolutionary calls for change.

2. Reagan, "Remarks at the Annual Convention."

Catholic Teaching on Communism

The first time communism was mentioned in a papal document was in Pope Pius IX's 1846 encyclical *Qui Pluribus*.[3] Two years before the publication of the 1848 Communist Manifesto,[4] "modernity" still featured as the most significant contending worldview. Communism was merely mentioned as an afterthought in a paragraph that deplored clerics following deceiving "charms and snares of pleasure." "To this goal," Pope Pius argued, "also tends the unspeakable doctrine of Communism . . . a doctrine most opposed to the very natural law. For if this doctrine were accepted, the complete destruction of everyone's laws, government, property, and even of human society itself would follow."[5] Pope Leo XIII advanced a more detailed critique of communism in his 1891 encyclical *Rerum Novarum*[6] in which he responded to the social question which had plagued industrial Western Europe in the late nineteenth century. He shared the communist diagnosis that the concentration of power and capital resulted in the division of society in some "very rich men" who are suppressing the masses of the working poor.[7] The pope's prescription, however, radically differed from communist theory. In Pope Leo's view, socialism undermines man's natural right to private property, falsely suggests that social classes are condemned to live in a situation of irreconcilable conflict, and wrongly intrudes into the private sphere of the family.

Until the 1917 Russian Revolution, communism merely posed a philosophical challenge to Catholicism. Only afterwards did it become a real threat. The civil wars in Mexico and Spain sparked communist persecution of the church and intensified anti-religious propaganda. By the end of the 1930s, Catholic leadership in the Soviet Union was largely nonexistent. All the bishops and most of the clergy had been removed.[8] The events in these three countries alerted the Holy See to the consequences of what might happen if socialists gained control over state institutions and spread their revolution around the world.

In 1937 Pope Pius XI responded to these developments by dedicating the encyclical *Divini Redemptoris* to the condemnation of "Bolshevistic

3. Pius IX, *Qui Pluribus*, n.p.
4. Marx and Engels, *The Communist Manifesto.*
5. Pius IX, *Qui Pluribus*, n.p.
6. Leo XIII, *Rerum Novarum.*
7. Ibid., para. 3.
8. Dunn, *Détente*, 13–14.

and atheistic Communism, which aims at upsetting the social order and at undermining the very foundations of Christian civilization."[9] Pope Pius XI attacked communism's commitment to atheism, its policies of state-sponsored violence toward the church, the collectivist reduction of individual personality to "a mere cog-wheel in the Communist system,"[10] as well as its disregard for Catholic family values. Under Pope Pius XI and his successor Pope Pius XII, Catholic-communist relations reached their antagonistic climax. As Stalinist regimes emerged in Central and Eastern Europe and as Mao Zedong celebrated his communist victory in the Chinese civil war, Pope Pius XII directed Holy See policy toward confrontation. This process culminated in an unforgiving 1949 decree against communism which excommunicated members or supporters of communist parties and those publishing, reading, writing, or disseminating communist propaganda.[11]

The intensity of Catholic-communist conflict decreased during the time of the pontificate of Pope John XXIII (1958–1963) and the Second Vatican Council (1962–1965). In his 1961 encyclical *Mater et Magistra*[12] Pope John reminded the church of the "fundamental opposition between Communism and Christianity."[13] Rather than exacerbating this opposition, he outlined a positive vision of social justice that strengthened the role of workers, welfare provisions, and called for a correction of global socioeconomic imbalances. In his 1963 encyclical, *Pacem in Terris*,[14] the pope made a consequential distinction between the "error as such" and the "person who falls into error." This distinction helped the Holy See to draw a line between "false" philosophies, and movements which may "draw their origin and inspiration from that philosophy." While the former are to be condemned, the latter may contain "good and commendable elements which do indeed conform to the dictates of right reason."[15] With this move, the pope legitimated dialogue and coexistence between the church and socialist regimes while maintaining that communism as a philosophy remained severely unjust.

9. Pius XI, *Divini Redemptoris*, para. 3.

10. Ibid., para. 10.

11. Kent, *Lonely Cold War*, 242–44.

12. John XXIII, *Mater et Magistra*.

13. Ibid., para. 34.

14. John XXIII, *Pacem in Terris*.

15. Ibid., paras. 158–59.

During the Second Vatican Council some cardinals sought the condemnation of communism and 334 council fathers signed a memorandum demanding that communism be condemned more explicitly. Yet they could not find a majority. Bishops from communist countries, including Cardinal Karol Wojtyła, were concerned that such a move would do more harm than good.[16] The council followed Pope John XXIII's pastoral approach by outlining what the church stands for, rather than what it condemns.[17] Yet the council also provided bishops with a formidable new tool to oppose communist oppression—religious freedom. With a separate declaration on religious liberty called *Dignitatis Humanae*,[18] church leaders could now oppose communism in the name of universal human rights rather than having to take recourse to particular Catholic arguments.

The Second Vatican Council, as well as the policies of Pope John XXIII and his successor, Pope Paul VI (1963–78), helped to move the framework of Vatican-communist relations "from containment to limited engagement."[19] The most important architect of the Vatican's emerging *Ostpolitik*, was Archbishop Casaroli who would later serve as Cardinal Secretary of State under Pope John Paul II. The archbishop was sent on several reconnaissance missions to Hungary and Czechoslovakia. His aim was to enable "sufficient religious support for the grand majority of Catholics . . . so that they would not need the courage to take recourse to 'illegal' and secret pastoral activities which some committed and courageous groups are engaging in."[20] A key characteristic of the new *Ostpolitik* pursued by Pope Paul VI and Archbishop Casaroli was "its emphasis on a 'step-by-step' approach and its moderation at the level of public rhetoric."[21] The new practice was underpinned by a belief that the socialist presence in Central and Eastern Europe was permanent for the foreseeable future and an assumption that without dialogue with socialist governments, the church might be unable to survive in a meaningful way.[22]

16. Luxmoore and Babiuch, *Vatican and the Red Flag*, 133.

17. Linden, *Global Catholicism*, 83; Luxmoore and Babiuch, *Vatican and the Red Flag*, 121–24.

18. Paul VI, *Dignitatis Humanae*.

19. Hehir, "Papal Foreign Policy," 30.

20. Casaroli, *Martirio Della Pazienza*, 38.

21. Weigel, *Final Revolution*, 75.

22. Hehir, "Papal Foreign Policy," 35.

The Holy See's *Ostpolitik* was controversial within the wider church. More confrontational bishops like the Hungarian Cardinal József Mindszenty[23] lost favor with the Vatican and were replaced by less outspoken bishops. Critics argued that the Vatican was "betraying" the underground churches by failing to condemn acts of persecution, by not extracting higher prices from the regimes, and by appointing more appeasing bishops.[24] On a more positive note, the Holy See's *Ostpolitik* helped to rejuvenate local hierarchies and fostered more direct contact between local bishops and the Vatican. Nevertheless, religious freedom in Central and Eastern Europe remained severely curtailed—above all in Czechoslovakia, the Soviet Union, and in Albania, the most atheistic of all socialist countries. Indeed, the aims behind papal *Ostpolitik* were limited. "Pope Paul was not so much seeking a *modus vivendi*, a way of living (perhaps even somewhat satisfactorily), with communist regimes," George Weigel clarifies, "he was trying to effect a *modus non moriendi*—a tolerable relationship with these regimes—so that the Church, even in a diminished or hard-pressed condition, would not die."[25]

In sum, while communism's commitments to historical materialism, collectivism, atheism, class struggle, and revolution are in conflict with the Catholic emphasis on private property, idealism, free will, individualism, and social reform, Catholic social doctrine allows the option of downplaying philosophical differences in the name of other goods such as dialogue, peaceful coexistence, or expediency. The political enmity between communist regimes and the Holy See is not predetermined.

John Paul II and Communism

Pope John Paul II steered away from both the confrontational approach of Pius XI and Pius XII, and the accommodating approach of John XXIII and Paul VI. He did not criticize communism with a view to present capitalism as a superior system and neither did he frame communism as a threat. Rather, the Polish pope viewed communism as a serious

23. Cardinal Mindszenty was given a life sentence at a 1949 show trial. Freed during the 1956 Hungarian Revolution, he sought political asylum at the US embassy in Budapest, where he lived for fifteen years. Pope Paul VI encouraged Mindszenty to resign from his office. In his memoirs, Mindszenty bitterly complained about the pope's lack of open support for the underground church. See Mindszenty, *Memoirs.*

24. Luxmoore and Babiuch, *Vatican and the Red Flag*, 188–89.

25. Weigel, *Final Revolution*, 88.

philosophical, moral, and anthropological mistake that was to be overcome by principled theoretical critique and practical commitment to the broader demands of the common good.

His 1981 encyclical *Laborem Exercens* commemorated the 90th anniversary of *Rerum Novarum* by discussing the concept of work. Pope John Paul directed his critique at the materialistic "error of economism" which consists of "considering human labour solely according to its economic purpose."[26] This fallacy is part of "various forms of capitalism - parallel with various forms of collectivism."[27] By identifying "economism" as his key target, John Paul took a different stance than standard Western Cold War narratives that saw communism as the problem for which capitalism was the solution. The problem with "economism" is that work fulfills more than an economic function.[28] The Holy Father illustrated this point by criticizing the Marxist concept of dialectical materialism. This notion holds that the economic base—the means and relations of production—is the driving force behind political, legal, and cultural developments. Dialectical materialism is incapable of "providing sufficient and definitive bases for thinking about human work, in order that the primacy of man over the capital, the primacy of the person over things, may find in it adequate and irrefutable *confirmation and support*." In dialectical materialism man "continues to be understood and treated, in dependence on what is material, as a kind of 'resultant' of the economic or production relations prevailing at a given period."[29]

Rather than being driven by a simplistic and crude "abhorrence" of communism, as conservatives like to argue,[30] the Holy Father appreciated worries about economic and political injustice, exploitation, and emancipation expressed by communist theorists. In the pope's view, the great burst of solidarity between industrial workers and their sympathies for socialist ideas was justified because the injustice of nineteenth-century capitalism "cried to heaven for vengeance." The pope believed it was an absolute imperative to counter the "*degradation of man as the subject of work*," as well as "the unheard-of accompanying exploitation in the field of wages, working conditions and social security."[31] He shared a strong

26. John Paul II, *Laborem Exercens*, para. 13.

27. Ibid., para. 7.

28. Ibid., para. 4.

29. Ibid., para. 13.

30. See, for example, Burleigh, *Sacred Causes*, 419.

31. John Paul II, *Laborem Exercens*, para. 8.

sense of moral indignation *vis-à-vis* the injustice and exploitation of this world.

In line with Catholic social doctrine, however, the pope could not condone communism's concept of class struggle. He underlined that he did not wish to deny the reality of diverging interests between labor and capital. Also, he did not "intend to condemn every possible form of social conflict" because "in the course of history, conflicts of interest between different social groups inevitably arise." But in the light of the common good and social solidarity, "this struggle should be seen as a normal endeavor 'for' the just good . . . it is *not* a *struggle 'against' others.*"[32] What John Paul criticized was unrestrained class struggle that goes against ethical and juridical limits, and that promotes partisan interests rather than the common good.

Any textual analysis of Pope John Paul's teaching on communism can only provide a springboard for a deeper contextual understanding of how the Holy See translated and lived out that teaching in his diplomatic and pastoral relations with Poland. The next section will examine how this teaching, situated in the broader context of Catholic social doctrine, was lived out during the most important diplomatic episodes involving the fate of Poland, Solidarity, and the Polish church from the pope's election in 1978 until the late 1980s.

Converting Communism in Poland

The 1979 Papal Visit

The first key issue between the Holy See and Poland following the 1978 election of Pope John Paul II was the Holy Father's desire to visit his home country. Papal visits can be a highly political affair, even though the Holy See usually stresses their "pastoral" and "non-political" nature. Yet the pope's personal background immediately raised expectations about the possible political impact on both sides of the Iron Curtain. A secret report by the East German intelligence service predicted that the pope "will represent the interests of the Catholic Church *vis-à-vis* the governments of socialist states more decisively than his predecessor . . . the pope

32. Ibid., para. 20.

will also take a stand for human rights, personal rights, human dignity, and religious freedom, as well as against discriminations."[33]

Original plans had foreseen that John Paul II would come to Poland in May 1979 to mark the 900th anniversary of the martyrdom of Saint Stanisław. This Catholic saint was killed by soldiers of the Polish King Bolesław II while saying mass and would later become a Polish "symbol of civic courage and moral resistance." The contemporary parallels made the Polish regime nervous. Polish leader Edward Gierek[34] received an agitated and bizarre phone call from Soviet leader Leonid Brezhnev[35] in early 1979 who told him that the previous Polish leader, Władysław Gomułka,[36] "was a better communist because he would not receive Paul VI in Poland, and nothing terrible has happened. The Poles have survived the refusal to admit a pope once; they'll survive it a second time." Brezhnev warned that the Polish regime might "regret it later" if they allowed Pope John Paul II into the country.[37] Not inviting Pope John Paul II was never a serious option for the Polish regime. Domestic pressure was simply too high. The Polish regime was interested in avoiding confrontation with the church "in the hope that the post-visit euphoria may calm some of Poland's present social tensions." The church, for its part, wanted to capitalize upon the post-election euphoria of Pope John Paul II "to ensure that the visit, the climax of the Polish Church's post-war history, will be suitably celebrated" and that the church's role in society will be strengthened.[38]

The timing of the papal visit was subject to intense diplomatic maneuvering. The Polish government did not agree to the initially proposed timeframe in May due to misgivings about a papal celebration of the anniversary of the martyrdom of Saint Stanisław. As a compromise, Warsaw offered a longer, nine-day visit in June instead. The Holy See accepted this compromise yet not without also pushing papal celebration of the feast of Saint Stanisław back to June. Monsignor Audrys Bačkis, under-secretary

33. Quoted in Koehler, *Spies in the Vatican*, 60–61.

34. Edward Gierek was leader of the Polish Communist Party from 1970 to 1980.

35. Leonid Ilyich Brezhnev was leader of the Communist Party of the Soviet Union from 1964 to 1982.

36. Władysław Gomułka was leader of the Polish Communist Party from 1956 to 1970.

37. Quoted in Luxmoore and Babiuch, *Vatican and the Red Flag*, 212–13.

38. Letter, British Embassy Warsaw to FCO, "Archbishop Casaroli's Visit to Poland, 22–26 March," April 6, 1979, Box "FCO 28/3801," TNA.

in the Holy See's Secretariat of State, noted tongue-in-cheek that a 900-year anniversary "perhaps merits extended celebration."[39] Even though the church thought that it had the regime's "tacit approval of the change in dates," the Polish authorities felt "double-crossed."[40]

Negotiations remained intense even beyond the question of the visit's timing. The Polish authorities requested advance copies of speeches that the pope intended to deliver for their approval. "This request has naturally been turned down flat," Monsignor Bačkis informed the British Legation to the Holy See.[41] The Vatican did not make any concessions over the pope's speeches. This would not, however, bar Polish state censorship from cutting out any papal references to Saint Stanisław in national media reports.[42]

A big concern was public safety. On this issue, the interests of the Polish government and the church converged. The state authorities understood that the church was "just as keen as they are to see that the visit is not marred by disturbances or violence of any kind." The Holy See, on its part, fully shared this concern and agreed with Warsaw that the responsibility for maintaining order and safeguarding against uncontrollable emotions or protests would be put into the hands of the Polish church.[43] When the Holy Father arrived in Warsaw, marshals appointed by the Polish church "were omnipresent and efficient." The organization of the pope's visit, especially the control of human crowds, was excellent and reflected unparalleled cooperation between church and state.[44]

The pope's statements and actions during the trip were a mix between an intention to primarily speak as a pastor and highly political interpretations of his statements and gestures. At a mass at Warsaw's Victory Square, the Holy Father famously cried out: "Christ cannot be

39. Letter, British Legation to the Holy See to FCO, "The Pope's Visit to Poland," May 21, 1979, Box "FCO 28/3801," TNA.

40. Letter, British Embassy Warsaw to FCO, "Archbishop Casaroli's Visit to Poland, 22–26 March," April 6, 1979, Box "FCO 28/3801," TNA. Eventually, the papal mass in honor of Saint Stanisław was celebrated on June 10, 1979 in Krakow.

41. Letter, British Legation to the Holy See to FCO, "The Pope's Visit to Poland," May 21, 1979, Box "FCO 28/3801," TNA.

42. "Vatican Radio Criticism of Polish Coverage," *BBC Summary of World Broadcasts*, June 7, 1979.

43. Letter, British Legation to the Holy See to FCO, "The Pope's Visit to Poland," May 21, 1979, Box "FCO 28/3801," TNA.

44. Telegram, British Embassy Warsaw to FCO, "The Pope's Visit: Impressions so far," June 4, 1979, Box "FCO 28/3801," TNA.

excluded from man's history anywhere in the world, from any geographical latitude or longitude . . . Without Christ it is impossible to understand the history of Poland."[45] During his final mass in Poland, in honor of Saint Stanisław, the pope begged his fellow Poles "once again to accept the whole of the spiritual legacy which goes by the name of 'Poland', with the faith, hope and charity that Christ poured into us at our holy Baptism . . . do not on your own cut yourselves off from the roots from which we had our origins."[46]

Content and presentation of the pope's message to the Polish church and nation were not confrontational. However, his sermons and speeches were charged with political sensitivity even as these implications remained subtle, opaque, or implicit. His claim that Polish history and society cannot be understood in isolation from Jesus Christ was viewed as an attack on the communist roots of the Polish regime.[47] The papal call that Poland was to "open the frontiers" referred to spiritual frontiers, but was equally interpreted to bear upon the country's political frontiers.[48] Moreover, the Holy Father's comment at Auschwitz that "one nation can never develop at the expense of another, by subordination, conquest, exploitation or death" referred to the Holocaust yet was also understood as a critical reference to Soviet hegemony over Poland.[49]

The papal visit was not a Catholic crusade or part of a larger Western scheme to undermine communism. In fact, the pope refrained from sharp and unjustified attacks, as the Polish ambassador to Italy acknowledged.[50] In the short-term there were no dramatic outcomes of the visit.

45. John Paul II, *Return to Poland*, 28.

46. Ibid., 174.

47. Telegram, British Embassy Warsaw to FCO, "The Pope's Visit: Impressions so far," June 4, 1979, Box "FCO 28/3801," TNA.

48. Telegram, British Embassy Warsaw to FCO, "The Pope's Visit: Conclusion," June 12, 1979, Box "FCO 28/3801," TNA.

49. Telegram, British Embassy Warsaw to FCO, "The Pope's Visit," June 8, 1979, Box "FCO 28/3801," TNA. "It is worth noting however," the same telegram continues, "that he chose to halt at the plaque commemorating Soviet citizens murdered in the camp to say 'We know all about the nation which it refers to. We know its contribution during the last terrible war for the freedom of nations. We must not remain indifferent upon passing by that board.'"

50. Telegram, "Polenbesuch von Papst Johannes Paul II," June 11, 1979, Box "ZA 132816, 214–651 Verhältnis Staat—Kirche in Polen," German Diplomatic Archives (AA).

The Holy See's foreign minister, Archbishop Achille Silvestrini, remained cautious about the future:

> The key to the long-term future outcome of the visit lay[s] with the Soviet Union. It was true that the visit had necessarily represented a confrontation between two ideologies. We must now wait to see whether the Soviets had learnt the lesson that religion is not an illusory and superstitious fruit of a social situation and that even in a Communist system it is possible to allow freedom, including religious freedom. If they drew this conclusion, the outcome of the visit would be positive. If, on the other hand, they had the illusion that they must and could, as a result of the visit, turn the screw, they would be confirming the fragility of their system . . . The Soviet Union should be clear that the Catholic Church wanted neither war nor destabilisation but believed there must be natural progressive change.[51]

Solidarity

Following the government's announcement of very significant meat price increases on July 1, 1980, strikes erupted throughout Poland. At the shipyards in Gdansk, Lech Wałęsa emerged as the charismatic and efficient leader of a nationwide workers' movement called Solidarity. Its demands included the right to strike, the right to form an independent trade union, the freeing of political prisoners, and freedom of the press and media. A seminal agreement with the Polish regime, the August 31, 1980 Gdansk Accord, recognized Solidarity as the first independent self-governing trade union based in a socialist country.[52] Until the imposition of martial law, Solidarity grew in strength until membership reached about eight million. The movement's success symbolized the moral corruption and economic decay of the socialist state.[53] The Catholic Church and John Paul II helped to create the supportive cultural and moral environment that allowed Solidarity to become as successful as it did. The Holy See supported the ideas, principles, and legitimacy of Solidarity. But it recommended a prudent and cautious approach in order to prevent a

51. Letter, British Legation to the Holy See to FCO, "Papal Visit to Poland," June 15, 1979, Box "FCO 28/3802," TNA.

52. The best general description of Solidarity remains Garton Ash, *Polish Revolution*.

53. Biskupski, *History of Poland*, 159–61; Davies, *God's Playground*, 482–85.

radicalization of Solidarity and political instability in Poland which could invite intervention by the Soviet Union. Whereas the pope's 1979 visit to Poland ignited moral hope in the country, the Holy See's broader aim was that such moral change did not have politically destabilizing effects. Hence, the Holy See and the Catholic Church simultaneously enabled and constrained Solidarity's emergence and evolution.

The primate of the Catholic Church in Poland, Cardinal Wyszyński, reacted cautiously to Solidarity's emergence. He did not want to distance himself from legitimate demands by his people. However, he was not sure whether Solidarity would become the church's faithful partner or a potential troublemaker. While Wałęsa's self-presentation as a pious Catholic reassured the leader of the Polish church,[54] Primate Wyszyński remained concerned about the reaction of Warsaw and Moscow. A US National Security Council (NSC) memorandum noted:

> Given its enormous prestige the Church and particularly Cardinal Wyszyński will play a crucial role in any settlement. While sympathizing with the workers, Wyszyński is clearly concerned that the strike may precipitate Soviet intervention and has indirectly sided with the government in an effort to try to defuse the crisis. But he is likely to exact a price for his support. Thus one outcome of the current unrest is likely to be a strengthening of the Church's role vis-à-vis the party and an expansion of its autonomy.[55]

The memorandum recommended that the White House "intensify contacts and consultations" with the pope who is "obviously a key actor, even behind the scenes."[56]

The Holy See hesitated in making a statement on the emergence of Solidarity. On August 18, 1980, the NSC observed that "the Vatican has said nothing publically" and that it had informed the US government that it was "very worried." If violence breaks out, the pope would be prepared to issue a public statement calling for restraint.[57] On August 20,

54. When Wałęsa signed the Gdansk Accord, he famously used a pen that had a huge and visible picture of the pope on it. See Paltrow, "Poland and the Pope," 12.

55. Memorandum, Steve Larrabee to Zbigniew Brzezinski, "The Polish Crisis and Beyond: Implications for US Policy," August 28, 1980, Box "National Security Affairs, Brzezinski Material, Country File, Poland, Box 65," Folder "Poland: 7–8/80," Jimmy Carter Presidential Library (JC).

56. Ibid.

57. Memorandum, Steve Larrabee to David Aaron, "SCC on Poland," August 19, 1980, NLC–15–40–8–3–0, JC.

1980, the pope ended his public silence before a crowd of 30,000 in St. Peter's Square by asking God to free the Polish "people from all evil and danger and [to] always defend all their good actions."[58]

The Soviet Union was acutely aware of the political implications of the pope's reaction to Solidarity. In September, Moscow used diplomatic channels to ask the Holy See "about using its influence to reduce tensions in Poland." The Soviets threatened "that they would intervene if the situation got out of hand." Cardinal Casaroli replied that "the Church considered the new situation 'irreversible' but it would do what it could to control it."[59] During a Warsaw Pact meeting that discussed the Polish question, Leonid Brezhnev argued that "a confrontation with the Church would only worsen the situation." The Soviet tactic was to "influence as far as possible the moderate circles within the Catholic Church . . . and keep them from closely aligning themselves within the extreme anti-socialist forces and those who desire the fall of socialism in Poland."[60]

On December 16, 1980, John Paul II dispatched a letter to Brezhnev to diplomatically ask him to refrain from any intervention in order to "dispel the actual tension." The pope also referred to Poland's occupation, to its six million casualties during the Second World War, and to the "solemn principles of the Helsinki Final Act," particularly the "principle of non-intervention in the internal affairs of each of the participating states." In his letter, the Holy Father explained the emergence of Solidarity "by the ineluctable necessity of the economic reconstruction of the country, which requires, at the same time, a moral reconstruction based on the conscious engagement, in solidarity, of all the forces of the entire society."[61] He received no reply from the Kremlin. As his private secretary, Stanisław Dziwisz, remembers, the Kremlin appeared like an "impenetrable wall."[62]

58. "Pope sings a hymn for his Poland," *The New York Times*, August 21, 1980.

59. Memo, "Additional Information Items," The Situation Room to Zbigniew Brzezinski, October 28, 1980, NLC-1-17-4-19-8, JC.

60. Wilson Center, "Stenographic Minutes."

61. Letter printed in Weigel, *Witness to Hope*, 406–7. "Recent disclosures also make it clear that the pope was seriously considering the possibility of returning to Poland to lead the national resistance should the Soviets invade," argues Biskupski, *The History of Poland*, 163. I found no supportive evidence for this claim.

62. Dziwisz, *Mein Leben*, 131. Stanisław Dziwisz was the personal secretary of Pope John Paul II throughout his entire pontificate. In 2005, following the pope's death, he was appointed Archbishop of Krakow and promoted to the rank of cardinal in 2006.

Whereas the Holy Father supported Solidarity's cause, Polish church leaders were walking on a tightrope by simultaneously lending "support both to Solidarity and to the Kania[63] regime." According to the CIA, the church had demands of its own such as larger access to the media, church construction, and expanded religious education, which created a "natural interest in encouraging a progressive, if cautious liberalization, and in exacting its own political price for the regime for its support." Some younger clergy "have questioned the wisdom of the strong support Cardinal Wyszyński was seen to have extended to the regime apparently at the expense of Solidarity." Yet the Cardinal fully enjoyed the pope's backing and continued playing "a moderating role toward the regime, the workers and the population at large."[64]

The Holy See's initial caution gave way to public support in January 1981 when the pope received Wałęsa in the Vatican for private conversation and public audience. Lech Wałęsa considered the pope's "public sanction" a "gift" for Solidarity.[65] In his public speech, the pope referred to the "memorable weeks" of the previous August and applauded the recognition of Solidarity by the Polish state. He praised Solidarity's efforts as "a common impulse to promote the moral good of society" and praised it as a movement *for* rather than *against* something.[66] The pope wished Wałęsa's delegation "courage" but also "prudence and moderation."[67] Wałęsa was grateful for the papal blessing but signaled that Solidarity was not a confessional trade union. While he accepted the Polish bishops' offer to pay for his trip, he refused to frame his visit as a "pilgrimage." Rather, he also accepted an invitation of the Italian confederation of trade unions. The Holy See, on its part, did not want to give the impression that the Polish Pope governed Poland from the outside. For this reason, the pope chose to give his speech to the Solidarity delegation in public in front of an official delegate of the Polish government.[68]

63. Stanisław Kania was leader of the Polish Communist Party from 1980 to 1981.

64. Central Intelligence Agency, "Poland's Prospects over the Next Six Months."

65. Wałęsa, *Way of Hope*, 164–65.

66. Ibid.

67. John Paul II, "Discorso del Santo Padre Giovanni Paolo II alla Delegazione del Sindacato Indipendente et Autonomo Polacco 'Solidarnosc.'"

68. Telegram, French Embassy to the Holy See to Foreign Ministry, "Lech Wałęsa au Vatican," January 16, 1981, Box "Europe, 1981–1985, Saint-Siège, Box 5503," Folder "11–5 Relations Saint-Siège—Pologne," AD. Mr. Rozalicz from the Polish Embassy to Italy showed himself "very satisfied" with the visit but preferred framing the visit as a "pilgrimage" in which the "religious" aspect of the program outweighed the

In sum, after initial hesitations, the Holy See reacted positively to the emergence of Solidarity. It put a particular emphasis on the non-use of violence, freedom of association, and the right of the Polish people to shape its own destiny. The relationship between the Holy See and Solidarity was also shaped by mutual appreciation and personal sympathy between John Paul II and Lech Wałęsa. Their different role understandings, however, did not allow for the formation of a deeper alliance. The Holy See's sympathies for Solidarity's cause were mediated by the principle of prudence. Papal diplomats stayed attuned to the skeptical position of Moscow. While the Holy Father did not shy away from sending Brezhnev a clear and principled letter defending Poland's sovereignty, he entrusted day-to-day relations with Solidarity to Cardinal Wyszyński, who wanted Solidarity to play a moderate rather than radical role.[69]

Martial Law

Poland was a crucial figure in the broader Cold War game of chess between the two superpowers. For Washington, Poland was a crack in the Iron Curtain that was to be widened without risking actual military conflict. For Moscow, the situation in Poland had become a risk to the maintenance of Soviet hegemony over Central and Eastern Europe. Food shortage and economic problems aggravated the domestic situation in Poland. In this delicate context, Solidarity was a "self-limiting

---

importance of contacts with Italian trade unions. He also claimed that the Minister-Counselor from the Soviet Embassy to Italy expressed his "satisfaction." See Letter, "Visite de M. Wałęsa à Rome: Point de vue du Ministre-Conseiller polonais," January 28, 1981, Ibid.

69. Ever since Carl Bernstein's 1992 "Holy Alliance" article, speculations about financial support by the Vatican abound. The Hungarian intelligence service reported that the Vatican bank (IOR) transferred the following sums to Solidarity: 1979–80: $15 million; 1980–81: $25 million; 1981–82: $25 million; $35 million previsioned for the 1982–83 period. The report explains the surge for the last period with the Vatican's collaboration with "American banks and other organizations" aimed at "activating subversive measures in Poland." This information is said to come from "competent Vatican sources." In the absence of any further proof, the reliability of this source remains questionable. Report, "Information der Sicherheitsorgane der UVR. Über das Programm der Vatikan-Bank zur Unterstützung der 'Solidarnosc,'" translated from Russian, Department X of the Ministerium für Staatssicherheit, November 9, 1982, Box "MfS HA XX/4 Nr. 462, BStU 0000220," Archives of the *Federal Commissioner for the Records of the State Security Service of the former German Democratic Republic* (BStU).

revolution."[70] Its leadership realized that the Polish government deliberately wanted to provoke Solidarity in order to entice violent action which they then would use as a convenient justification for an even more violent clampdown. As a mass movement, Solidarity's leaders inevitably had to deal with internal tensions, fragmentation, and pressure from below that led to stronger demands for democratically elected local governments and for more decision-making power over Poland's economic and social policy. Faced with a worsening economic situation, Solidarity's self-discipline declined, leading to ever stronger calls for free elections and nationwide strikes.[71]

In the Silesian town of Bielsko-Biała, an unauthorized strike paralyzed the entire region. Tension only decreased after a compromise negotiated by Bishop Bronislaw Dąbrowksi.[72] In this heated context, Cardinal Wyszyński became ever more concerned about Solidarity's radicalization.[73] Fearing spontaneous outbursts of popular protest without wanting to turn a blind eye to underlying social injustice, the Polish bishops reiterated their call for dialogue between the regime and Solidarity in line with the 1980 Gdansk Accord.[74] On March 19, three Solidarity activists were badly beaten by Polish policemen in the town of Bydgoszcz and the Polish regime almost provoked Solidarity to a national insurrection.[75] The Holy Father sent a message to Cardinal Wyszynski to express his concern. He expressed his belief that Poles wanted "to work and not to strike" and recommended "reciprocal understanding, dialogue, patience, and perseverance" in line with the principles of the Gdansk Accord.[76]

70. Ascherson, *Polish August*; Staniszkis, *Poland's Self-Limiting Revolution*.

71. Garton Ash, *Polish Revolution*, 297–307. See also Davies, *God's Playground*, 488–89.

72. Garton Ash, *Polish Revolution*, 148–49. Bishop Dąbrowksi was Auxiliary Bishop of Warsaw from 1961 to 1997 and promoted to Titular Archbishop in 1982.

73. Telegram, French Foreign Ministry to French Embassy to the Holy See et al, "L'Église Polonaise et la situation en Pologne," February 5, 1981, Box "Europe, 1981–1985, Pologne, Box 5418," Folder "2–14 Crise Polonaise (avant le 13 Dec 1981), Position de l'Église Polonaise," AD.

74. Letter, French Ambassador to Warsaw to French Foreign Minister, "Communiqué de l'Épiscopat polonais," February 10, 1981, Box "Europe, 1981–1985, Pologne, Box 5418," Folder "2–14 Crise Polonaise (avant le 13 Dec 1981), Position de l'Église Polonaise," AD.

75. Garton Ash, *Polish Revolution*, 158–68.

76. John Paul II, "Messaggio del Santo Padre Giovanni Paolo II al Primate di Polonia," n.p.

The Polish church was temporarily weakened by the death of Cardinal Wyszyński on May 29, 1981, and shocked by Mehmet Ali Ağca's near-fatal assassination attempt of Pope John Paul II on May 13, 1981.[77] As primate, Wyszyński had shaped relations between the Polish church and the government since his appointment in 1948. His successor, Archbishop Józef Glemp, struggled to emulate Wyszyński's unique style that combined principled anti-communism and political prudence. Archbishop Glemp presided over the opening mass of Solidarity's first national congress in September 1981.[78] However, he insisted on the autonomy of the church which should not become "a tool for the state nor for Solidarity." For this reason, the church could help Solidarity only "when possible and appropriate."[79] Not all papal diplomats in the Holy See's Secretariat of State viewed Glemp's presence at the Solidarity congress positively. Some feared his attendance would be interpreted as a "blessing" for all decisions the congress might take.[80]

Soviet pressure on the Polish government was intense. Solidarity posed an unacceptable challenge to the legitimacy and stability of the socialist bloc. Moscow wanted Warsaw to "solve" the problem and by December 1980 a military invasion seemed imminent. The Polish party leader, Stanisław Kania, was able to persuade the Soviet Union from refraining to intervene.[81] In October 1981, Kania was replaced by General Wojciech Jaruzelski who argued that domestic imposition of martial law was a "lesser evil" than the international alternative of Soviet intervention. But Jaruzelski was reluctant to impose martial law without a Soviet guarantee that its troops would intervene if martial law failed. Soviet leaders were unwilling to provide Jaruzelski with such a guarantee though. "Far from having 'saved' Poland from a Soviet invasion," Mark

77. For a discussion of the assassination attempt see Alexiev, *Kremlin and the Pope*; Bernstein and Politi, *His Holiness*, 291–308. The most widely believed theory holds the Bulgarian secret service responsible. This organization did the dirty work for the Soviet KGB.

78. Garton Ash, *Polish Revolution*, 280.

79. Interview in *Le Figaro*, "L'Église ne sera ni un instrument ni pour l'État ni pour Solidarité," September 15, 1981. See Box "Europe, 1981–1985, Pologne, Box 5418," Folder "2–14 Crise Polonaise (avant le 13 Dec 1981), Position de l'Église Polonaise," AD.

80. Telegram, French Embassy to the Holy See to Foreign Ministry, "Le Saint-Siège et la Pologne," October 7, 1981. In Box "Europe, 1981–1985, Pologne, Box 5418," Folder "2–14 Crise Polonaise (avant le 13 Dec 1981), Position de l'Église Polonaise," AD.

81. Garton Ash, *Polish Revolution*, 357–60.

Kramer highlights, "Jaruzelski was desperately promoting the very thing he now claims to have prevented."[82] General Jaruzelski imposed military dictatorship and martial law on Sunday morning, December 13, 1981. By imprisoning the leadership of Solidarity, imposing curfews, curtailing civil liberties, and arresting thousands of citizens without due process, the Polish regime had declared war on its own people.

Archbishop Glemp's immediate reaction was very restrained. Quoting Glemp's Sunday sermon which followed the imposition of martial law, Timothy Garton Ash notes, "The authorities consider that the exceptional nature of martial law is dictated by a higher necessity, it is the choice of a lesser rather than a greater evil. Assuming the correctness of such reasoning the man in the street will subordinate himself to the new situation." Clearly, Glemp wanted to prevent bloodshed by all means. "There is nothing of greater value than human life. That is why I, myself, will call for reason even if that means I become the target of insults. I shall plead, even if I have to plead on my knees: Do not start a fight of Pole against Pole." Garton Ash also notes that the sermon played an important "part in reducing the immediate (passive) resistance to martial law, and that the Primate's words were bitterly resented by many Christian Poles who were, at that moment, preparing to risk their own lives for what they considered greater values."[83]

In Rome, the pope was surprised and worried.[84] During his public Angelus prayer he reminded the world that "there cannot be any more shedding of Polish blood because too much blood has already been shed during the Second World War."[85] Three days later the Holy Father called for a "return to the road to renewal built through dialogue, with respect for the rights of every man and every citizen. This road is obviously not an easy one but it is not impossible." John Paul II admonished the Polish authorities to reestablish dialogue and not to use violence.[86]

Eastern European intelligence services assumed the pope did not want to exacerbate internal tensions in Poland.[87] Instead, the Holy See

82. Kramer, "Jaruzelski," 10.

83. Garton Ash, *Polish Revolution*, 280.

84. Dziwisz, *Mein Leben*, 145.

85. John Paul II, "Angelus," n.p.

86. John Paul II, "Udienza Generale, December 16, 1981," n.p.

87. Report, "Information der Sicherheitsorgane der UVR. Über westliche Reaktionen auf die Ereignisse in Polen," translated from Russian, Department X of the Ministerium für Staatssicherheit, December 28, 1981, Box "MfS HA XX/4 Nr. 462, BStU 000021," BStU.

sent Archbishop Luigi Poggi[88] on a reconnaissance mission to Poland to deliver a papal letter to General Jaruzelski. The Holy Father appealed for ending the state of emergency and resuming peaceful dialogue. Copies of the letter were forwarded to Lech Wałęsa, Archbishop Glemp, and all governments that signed the 1975 Helsinki Final Act.[89]

Archbishop Poggi came back from Poland with the conviction that General Jaruzelski's intention to prevent worse things from happening was sincere.[90] While Poggi believed that consequences were "much less tragic" than presented by Western media, he nonetheless reported 4,200 political internments and seven deaths back to Rome. While the Polish bishops were united in their desire for an end of martial law, their outspokenness varied. Cardinal Franciszek Macharski, the pope's successor as Archbishop of Krakow, for example, was considerably more candid than Archbishop Glemp as he compared martial law to the German occupation of Poland during the Second World War.[91]

In January 1982, during his annual speech to the diplomatic corps accredited to the Holy See, John Paul II deplored the "state of war" and the "detention of thousands of citizens" in Poland. The pope said he "could not remain silent" when inviolable human rights were at stake. He underlined his conviction that every people had the right to choose freely its own destiny and form of government in accordance with justice, respect for life, religious freedom, and human rights. In a thinly veiled attack on Soviet hegemony, the Holy Father said that no people should be subordinated or become an instrument of another state. The historical

88. Archbishop Poggi was a papal career diplomat. From 1975 to 1986 he was responsible for the Vatican's working relations with Poland. In 1989, full diplomatic relations were reestablished.

89. Telegram, French Embassy to the Holy See to Foreign Ministry, "Message du Pape au Général Jaruzelski," December 22, 1981, including full transcript of letter by Pope John Paul II to General Jaruzelski, dated December 18, 1981, and transmitted to the French Embassy by Archbishop Silvestrini, Box "Europe, 1981–1985, Pologne, Box 5422," Folder "2–14 Réactions des Pays d'Europe Occidentale à l'État de siège en Pologne—Saint-Siège," AD.

90. After their hour-long "very open" conversation, the French ambassador to the Holy See noted that even Poggi seemed "not completely convinced" by this explanation.

91. Telegram, French Embassy to the Holy See to Foreign Ministry, "Entretien avec Mgr Poggi," December 29, 1981, Box "Europe, 1981–1985, Pologne, Box 5422," Folder "2–14 Réactions des Pays d'Europe Occidentale à l'État de siège en Pologne—Saint-Siège," AD.

separation of world politics into hegemonic spheres had no normative justification.[92]

Overall, concern about Soviet invasion, state repression, and social order colored the cautious position of Archbishop Glemp. The Holy See did not criticize Glemp or distance itself from Glemp's advice to the Polish people. Yet the pope's letter to Jaruzelski and his speech to the diplomatic corps accredited to the Holy See stressed that there was no justification for martial law. The dialogue process had to continue, political prisoners had to be freed, and martial law had to end. Both Archbishop Glemp and Pope John Paul II were aware of the need to encourage the people while preventing worse forms of violence. Being responsible for keeping up relations with the local government, however, Archbishop Glemp preferred to err on the side of caution, whereas the pope was willing to express his moral concerns more directly.

Economic Sanctions

The Reagan administration followed the events in Poland with interest and concern. President Reagan appointed his personal friend William A. Wilson to be his Rome-based personal envoy to the Holy See. Frequent high-level messages were sent back and forth between Washington and the Vatican. To build up pressure, the White House imposed economic sanctions both on Poland and the Soviet Union following the imposition of martial law. Measures aimed at Poland involved the suspension of shipments of agricultural and dairy products, the halting of credit lines, the suspension of Polish civil aviation landing rights in the US, and the suspension of Polish fishing rights in US waters. Sanctions toward the Soviet Union included the suspension of US landing rights of the Soviet airline Aeroflot, the closure of the Soviet Purchasing Commission, the suspension of the issuance or renewal of licenses for the export of high-technology materials to the Soviet Union, the postponement of negotiations of a long-term grains agreement, the suspension of a new US-Soviet maritime agreement, and a complete review of all US-Soviet exchange agreements.[93]

92. John Paul II, "Discorso Di Giovanni Paolo II Al Corpo Diplomatico Accreditato Presso La Santa Sede, January 16, 1982," para. 7.

93. Reagan, "Statement on U.S. Measures."

President Reagan's intention was "to send a strong message of condemnation in order . . . to deter Soviet involvement in the repression of the Polish reform movement and to try to deter them from further aggressive moves."[94] The Western European allies of the United States were not convinced about the need to forbid valuable exports of high-technology materials such as oil and gas equipment. The French signed a major pipeline contract with the Soviet Union in January 1982, and the United Kingdom and Germany expressed their concern once they understood that the White House intended to apply the sanctions retroactively which required them to break contracts already concluded.[95]

Part of the Reagan administration's Poland strategy was to get the Holy See to put moral pressure on Western European governments so they would support US economic sanctions. Since "Western unity on such a program of sanctions was crucial," President Reagan asked for the pope's "assistance in using your own suasion throughout the West in an attempt to achieve unity on these needed measures." Furthermore, the president hoped the pope would use his "influence with the Church in Poland to help persuade the Polish authorities promptly to lift martial law, release all detainees, and resume the dialogue with Solidarity." In a latent side-attack on Archbishop Glemp, the president opined that those "who urge only patience and understanding for the Jaruzelski regime condemn the Polish people to a military dictatorship."[96]

In his reply, John Paul II did not provide a direct answer to the President's request for moral support. Instead, he referred to the defense of fundamental principles of international relations such as the peaceful coexistence of nations and human rights. With regard to the church's own endeavors, the Holy Father argued that they reflect

> the mission of the Catholic Church, not only because she is profoundly involved in the history and reality of national life but also because she cannot keep silent and must duly bear witness when human rights and fundamental freedoms are violated, especially in such a radical way . . . It is therefore natural, and profoundly just, that in its painful experiences the Polish Nation

94. Dobson, "Reagan Administration," 543.

95. Ibid., 543–44.

96. Telegram, White House Situation Room to US Embassy Rome, "Presidential Letter to the Pope on Poland," December 30, 1981, Box "Executive Secretariat, NSC: Head of State File, Box 41," Folder "The Vatican: Pope John Paul II—Cables [1 of 2]," RR.

> should find solidarity on the part of all the nations and peoples that are rightly anxious that these fundamental principles should be introduced into and safeguarded in social and international life. And it is equally understandable that those who are most involved and who most directly share in the drama of Poland are in the first place the peoples of Europe, those with a European tradition and special European links—those who are closest in our outlook, history and culture. The solidarity expressed by individuals, social groups and peoples is certainly the very same that inspires the attitudes assumed by many Governments, like your own, on the international level—attitudes which are not directed against the life and development of Poland, but which intend to support her people's aspiration for freedom. This common action among all peoples that have moral values at heart is supported by the Holy See in the sphere of its competence and in a manner corresponding to its mission, which does not have a political character.[97]

Archbishop Silvestrini personally handed this papal letter to Michael Hornblow, the assistant of President Reagan's envoy to the Holy See. He noted that press reports suggesting the Holy See disapproved of US sanctions against Poland and the Soviet Union were false. Whereas the United States must operate "on the political plane," the Holy See "operates on the moral plane." In the case of Poland the two planes were "complementary because both the Holy See and the United States have the same objective—the restoration of liberty to Poland."[98] On this basis, William P. Clark, the US National Security Advisor under President Reagan and a devout Catholic, briefed the president that the pope had made it "clear that he supports your measures against the Polish government and the Soviet Union and considers them complementary to the moral pressure which he is bringing to bear."[99] In a news conference, President Reagan

97. President Reagan's envoy to the Holy See gave a copy of the letter to the French ambassador of the Holy See. The letter is still classified in the Reagan Presidential Library but I found a declassified copy in the French diplomatic archives. See "Lettre du Saint-Père au Président Reagan," French Ambassador to the Holy See to the French Foreign Minister, January 26, 1982, Box "Europe, 1981–1985, Pologne, Box 5422," Folder "2–14 Réactions des Pays d'Europe Occidentale à l'État de siège en Pologne—Saint-Siège," AD. The pope's letter is dated January 4, 1982.

98. Telegram, US Vatican Office via Department of State to the White House Situation Room, "Letter from Pope John Paul II to President Reagan," January 6, 1982, Box "Executive Secretariat, NSC: Head of State File, Box 41," Folder "The Vatican: Pope John Paul II—Cables [1 of 2]," RR.

99. Memorandum, William P. Clark to President Reagan, "Reply from the Pope

thus did not hesitate to inform the press that he has "had a lengthy communication from the pope. He approves what we have done so far; he believes that it has been beneficial."[100]

This public statement went too far for the Holy See. Its press office, in a rare step, issued a public clarification the following day. It stressed the Holy See's general support for "common action among all peoples that have moral values at heart" with a view to promote Poland's freedom. Refusing to provide specific support for US economic sanctions, the statement stressed that the Holy See had to act "according to its sphere of competence and in a manner compatible with its non-political mission."[101] Publicly, the Holy See abstained from taking a position on the sanctions issue with the argument that it lacked the political competence of doing so. Privately, however, Archbishop Silvestrini expressed doubts about the efficacy of sanctions, fearing that they would hurt the Polish people more than the government.[102]

Presidential envoy William Wilson followed up with Cardinal Casaroli to request Vatican approval of America's Poland strategy. He complained that "some European countries have been citing Vatican support as a justification for their passive policies with regard to Poland." The Holy See should not "allow itself to be used by these other countries to justify their inaction." Wilson regretted that the "Vatican press statement of January 20 has been interpreted by the press as implying Vatican disapproval of United States sanctions toward Poland and the Soviet Union. It has also been used by Soviet propaganda agencies to suggest there is disagreement between the Vatican and the United States on Poland." Wilson apologized that "the President's statement was meant to suggest that the United States and the Vatican had the same general objectives with regard to Poland. It was unfortunate that the press had only focused on the economic sanctions issue."[103]

---

on Poland," January 11, 1982, Box "Executive Secretariat, NSC: Head of State File, Box 41," Folder "The Vatican: Pope John Paul II (8107378–8200051)," RR.

100. Reagan, "The President's News Conference," n.p.

101. Telegram, French Embassy to Holy See to Foreign Ministry, "Communiqué du Vatican," January 21, 1982, Box "Europe, 1981–1985, Pologne, Box 5422," Folder "2–14 Réactions des Pays d'Europe Occidentale à l'État de siège en Pologne—Saint-Siège," AD.

102. Telegram, "Pologne, entretien avec Mgr. Silvestrini," French Embassy to the Holy See to Foreign Ministry, January 20, 1982, Box "Europe, 1981–1985, Pologne, Box 5422," Folder "2–14 Réactions des Pays d'Europe Occidentale à l'État de siège en Pologne—Saint-Siège," AD.

103. Telegram, William Wilson to Department of State, "Poland—Meeting with

When the pope consequently granted a personal audience to Wilson, he expressed his concern that the Polish people "will not allow themselves to be kept under this type of pressure for a prolonged period of time." Yet, when pressed by Wilson about what could be done to release this pressure, "he simply looked at the ceiling and after a few moments started the conversation off in another direction." Wilson then conveyed the president's regret about "any possible embarrassment." The pope cut Wilson off, saying there was "no problem" and that the White House and the Holy See are "in complete accord" on the broad issues and principles. Wilson left the conversation with the impression that both the pope and the Polish people "understand and agree with the purposes of the sanctions" even though they create some hardships."[104]

The Holy See's doubts about the sanctions increased over time though. The major church critic of the sanctions was Archbishop Glemp. US intelligence reports maintained that he "has remained steadfastly opposed—publicly at times—to Western sanctions, arguing that the nation and the economy were exhausted by the prolonged crisis and that lifting them would benefit the people and the country more than the regime."[105] Briefing points for a lunch between President Reagan and Archbishop Glemp scheduled for October 15, 1982, revealed the extent of US concern about Glemp. Any critical remarks by the Polish primate just two weeks before the 1982 US congressional elections "would have a very bad effect at this sensitive time." "Of course, we can't muzzle the Archbishop," Wilson briefed the White House from Rome, "but he should be cautioned."[106]

During the pope's second visit to Poland, in June 1983, General Jaruzelski complained about Western hostility. The pope responded by explaining that these sentiments were a reaction to human rights abuses by the Polish regime rather than an act of aggression against the Polish

Cardinal Casaroli 1/27/82," January 27, 1982, Box "Peter R. Sommer Files, Box 6," Folder "Vatican 1983–84 (9 of 10) Box 90587," RR. The responses by Cardinal Casaroli are still classified.

104. Telegram, William Wilson to Department of State, "Audience with the Pope—1/29/82," January 29, 1982, Box "Peter R. Sommer Files, Box 6," Folder "Vatican 1983–84 (9 of 10) Box 90587," RR.

105. Central Intelligence Agency, "Poland's Prospects over the Next 12 to 18 Months," 9.

106. Memorandum, "Call from US Rep to Vatican Bill Wilson," September 23, 1982, Box "Peter R. Sommer Files, Box 6," Folder "Vatican 1983–84 (6 of 10) Box 90587," RL. According to handwritten notes on the memorandum, however, the Glemp visit was called off on September 30, 1982, for unspecified reasons.

people. The Polish regime had to make "concrete gestures" to deserve a revision of Western sanctions policy, the pope argued.[107] Even after the Polish regime announced the official end of martial law on July 22, 1983, the Holy See was still not forthcoming with a favorable comment for Poland's wish of further relaxation of US sanctions. According to Archbishop Poggi, the Holy See needed more "time for reflection" to wait for the reaction of the Polish people and to get a sense of the legal consequences the lifting of martial law would have on matters of interest to the Polish church such as education.[108]

It was Lech Wałęsa's own first public criticism of Western sanctions that brought about a change in the Vatican's position. Toward the end of 1983, Wałęsa argued that the sanctions had outlived their utility and had become a propaganda tool for the government in Warsaw.[109] In a conversation with Wilson, Archbishop Silvestrini showed sympathy for Wałęsa's position and believed that the "situation in Poland has changed":

> Wałęsa's declarations indicate a certain change in Polish public opinion on economic sanctions. Before, Polish public opinion saw the sanctions as a measure against the regime. Wałęsa also saw them as justified in their time. Today, given the abnormal situation in Poland, Wałęa sees them causing harm to the basic condition of the people . . . The Holy See realizes that the sanctions have a just purpose but they are doing harm to the people.[110]

107. Memorandum, Italian Permanent Representation to NATO, "Visite du Pape en Pologne—Evaluations du Saint-Siège," July 5, 1983, on the basis of information provided by a "high-ranking personality" of the Vatican. As the French ambassador to NATO notes in an accompanying memorandum, the views reflect the opinions of Archbishop Silvestrini. See Letter, French Ambassador to NATO to French Foreign Minister, July 12, 1983, Box "Europe, 1981–1985, Saint-Siège, Box 5503," Folder "11–5 Relations Saint-Siège—Pologne," AD.

108. Telegram, French Embassy to the Holy See to Foreign Ministry, "Pologne—Entretien avec Mgr. Poggi," July 27, 1983, Box "Europe, 1981–1985, Pologne, Box 5431," Folder "2–14 Suites de la levée de l'état de siège—réactions des pays d'Europe sauf est," AD.

109. Memorandum, Paula Dobriansky to Robert C. McFarlane, "Poland: Next steps," December 6, 1983, Box "Paula J. Dobriansky Files, Box 3," Folder "Poland—Memoranda, 1981–83 [December 1983]," RR.

110. Telegram, William Wilson to Department of State, "Vatican views on Wałęsa's sanctions statement," December 23, 1983, Box "Paula J. Dobriansky Files, Box 3," Folder "Poland: Memoranda 1984–85 [January 1984]," RR.

Silvestrini underlined "the danger of future suffering if the present situation continues." Wilson reported to Washington that the Vatican message "to lift the sanctions is unmistakable."[111]

The US would not entirely lift economic sanctions against Poland until 1987. During a special White House ceremony on February 19, 1987, President Reagan mentioned the position of both the Polish church and Solidarity in support of his decision to lift sanctions.[112] Ironically, he did not mention that both the Vatican and Cardinal Glemp had already been pushing for a progressive, if not complete, lifting of the sanctions since the end of 1983 on the grounds that they hurt the people and that they made Poland only more dependent on the Soviet Union.[113]

Toward 1989

Pope John Paul II was keen on revisiting his beloved Poland to renew the hope of his compatriots despite the Roman Curia's skepticism about a papal visit to a country still under martial law. In the end, the pope's personal wish made the difference.[114] Tough bargaining between the Vatican and Warsaw preceded the pope's second trip to Poland. A planned return to Poland in August 1982 for the 600th anniversary of the Black Madonna of Jasna Gora was ruled out because the imposition of martial law was still too recent.[115] The 1983 papal visit was announced in Warsaw by the Polish government and Primate Glemp on November 8, 1983. Announced two days before a nationwide strike organized by the underground leaders of Solidarity, the "permission for the pope's return appeared to be a

111. Ibid.

112. Reagan, "Statement on the Lifting of Economic Sanctions against Poland," n.p.

113. Telegram, French Embassy to the Holy See to Foreign Ministry, "Pologne," October 13, 1984, Box "Europe, 1981–1985, Pologne, Box 5431," Folder "2–14 Suites de la levée de l'état de siège—réactions des pays d'Europe sauf est," AD.

114. Telegram, French Embassy to the Holy See to Foreign Ministry, "Visite du Pape en Pologne," June 14, 1983, Box "Europe, 1981–1985, Saint-Siège, Box 5503," Folder "11–5 Saint-Siège Visite de Jean Paul II en Pologne 16–23 juin 1983," AD.

115. Kohan, "Return of the Native," n.p. The Hungarian intelligence service reported that Cardinal Casaroli, together with a number of Polish bishops, opposed an earlier papal visit in 1982 for its potentially destabilizing effect. Report, "Information der Sicherheitsorgane der UVR. Über die Meinung von Kreisen des Vatikans zum geplanten Besuch des Papstes in Polen," translated from Russian, Department X of the Ministerium für Staatssicherheit, March 25, 1982, Box "MfS HA XX/4 Nr. 407, BStU 000051,," BStU.

move on the part of the authorities to give the Polish people an emotional release—something to look forward to—and another reason not to join Solidarity's demonstrations."[116] The Holy See, for its part, remained committed to three objectives—end to martial law, general amnesty for political prisoners, and resumption of dialogue between Solidarity and the government on the basis of the 1980 Gdansk Accord. The Holy Father did not insist, however, on these three demands as a precondition for a visit to Poland. Rather, he thought that the potential benefits of a papal visit to his home country outweighed the political risks.

The pope's second trip to Poland took place from June 16–23, 1983. At the welcome ceremony, the pope said his visit was motivated both by a personal desire and by his "special responsibility as bishop of Rome."[117] He expressed his particular affection for those who were suffering and asked all detainees to be close to him in spirit.[118] During a memorial mass for Cardinal Wyszyński, the Holy Father expressed his gladness to be "together with all my compatriots—especially those who are most acutely tasting the bitterness of disappointment, humiliation, suffering, of being deprived of their freedom, of being wronged, of having their dignity trampled upon." Under applause from the congregation, the pope thanked God that Wyszynski had been spared the sad events surrounding martial law.[119]

In a long meeting with General Jaruzelski in Warsaw's Belvedere Palace, the general "seemed uncomfortable with his guest . . . his hands trembled nervously." In his speech, Jaruzelski implied that martial law had forestalled a Soviet invasion of Poland and promised to end it as soon as the domestic situation allowed it. The Holy Father admonished Jaruzelski to go back to the *status quo ante*. He hoped that "social reform . . . according to the principles painstakingly worked out in the critical days of August 1980 . . . will gradually be put into effect" and argued that liberalization would help end Poland's international isolation and lead to improved relations "above all with the United States."[120]

The strategy of the Polish regime during the pope's visit was to cast his visit as a sign of gradual "normalization" in Poland. The government

116. Kifner, "Pope will Visit Poland next June, Warsaw and Primate Announce," *The New York Times*, November 9, 1983.

117. John Paul II, "Ceremonia di Benvenuto," para. 1.

118. Ibid., para. 3.

119. Kohan, "Return of the Native," n.p.

120. Ibid., n.p.

stressed the improvement of church-state relations and rhetorically reasserted its commitment to reform.[121] Jaruzelski thought he could "rehabilitate Poland in the eyes of the world." On the eve of John Paul's return to Rome, he traveled to Krakow for a second surprise meeting with the pope to "garner what prestige he could from the papal visit."[122] Unwilling to be used by Jaruzelski, John Paul II also insisted on a private meeting with Wałęsa, who was held captive by the state. The meeting took place at a secret location in the Tatra Mountains. While the content of their talk remains unknown, the meeting symbolized John Paul's belief that "Polish conditions were not solely as the regime had defined them."[123]

East German intelligence reports suggested that the pope walked at the "outer limit of full confrontation, even if it did not aim at beginning a war. The church will put itself on top of the counter-revolution." While there were no street demonstrations, the pope "declared the government to be unable to comprehend and govern the country" and "mentioned imperialistic states as a positive example to follow."[124] The East German military attaché in Warsaw informed East Berlin that the pope's "propagation of Catholicism, especially of its social thought" had a "distinct political character" by stressing the unity between "Polishness" and "Catholicism" and by "defaming" socialism as a "source of all evil." While the visit did not pose any "immediate counterrevolutionary threat," the danger resided in the "politically corroding long-term effect" of strengthened Catholicism.[125]

Despite their usual emphasis on the pastoral motivations of Holy See diplomacy, papal diplomats privately conceded that the pope's trip had a political impact, above all by confirming the continued validity of the Gdansk Accord. As Archbishop Silvestrini put it, the papal visit was difficult since the Holy Father had to meet popular expectations without engaging in direct conflict with the regime.[126] The Holy See evaluated

121. Luxmoore and Babiuch, *Vatican and the Red Flag*, 249.

122. Kohan, "Poland," n.p.

123. Luxmoore and Babiuch, *Vatican and the Red Flag*, 250.

124. Letter, Gen. Oberst Erdmann to Ministry for Foreign Trade, Department XVIII of the Ministerium für Staatssicherheit, June 27, 1983, Box "MfS HA XVIII Nr. 6461, BStU 000019–21," BStU.

125. Report, "Der programmatische Charakter der Predigten des Papstes während seiner Visite in der VRP 1983," June 30, 1983, Box "MfS HA I Nr. 14150 Teil 1 von 2, BStU 000218–220," BStU.

126. Telegram, French Ambassador to the Holy See to Foreign Ministry, "Premières

the outcome of the visit positively as it reaffirmed the church's authority in Poland.[127] With regard to its long-term consequences, the Holy See waited for the promised general amnesty and for seeing what "normalization" would really mean for the life of the Polish church.

Following the pope's return to Rome, the *L'Osservatore Romano* published an editorial piece by Father Virgilio Levi that claimed that Lech Wałęsa "had to meet the Holy Father as a private person in a secret manner without demanding to count any longer in the present phase of life in his country . . . Officially Lech Wałęsa once more leaves the scene," reasoned Father Levi and claimed "that he has lost his battle."[128] The pope was "irritated" and informed the Polish Bishops' Conference that he did not share these views.[129] A "high-ranking" Vatican source told the French ambassador to the Holy See that the piece was authorized by "nobody and without any motive" but was a personal vendetta by Father Levi who had unsuccessfully aspired to the directorship of the *L'Osservatore Romano*.[130] Be this as it may, Levi's resignation signaled that the Holy See did not wish to take too much distance from Lech Wałęsa and the larger moral struggle he represented.

A long and arduous road connected the papal trips of 1979 and 1983 with the 1989 fall of the Iron Curtain. Whereas the church and Solidarity had hoped for normalization in Poland following the official end of martial law in 1983, the situation on the ground resembled more a Soviet type of normality rather than a gradual progression toward liberal democracy. Pessimism, economic stagnation, and hopelessness ruled the country. Primate Glemp continued to pursue his cautious approach, preferring

réactions de la Curie Romaine sur le Voyage du Pape en Pologne," June 23, 1983, Box "Europe, 1981–1985, Saint-Siège, Box 5503," Folder "11–5 Saint-Siège Visite de Jean Paul II en Pologne 16–23 juin 1983," AD.

127. Memorandum, "Visite du Pape en Pologne—Evaluations du Saint-Siège," July 12, 1983, Box "Europe, 1981–1985, Saint-Siège, Box 5503," Folder "11–5 Relations Saint-Siège—Pologne," AD.

128. "Vatican newspaper says Wałęsa has lost his battle with regime," *The New York Times*, June 25, 1983.

129. Telegram, French Ambassador to the Holy See to Foreign Ministry, "Démission du rédacteur en chef de L'Osservatore Romano," June 27, 1983, Box "Europe, 1981–1985, Saint-Siège, Box 5503," Folder "11–5 Saint-Siège Visite de Jean Paul II en Pologne 16–23 juin 1983," AD.

130. Memorandum, "Visite du Pape en Pologne—Evaluations du Saint-Siège," July 5, 1983, Box "Europe, 1981–1985, Saint-Siège, Box 5503," Folder "11–5 Relations Saint-Siège—Pologne," AD.

dialogue with Jaruzelski over a policy of cultural resistance, as demanded by some of the younger, more radical Polish clergy. Vatican officials were increasingly unhappy about Primate Glemp, believing he might have gone too far with his non-confrontational attitude. Papal diplomats at the Secretariat of State reportedly considered him to be "an intelligent man, but too weak" and too easily impressed by General Jaruzelski.[131]

Pope John Paul II and Cardinal Glemp assumed two different postures. Pope John Paul took a forward-looking moral perspective which posited Europe's cultural, historical, and spiritual unity from the Atlantic to the Ural Mountains. The division of Europe, as triggered by the Yalta summit, was anachronistic from his point of view. The primate, who was in charge of day-to-day relations with the government, took a short-term pragmatic perspective that accepted and worked with the existing government. Cardinal Glemp was convinced that, for the time being, Poland would remain a member of the Warsaw Pact and that General Jaruzelski was better than possible alternative leaders who might pursue a more hostile approach.[132] Even if he personally might have preferred a tougher tone *vis-à-vis* Jaruzelski, the pope continued giving Cardinal Glemp a considerable margin for discretion for shaping relations with the government as the Polish church leader deemed it fit.

A different reaction to the "normalization" in Poland was exemplified by younger and more radical priests such as Father Jerzy Popiełuszko. The young priest from Warsaw personified a more outspoken way of cultural resistance to the regime than the approach adopted by Cardinal Glemp. The priest's masses and his message of non-violent resistance attracted thousands of people. In contrast to Cardinal Glemp's diplomatic style, Father Popiełuszko outlined a clearer moral choice to the Polish people: "Which side will you take? The side of good or the side of evil? Truth or falsehood? Love or hatred?"[133] On October 19, 1984, Fr. Popiełuszko was abducted and killed by officers of the Polish secret police. The pope condemned his disappearance as an "inhuman action that constitutes an act of tyranny against a priest and a violation of the dignity and the inalienable rights of the human person."[134]

131. Letter, French Ambassador to the Holy See to Foreign Ministry, "L'hiver polonais," January 25, 1984, Box "Europe, 1981–1985, Saint-Siège, Box 5503," Folder "11–5 Relations Saint-Siège—Pologne," AD.

132. Ibid.

133. Weigel, *Witness to Hope*, 460.

134. John Paul II, "Udienza Generale, October 24, 1984," n.p.

Following the line of the Polish bishops, however, the Holy See refrained from further escalation for the sake of maintaining working relations with the Polish government. In its assessment, the assassination was a deliberate attempt to provoke the church to make the strained relations between the church and the state even more difficult. As far as Monsignor Bačkis was concerned, the assassination of Father Popiełuszko was orchestrated by ultra-radical communists "with the blessing of an external actor who resides outside of Poland" with the purpose of "throwing a cadaver between the state and the church."[135]

In 1987, the pope visited Poland for the third and last time before the end of the Cold War. By praying at the tomb of Father Popiełuszko, he demonstrated his respect for the courage of this young priest. The Holy Father continued encouraging change through emphasizing human rights and affirming that the values of Solidarity remained intact and valid. As in 1983, political observers and some church circles wondered whether the pope's pilgrimage would "not merely give a propaganda boost to Jaruzelski's regime."[136] Through symbolic gestures, the Holy Father managed to resist General Jaruzelski. John Paul II maintained that the regime's demand for social peace was not enough. The state had to exist for society rather than *vice versa*. In a reference to the free West, John Paul quoted *Gaudium et Spes*: "One must pay tribute to those nations whose systems permit the largest possible number of citizens to take part in public life in a climate of genuine freedom."[137]

Conclusion

If Catholic teaching on peace provided the key theme for Pope Paul VI's promotion of peace during the Vietnam War, Catholicism's normative critique of communism was the guiding theme behind Pope John Paul

135. Telegram, French Embassy to the Holy See to Foreign Ministry, "Assassinat du P. Popieluszko," October 31, 1984, Box "Europe, 1981–1985, Pologne, Box 5431," Folder "2–14 L'enlèvement de l'Abbé Popieluszko et son assassinat le 19 Oct 1984," AD. Evidence suggests the killing was plotted by hawkish forces within the Polish Communist Party, possibly with support from the KGB, to embarrass Jaruzelski and provoke a new round of unrest that could justify further state repression. International and domestic pressure forced the Polish government to authorize a public trial, leading to the conviction of the three responsible police officers.

136. Luxmoore and Babiuch, *Vatican and the Red Flag*, 283.

137. Weigel, *Witness to Hope*, 544.

II's attempt to convert Poland from communism. Crucially, however, constant emphasis was given to positive affirmation of human rights, religious freedom, and the sovereign equality of nations rather than to a negative critique or demonization of communism. Catholic defense of human rights, especially the right to form trade unions, helped legitimate Solidarity. A focus on religious freedom helped the Polish church to present Christianity—rather than socialism—as the core of Polish identity. Catholic social doctrine's view on the sovereign equality of nations became a critique of Soviet hegemony over Central and Eastern Europe.

However, Catholic teaching on communism legitimates a variety of different options ranging from a position of total yet non-violent confrontation to constructive cooperation. To understand the way the Holy See lived out its norms on communism in its relationship with Poland, it is imperative to stress the Holy See's will to play a purely moral as opposed to political role, its strategic preference for prudence, and the personal Polish background of Pope John Paul II.

The Holy See aspires to present its role in global politics as being of a purely moral nature, with a view to stay above geopolitical divides and party politics and to promote Catholic social doctrine and natural law in a universally acceptable manner. In the previous chapter, this mediating factor was present when Pope Paul VI resisted US diplomatic pressure by refusing to side publicly with the White House during the Vietnam War. In the Polish case the Holy See's defensive stress of its moral role came across even stronger. Unlike Cardinal Casaroli, Cardinal Glemp, and papal diplomats, the Holy Father refrained from engaging in overly political analysis. His private diplomatic conversations as well as his public messages were full of references to key principles of Catholic social doctrine, particularly solidarity and human rights. The Holy See's commitment to playing a moral role also helps us understand its refusal to bless or criticize US economic sanctions against Poland and the Soviet Union despite diplomatic pressure coming from both Washington and Warsaw.

The Holy See also lived out Catholic teaching on communism rather prudently *vis-à-vis* the Polish regime, Solidarity, and the Reagan administration. Prudential considerations frequently served as a break on the intensity of the Holy See's statements and positions. During his papal visits, John Paul II made positive proposals for social justice rather than condemning communism. He proposed human rights, the right of Solidarity's existence, religious freedom, and social justice. He did not engage in inflammatory Cold War rhetoric. During the emergence of

Solidarity, throughout martial law, and in the years leading up to 1989, Vatican policy was guided by a balanced approach that would defend the legitimate cause of Solidarity but also promote moderation and caution lest to provide Warsaw or Moscow with excuses for violent crackdowns.

Similar to Pope Paul VI's peace diplomacy during the Vietnam War, but in sharp contrast to the UN conferences in Beijing and Cairo that will be discussed in the next chapter, the Holy See gave local bishops, clergy, and laypeople a considerable margin of discretion to live and apply Catholic social doctrine in accordance with local circumstances. Unlike Pope Pius XII, Pope John Paul II did not condemn Catholics in communist lands to become martyrs. Rather, he proposed an alternative—a Catholic—vision of the good life, stressed moral principles, and defended Solidarity and the 1980 Gdansk Accord. The pope maintained close personal ties to his people but was equally keen on engaging Polish leaders in personal dialogue.

The personal background of Pope John Paul II also affected the way the Holy See lived out Catholic teaching on communism toward Poland. John Paul II looked at the history of Poland as a history of suffering. On numerous occasions, he referred to the six million Poles who had lost their lives during the Second World War and German occupation. National self-determination, as a principle of both international law and Catholic social doctrine, played a great role in the pope's mind. This was a striking contrast to Pope Paul VI's reaction to the Vietnam War in which Catholic anti-communism marginalized any appreciation for Vietnamese self-determination. Pope John Paul II referred to the principle of self-determination to deter Soviet aggression in the period leading up to martial law. The Holy Father also used it to call for Polish "cultural self-determination" *vis-à-vis* the socialist government to strengthen the Catholic identity of the nation. As a Pole, John Paul II could connect to his audience much better and more intimately than any non-Polish pope could ever have done.

To conclude, the Holy See opted for a prudent approach to the series of social, political, and diplomatic crises that occurred in Poland. There was at best only a temporary convergence of interests between Washington and the Holy See rather than a deeper alliance based on shared values and principles. Even though the Holy See harbored friendly feelings for the Reagan administration and Solidarity, it cautiously guarded its independence from both. In a very tense period of the Cold War era, the Holy See refrained from frantically demonizing or constantly criticizing the communist "Other." This was a profound difference to President Reagan's "peace through strength" approach that attached a lot of value to inflammatory rhetoric and military build-up. The Holy See had no interest in escalating conflict. In fact, it maintained a critical posture toward communism and continued support for Solidarity without promoting a Western victory or risking a deterioration of East-West relations.

6

Lamenting Liberalism in Cairo and Beijing

Introduction

With the fall of the Iron Curtain in 1989 and the emancipation of Central and Eastern Europe from socialist rule, Western liberal democracy was praised as the model to be emulated by the rest of the world.[1] Whereas the West had hailed John Paul II for his contribution to the downfall of socialist regimes in Europe and authoritarian regimes in South America,[2] his ardent criticism of Western liberal societies, especially with regard to sexual ethics and family values, were now viewed as an unpleasant surprise. The same tradition which the pope drew upon in his critique of communism was suddenly denounced as scandalous and outdated by liberals and feminists alike. The secularization of Western elites, the 1992 election of US President Clinton, whose pro-choice abortion agenda was well known, and the pope's critique of a Western "culture of death," alienated the Holy See from the US government and liberal Western public opinion. After the disappearance of the specter of communism from Central and Eastern Europe, liberal secular relativism replaced communism as the Holy See's main "Other" in global politics.

A series of major UN conferences in the 1990s created a platform for the Holy See to put its critique of ethical relativism into diplomatic practice. The 1992 Earth Summit in Rio (UN Conference on Environment and Development), the 1993 World Conference on Human Rights

1. Fukuyama, *End of History*.

2. Philpott, "Catholic Wave."

in Vienna, the 1994 UN International Conference on Population and Development (ICPD), the 1995 World Summit for Social Development in Copenhagen, and the 1995 Fourth World Conference on Women (FWCW) in Beijing aimed at creating a holistic global consensus on several core aspects of development. Even though the final documents of these conferences were action plans rather than legally binding treaties, they constituted globally accepted norms and principles. Hence, the UN conferences of the 1990s were an important supranational forum which stipulated blueprints for actions and generated fierce negotiations about what norms constitute good global development.[3]

At both the 1994 ICPD in Cairo and the 1995 FWCW in Beijing, the Holy See only joined the international consensus in a partial manner, registering major reservations in the final conference documents. At both conferences, contending visions on sexuality, health, and development were advanced by the Holy See—supported to varying degrees by Muslim states and South American governments—against coalitions consisting of the US, the EU, and feminist NGOs. But by partially joining the consensus of Cairo and Beijing, the Holy See showed it wanted to constructively engage with and shape the outcome of the ICPD and the FWCW rather than boycott or sabotage the conferences.

Catholic Teaching on Abortion and Contraception

The Old Testament has nothing to say on abortion.[4] The New Testament contains "no direct and explicit calls to protect human life at its very beginning, specifically life not yet born." Expecting such a prohibition would be anachronistic since "the mere possibility of harming, attacking, or actually denying life in these circumstances [was] completely foreign to the religious and cultural way of thinking of the People of God."[5] The early church fathers, in opposition to existing abortion practices in the Greco-Roman world, developed a strong moral opposition to abortion which they began to frame as a sin forbidden by the fifth commandment "Thou shalt not kill." In order to maintain that abortion amounts to homicide, Saint Augustine affirmed that the unborn fetus already had been given a soul by God.[6] Only abortion after the moment of "ensoulment"

3. Buss, "Robes, Relics and Rights," 143.

4. Noonan, "Abortion and the Catholic Church," 67.

5. John Paul II, *Evangelium Vitae*, para. 44.

6. He remained agnostic about the exact moment "ensoulment" took place.

was covered by the fifth commandment, he argued. Hence, by the fifth century, Catholic teaching on abortion had been clearly set out. The early church fathers did not seek justifications that would have endorsed abortion in extraordinary circumstances. However, "there was a distinction accepted by some as to the unformed embryo, some consequent variation in the analysis of the sin, and local differences in the penance necessary to expiate it."[7]

One of the most important references in the history of Catholic teaching on abortion is the work of Saint Thomas Aquinas. In contrast to Saint Augustine, Saint Thomas argued that ensoulment did not take place at conception. Until there is "sensation and movement" there is only "seed" rather than "man." Abortion before ensoulment amounted to contraception. As such it was prohibited as well. Saint Thomas did not explicitly deal with the question of whether abortion was justifiable in order to save the life of the mother. In theory, it is possible to construct a favorable response to this question if one takes recourse to his principle of double effect. The good intention of saving one's life, such an argument would go, justifies the unintended consequence of the aborted life of the unborn. However, such a claim depends on how much importance one attaches to Saint Thomas's prohibition that "in no way is it lawful to kill the innocent." While it "cannot be said definitively how Thomas would have answered in these cases or in the case of therapeutic abortion to save the mother's life," James T. Noonan argues, a theoretical "basis for weighing the life of the embryo against other values had been laid."[8]

Drawing upon the tools of casuistry, some theologians began to question the absolute prohibition on abortion. The Jesuit Thomas Sánchez (1550–1610) justified abortion in order to save the life of the mother. Once the life of the mother was allowed to be weighed against the embryo's life, complex casuistic arguments emerged. In the following centuries, however, papal teaching would develop "to an almost absolute prohibition on abortion."[9] Reacting to the legalization of abortion in the Soviet Union, Pope Pius XI in his 1931 encyclical *Casti Conubii* firmly spoke out against "medical, social, or eugenic 'indication.'" He condemned abortion as "direct murder of the innocent" which "is against the precept of God and the law of nature: 'Thou shalt not kill.'"[10] This core

7. Noonan, "Abortion and the Catholic Church," 89–97.

8. Ibid., 104.

9. Ibid., 113.

10. Pius XI, *Casti Conubii*, paras. 63–64.

message continues to set the tone for Catholic teaching on abortion up to the current day.

The Second Vatican Council dealt with abortion only very briefly. *Gaudium et Spes* (1965) mentioned abortion only twice. Firstly, it listed abortion in a longer list of "infamies" that are "opposed to life" such as "murder, genocide, abortion, euthanasia or wilful self-destruction."[11] Secondly it condemned abortion and infanticide as "unspeakable crimes."[12] Pope Paul VI's 1968 encyclical *Humanae Vitae* specified that "the direct interruption of the generative process already begun and, above all, all direct abortion, even for therapeutic reasons, are to be absolutely excluded as lawful means of regulating the number of children."[13] The only two exceptions that survived the tightening of Catholic teaching were the cases of an ectopic pregnancy and a cancerous uterus. In both cases, "indirect" abortion is permissible even if medical procedures result in the loss of the unborn child.[14]

The church's teaching on contraception is also very complex and the result of a 2,000-year-long theological debate, encounters with other cultures, and internal power struggles. The Old Testament attached a lot of importance to the production of offspring. The New Testament, on the other hand, praised voluntary celibacy for the sake of God's kingdom, as practiced by Jesus Christ and Saint Paul. Apart from the latter's condemnation of "unnatural" sexual practices, the New Testament did not explicitly refer to birth control methods. In contrast to a negative attitude toward human sexuality by Gnostic thinkers, early church fathers such as Clemens of Alexandria emphasized the procreative function of sexuality in a positive light.[15]

Saint Augustine articulated the most important early expression of Christian opposition to contraception. Challenging Manichaeism's[16] appraisal of sex without offspring, he condemned contraception by defining good sexual intercourse strictly in relation to the possibility of begetting children. Augustine dismissed sexual relations which were purely

11. Paul VI, *Gaudium et Spes*, para. 27.

12. Ibid., para. 51.

13. Paul VI, *Humanae Vitae*, para. 14.

14. On the theological debate about these exceptions see Noonan, "Abortion and the Catholic Church," 39–42.

15. Jütte, *Lust ohne Last*, 36–47.

16. Manichaeism was founded by the Persian prophet Mani (216–76). Its worldview posited a fundamental dualist struggle between good and evil. Saint Augustine adhered to Manichaeism before his conversion to Christianity.

intended for pleasure and dismissed contraceptive or abortive measures as "cruelful lust." "With Augustine," Robert Jütte argues, "the Christian ban on contraception adopts its classical justification and form."[17] In the Middle Ages, teaching on contraception became even stricter. Practices such as *coitus interruptus*, oral sex, and anal sex were all punished by several years of penitence. The church's fight against Catharism, a religious sect which valued sexual desire rather than procreation, helped to reify the church's infamous "theology of the sinful flesh." During the Reformation, Martin Luther was one of the first major theologians to assert that sexual pleasure within marriage could have a positive function. However, even Luther did not attach intrinsic value to sexual pleasure but only saw it as a "cure" for temptations to break the rule of chastity.[18]

Following the liberalization of civil laws on birth control in most Western countries in the nineteenth century, the Catholic Church became one of the last major societal forces to uphold the ban on artificial contraception. In *Casti Conubii*, Pope Pius reacted to the Anglican Church's decision to relax existing prohibitions on birth control methods. The pope asserted that the "conjugal act is destined primarily by nature for the begetting of children, those who in exercising it deliberately frustrate its natural power and purpose sin against nature and commit a deed which is shameful and intrinsically vicious."[19]

The Second Vatican Council did not deal with the delicate issue of birth control. In 1963, Pope John XXIII created a "Pontifical Commission on Population, Family, and Birth-rate." Pope Paul VI would later instruct its members to re-examine the issue of contraception and to assess whether or not Catholics could legitimately use the birth control pill which had entered the global market in the 1960s. The commission's "majority report" concluded that the "licitness of a contraceptive intervention . . . can be affirmed in continuity with the Church's tradition and the supreme Magisterium's declarations about the goods of matrimony." It proposed that the Holy Father should soon speak out on the topic.[20] Cardinal Alfredo Ottaviani, the powerful conservative prefect of the Congregation of the Doctrine of Faith, was alarmed about this recommendation. He commissioned a US member of the papal commission,

17. Jütte, *Contraception*, 25–26.

18. Ibid., 75–89.

19. Pius XI, *Casti Conubii*, para. 54.

20. "About John C. Ford, S.J." (n.p.) on website in memory of John C. Ford that also contains other illuminating documents relating to the papal birth control commission.

Father John C. Ford, to prepare a critical rebuttal.[21] Against the hopes of a vast majority of Catholics and theologians in Western Europe and the US, Ford's "minority" view prevailed.

In *Humanae Vitae*, Pope Paul VI vigorously defended the teaching of *Casti Conubii.* Alluding to the commission's "majority report" which had been leaked to the press, the pope stated that he did not consider its conclusions "definitive and absolutely certain."[22] It was not enough that the "totality of married life"[23] was ordered toward procreation, as liberal Catholics would argue. Rather, "each and every marital act must of necessity retain its intrinsic relationship to the procreation of human life."[24] The pope prohibited "any action which either before, at the moment of, or after sexual intercourse, is specifically intended to prevent procreation—whether as an end or as a means."[25] He only permitted the "natural cycle" method of contraception.[26] The Holy Father anticipated widespread resistance; but he called upon Catholics to respond to the church's teaching on contraception heroically and with self-discipline. For those who believed that the Second Vatican Council would usher in a liberalization of the church's teaching on sexual ethics, *Humanae Vitae* was a sobering turning point.

John Paul II on Abortion and Contraception

Thanks to his pastoral work with young people as a priest, Pope John Paul II was well aware of the moral difficulties many Catholics had with the sexual ethics of their church. Unlike so many liberal Catholic priests who either objected to the teaching of *Humanae Vitae* or withdrew into a "don't ask/don't tell" position, the Holy Father wrote extensively on the topic of human sexuality and marriage. Entering into "one of the minefields of contemporary Catholic life," the then Auxiliary Bishop Karol Wojtyła defended traditional Catholic teaching from a personalist perspective. He emphasized the need of "loving rather than using" other

21. See "About John C. Ford, S.J." See also Slevin, "New Birth Control Commission Papers" as well as Kaiser, *Encyclical That Never Was*, and McClory, *Turning Point.*

22. Paul VI, *Humanae Vitae*, paras. 5–6.

23. Ibid., para. 3.

24. Ibid., para. 11.

25. Ibid., para. 14.

26. Ibid., para. 16.

people, and affirmed that the natural cycle method was the only morally appropriate method of birth regulation.[27]

As Bishop of Rome, Pope Wojtyła made Catholic teaching on sexuality and marriage a pastoral priority of his early pontificate. In the course of 129 weekly general audiences, spread over four years, he developed his "Theology of the Body." The pope meditated on the corporal embodiedness of the human person and the connection between the unitive and the procreative functions of marriage. He shifted the moral focus away from the question "What am I forbidden to do?" to "How do I live a life of sexual love that conforms with my dignity as a human person?"[28] Notwithstanding his attempt to propose a positive portrayal of sexual ethics, the pope's official teaching on abortion and contraception fully reaffirmed traditional Catholic positions. The 1981 Apostolic Exhortation *Familiaris Consortio* deplored that Catholic family life was under threat due to a "growing number of divorces; the scourge of abortion; the ever more frequent recourse to sterilization" as well as "the appearance of a truly contraceptive mentality."[29]

By the time of the UN conferences in Cairo and Beijing in the mid-1990s, the pope's critique of Western liberal culture had reached its climax. Understanding that the "Church's Magisterium is often chided for being behind the times and closed to the promptings of the spirit of modern times," the pope purposefully called upon the church to deliberately "swim against the tide." His 1994 *Letter to the Families* emphasized the importance of "responsible fatherhood and motherhood." Sex had to retain its intrinsic linkage with procreation so that no person can "hide behind expressions such as: 'I don't know,' 'I didn't want it,' or 'you're the one who wanted it'" when a child is conceived.[30]

His 1995 encyclical *Evangelium Vitae* was a theological attack on threats to human life. The pope deplored how

> broad sectors of public opinion justify certain crimes against life in the name of the rights of individual freedom, and on this basis they claim not only exemption from punishment but even authorization by the State, so that these things can be done with

27. Weigel, *Witness to Hope*, 140–44. See also John Paul II, *Love and Responsibility*.

28. Weigel, *Witness to Hope*, 334–43.

29. John Paul II, *Familiaris Consortio*, para. 6.

30. John Paul II, "Letter to Families," para. 12.

> total freedom and indeed with the free assistance of health-care systems.[31]

Moreover, John Paul II was upset about the larger moral problem "that conscience itself, darkened as it were by such widespread conditioning, is finding it increasingly difficult to distinguish between good and evil in what concerns the basic value of human life."[32] In the year following the heated abortion debates in Cairo, the pope claimed that a "culture of death" that privileged efficiency over loving acceptance was darkening Western society "to the point of damaging and distorting, at the international level, relations between peoples and States."[33] The Holy Father noted that this Western "culture of death" paradoxically coexists with a strong liberal human rights rhetoric. He blamed exaggerated individualism, utilitarianism, a disconnect between freedom and truth, secularism, and practical materialism for this "remarkable contradiction."[34] On a more positive side, however, Pope John Paul also praised the global anti-war movement, the opposition to the death penalty, and the growing global concern about the environment as "signs of hope."[35] Despite a sharper rhetoric, there remained enduring convergences between Catholic social doctrine and contemporary Western liberal projects even if they were not necessarily in the spotlight of public attention.

John Paul II contrasted the Catholic concept of "responsible parenthood" with a growing "contraceptive mentality" which, he contended, did not reduce the need for abortion but actually helped making abortion a "temptation" once unwanted life is conceived. Even though abortion and contraception are "specifically different evils" they are "often closely connected" because they are both rooted in a "hedonistic mentality unwilling to accept responsibility in matters of sexuality, and they imply a self-centered concept of freedom, which regards procreation as an obstacle to personal fulfilment. The life which could result from a sexual encounter thus becomes an enemy to be avoided at all costs, and abortion becomes the only possible decisive response to failed contraception."[36]

31. John Paul II, *Evangelium Vitae*, para. 4.
32. Ibid., para. 4.
33. Ibid., para. 12.
34. Ibid., paras. 18–24.
35. Ibid., paras. 18–27.
36. Ibid., para. 13.

Finally, on the topic of abortion, the pope invoked his highest teaching authority, declaring

> that direct abortion, that is, abortion willed as an end or as a means, always constitutes a grave moral disorder, since it is the deliberate killing of an innocent human being. This doctrine is based upon the natural law and upon the written Word of God, is transmitted by the Church's Tradition and taught by the ordinary and universal Magisterium . . . No circumstance, no purpose, no law whatsoever can ever make licit an act which is intrinsically illicit, since it is contrary to the Law of God which is written in every human heart, knowable by reason itself, and proclaimed by the Church.[37]

To sum up, Pope John Paul II continued and actually reified the traditional Catholic ban on contraception and abortion even as he tried to move away from a negative theology of the sinful flesh toward a positive theology of the body. He neither saw a possibility nor a necessity to change Catholic teaching. Rather, he presented a sharp contrast between a secular, Western, liberal "culture of death" and an alternative "culture of life" based on the Gospel and natural law.

Criticizing Abortion and Contraception in Cairo

The ICPD took place in Cairo from September 5–13, 1994. It was the third major UN conference on the topic of population following the 1974 World Population Conference in Bucharest and the 1984 International Conference on Population in Mexico City. The purpose of the Cairo conference was to form a new international consensus on population policy that would move away from a top-down approach with predefined population targets, to a bottom-up approach focusing on the needs of the human person. The lengthy preparatory process began in 1989 and covered more than twenty meetings, climaxing in three meetings of the Preparatory Committee held in New York.[38] The UN's decision to create an entirely new consensus rather than simply reevaluate and update previous action plans agreed upon in Bucharest and Mexico, created an opportunity for different players to push their respective agendas. The

37. Ibid., paras. 57, 62.

38. PrepCom I in March 1991, PrepCom II in May 1993, and PrepCom III in April 1994. See Singh, *Creating a New Consensus on Population*.

final outcome of the preparatory process was a 113-page Draft Program of Action that was submitted for discussion, negotiation, and approval by the ICPD.[39] Even though a consensus was reached on 90 percent of the draft action program, the remaining 10 percent of controversial content caused a lot of furor, particularly on the issue of abortion.

In 1993, the incoming Clinton administration reversed President Reagan's "Mexico City policy" that prevented the US Agency of International Development to fund NGOs that help perform or promote information on abortion. This reversal transformed the international balance of power in favor of easier access to abortion. With President Clinton's liberal views on abortion and contraception, pro-choice NGOs received a boost in their finances, morale, and expectations. The International Federation of Planned Parenthood (IFPP) and the United Nations Population Fund, whose funding the Reagan administration previously had cut off, were now promised renewed financial support by the US government.[40] In March 1993, a leaked US cable revealed that the Clinton administration believed that "access to safe, legal and voluntary abortion" was a "fundamental right of all women."[41] In the course of the preparatory phase, the US backed down from this assertion but nevertheless pushed for granting women access to "the full range of reproductive health care services, including abortion."[42] The Holy See was alarmed.

The NGO gathering held alongside the Cairo conference attracted over 4,200 representatives of over 1,500 NGOs from 133 countries.[43] During the preparatory phase, their activities would include networking, media relations, lobbying government delegations, and placing representatives as members of national delegations.[44] Major feminist groups formed an effective "Women's Caucus" that successfully lobbied for women's issues during the preparatory process, especially for access

39. United Nations, "Draft Programme of Action of the International Conference on Population and Development."

40. McIntosh and Finkle, "Cairo Conference," 239–42.

41. Ibid., 245–46.

42. Mann, "The Front Lines of the Population War," *The Washington Post*, August 31, 1994. The quotation is from former Senator Timothy Wirth who was in charge of the US negotiation team during the Cairo process.

43. Singh, *Creating a New Consensus*, 129.

44. Higer, "International Women's Activism"; McIntosh and Finkle, "Cairo Conference," 235–39.

to contraceptives and safe abortion.[45] The President of the IFPP, the Ghanaian Fred Sai, was elected Chairman of PrepCom II. As leader of the world's most prominent pro-choice movement he was a thorn in the side of the Holy See. The papal delegates became increasingly alarmed by the strength of the mostly secular pro-choice NGO movement. A confidential report of the Holy See's delegation to PrepCom II deplored the absence of NGOs which "were supportive of the position of the Holy See and capable of effectively articulating that position . . . This is a shortcoming which should immediately be addressed."[46]

The convergence of interests between the US, the IPFF, and the international women's movement on the issues of contraception and abortion troubled the Holy See. Its "non-member state" permanent observer status at the UN allowed the Holy See to fully participate in the ICPD process. This is because international UN conferences are open to all interested "states" rather than simply to UN member states. While the Holy See does not have the right to vote in the UN General Assembly, it has full voting rights during UN conferences. "The UN's commitment to consensus provides the Holy See with a quasi-veto at conferences," explained Yasmin Abdullah, "the adoption of any measure is substantially contingent upon Vatican approval."[47]

Having already abstained from joining the international consensus at the 1974 Bucharest and the 1984 Mexico City population conferences, it was highly questionable whether the Holy See would join the Cairo consensus at all. In the final draft document, the Holy See saw numerous threats to Catholic family values and human life, especially in attempts to define the "reproductive freedom" of women in a way that included

45. Higer, "International Women's Activism," 132–38.

46. "Report of the Delegation of the Holy See to the Second Session of the Preparatory Committee for the International Conference on Population and Development," undated, Box "2108/C398–1992 ONU.Conferenze International Conference on Population and Development, Il Cairo: 5–13 Sett, 1994 (Draft Final Document, Documenti vari della Conferenza, Report of the International Conference)," Folder "Cairo Prep Conf Statements," Documentation Center of the Pontifical Council for Justice and Peace (PCJP). The same report also asserts that Chairman Fred Sai's "opposition to the Holy See is well known."

47. Abdullah, "Holy See at United Nations Conferences," 1837–44. Her article challenges the legitimacy of the Holy See's status at the UN and provides an academic elaboration of political arguments that feminists had continuously made against the Holy See during both the Cairo and the Beijing process.

access to abortion services.[48] During the negotiation process, the Holy See could count on Central and South American countries—from Guatemala, Nicaragua, Honduras, Chile, and Argentina—whose traditional Catholic electorates predisposed their governments to supporting the position of the Vatican.

The Holy See identified Muslim governments as other potential partners for fighting abortion, defending religious values, and promoting traditional family values. During PrepCom II, the Holy See delegation noted that whereas "Muslim countries tend to be very protective of the rights of parents over the education and upbringing of children, they did not tend to be highly vocal in this." Most Arab delegations only displayed "a certain sympathy" toward the Holy See without being under more explicit instructions from their respective governments.[49] The Holy See therefore intensified dialogue in the run-up to Cairo by engaging several Muslim countries in diplomatic dialogue, including Libya and Iran.[50]

While the liberal Western press warned of a new "holy and explosive alliance,"[51] the convergence of interests between the Holy See and Muslim states was limited to a shared rejection of abortion as a method of family planning and an insistence that sexual activity should be confined to marriage. In contrast to the Vatican, the latter supported the use of contraceptives and contraception and permitted abortion in well-defined situations.[52] Cardinal Renato Martino[53] who was in charge of the Holy See delegation at the ICPD remembers that he "had the best dialogue

48. Sodano, "Address by His Eminence Angelo Cardinal Sodano."

49. "Report of the Delegation of the Holy See to the Second Session of the Preparatory Committee for the International Conference on Population and Development," undated, Box "2108/C398–1992 ONU.Conferenze International Conference on Population and Development, Il Cairo: 5–13 Sett, 1994 (Draft Final Document, Documenti vari della Conferenza, Report of the International Conference)," Folder "Cairo Prep Conf Statements," PCJP.

50. Tagliabue, "Vatican Seeks Islamic Allies in U.N. Population Dispute," *The New York Times*, August 18, 1994.

51. Cruise O'Brien, "A Holy and Explosive Alliance," *The Independent*, August 26, 1994. See also "Holy Alliance," *The Globe and Mail*, August 30, 1994; Fisk, "'Holy Alliance' Tries to Wreck Birth-Control Conference," *The Independent*, August 31, 1994.

52. Bowen, "Abortion, Islam, and the 1994 Cairo Population Conference," 178–80.

53. Renato Raffaele Martino was appointed the Holy See's Permanent Observer at the United Nations in New York in 1986. In 2002, he became President of the Pontifical Council for Justice and Peace (until 2009), and was elevated to the rank of cardinal. In addition, he also served as President of the Pontifical Council for the Pastoral Care of Migrants and Itinerant People between 2006 and 2009.

with the Muslims" even though, he admits, Muslim governments were perhaps more interested in the political opportunity of bandwagoning with the Vatican in order to criticize the West than in the moral merits of the underlying theological arguments.[54]

Given the procedural nature of international conferences, the Holy See had to operationalize its deeper theological concerns by identifying which phrases and suggestions—referred to as "language" in UN jargon—were unacceptable and which ones were desirable. Negotiations inside and outside preparatory conferences aimed at finding a consensus on the structure and content of the draft action program. Controversial language was bracketed and left for negotiation during the ICPD itself. The Holy See's assessment of the emerging draft document was very negative. Pope John Paul II thought the Cairo draft was a "disturbing surprise." He had the "troubling impression" that the document was imposing "a life-style typical of certain fringes within developed societies, societies which are materially rich and secularized."[55] The Holy See's critique focused on various issue areas.

Abortion was the priority issue for the Holy See. The Holy See did everything it could to undermine efforts that pushed for wider access to, or even an international right to, abortion. "We had to promote life first," Archbishop Martino is still convinced. "If we don't promote life, all the rest is nothing."[56] The Holy See opposed attempts to insert abortion into the conference text as a "means of family planning" or as a part of women's health. In fact, the Holy See's delegation to PrepCom II warned that the "continually re-proposed entree for abortion as an agenda item for the ICPD is as a public health issue wherein women are said to be subjected to 'unsafe' abortions when they wish to exercise their 'human right' to terminate their pregnancies." The Holy See objected to the consideration of abortion as an integral part of "reproductive health."[57] It also

54. Personal interview with Cardinal Renato Martino, President-Emeritus of the Pontifical Council for Justice and Peace, Vatican, March 17, 2012; Bowen, "Abortion, Islam, and the 1994 Cairo Population Conference," 178–80.

55. John Paul II, "Letter of His Holiness Pope John Paul II to the World's Heads of State," n.p.

56. Personal interview with Cardinal Renato Martino, President-Emeritus of the Pontifical Council for Justice and Peace, Vatican, March 17, 2012.

57. "Report of the Delegation of the Holy See to the Second Session of the Preparatory Committee for the International Conference on Population and Development," undated, Box "2108/C398–1992 ONU.Conferenze International Conference on Population and Development, Il Cairo: 5–13 Sett, 1994 (Draft Final Document, Documenti

disagreed with a compromise proposal that held that in circumstances where abortion is legal, it should be safe.

In the Vatican's view, the health risks posed by illegal abortion in no way justified the death of the unborn person. It feared that the new buzz word "reproductive health" implied a right to abortion since the concept was defined as "rights . . . to safe, effective, affordable and acceptable means of fertility regulation of their choice." The World Health Organization's official definition of "fertility regulation," the Holy See pointed out, includes abortion. For this reason it bracketed all references to "reproductive health" during the drafting process. Moreover, the Holy See pushed for upholding recommendation 18(e) of the 1984 Mexico City Population Conference which asserted that "abortion should in no case be promoted as a means of family planning."[58] Of course, pro-choice forces would bracket this recommendation during the preparatory negotiations.

In line with its traditional teaching, the Holy See opposed the promotion of artificial contraceptives. The Holy Father warned the ICPD's Secretary General, Nafis Sadik, that the separation of "the unitive and procreative dimensions of marital intercourse" was "contrary to the moral law" as "inscribed on the human heart."[59] Supporting or even simply condoning the use of contraceptives, the Holy See warned, could increase sexual promiscuity among adolescents. At every relevant occasion during the preparatory process the Holy See instead advocated responsible parenthood. This concept grants spouses the autonomy to make decisions "concerning the spacing of births and the number of children" yet only endorses natural methods of fertility regulation.

Internal deliberations show that the Holy See delegation to PrepCom II was aware that "there can be no fully satisfactory 'win'" on the contraception issue due to the "'common wisdom' currently pushed by the Western media that the primary solution to the world's economic, social, [and] environmental problems is contraceptive." Realizing that negotiating an outright rejection of artificial contraceptive methods

---

vari della Conferenza, Report of the International Conference)," Folder "Cairo Prep Conf Statements," PCJP.

58. Navarro-Valls, "Briefing by Dr. Joaquín Navarro-Valls, Director of the Holy See Press Office, on the Draft Program of the International Conference on Population and Development," 304–5.

59. John Paul II, "Message of His Holiness Pope John Paul II to Mrs. Nafis Sadik," para. 5.

would be impossible, the Holy See's pragmatic strategy was to dilute the dominant draft language by replacing "contraceptive" language with "responsible planning of family size and spacing of births" or simply with "family planning."[60]

The Holy See believed that the draft document was also a dangerous threat for Catholic family values. Particularly, it objected to a prevailing "tendency to qualify the term family with phrases like 'in all its forms' and to refer to the family not as 'the' but only as 'a' basic unit of society, thereby denigrating the special recognition which the family deserves." The Holy See regretted that "an institution as natural, fundamental and universal as marriage is practically absent" from the draft.[61] In addition, the Holy See also actively lobbied for parental control over the education of adolescents, especially with regard to sexual education.

The Holy See's negotiating position during the preparatory process went well beyond abortion, contraception, and family values as it also stressed the question of international migration and the well-being of asylum seekers, migrants, and refugees. It asked for recognition of "the right to family reunification" and for better "access to citizenship and its benefits for those who have resided for a long time in the host country, and especially for the second generation of migrants who have grown up there."[62] Moreover, the Holy See argued for a stronger emphasis on development.[63] The Holy See's interest in championing the rights of migrants and making globalization work better for the global poor remained overshadowed, though, by the quarrel over abortion, contraception, and family values.

The global media was only too keen to magnify the conflict. Liberal newspapers such as *The New York Times*, *The Guardian*, *The Washington Post*, or *The Independent* continuously insinuated that a "fundamentalist"

60. "Report of the Delegation of the Holy See to the Second Session of the Preparatory Committee for the International Conference on Population and Development," undated, Box "2108/C398–1992 ONU.Conferenze International Conference on Population and Development, Il Cairo: 5–13 Sett, 1994 (Draft Final Document, Documenti vari della Conferenza, Report of the International Conference)," Folder "Cairo Prep Conf Statements," PCJP.

61. There was no sustained controversy surrounding same-sex marriage during the Cairo process—such battles have been more characteristic of the twenty-first century than the early 1990s. See Holy See, "National Report of the Holy See," 853.

62. Ibid., 853.

63. Tauran, "Statement by His Excellency Archbishop Jean-Louis Tauran, Secretary for Relations with States of the Holy See: The Position of the Holy See."

Vatican turned the Cairo conference into a battleground on abortion. The Vatican's counternarrative, as reflected in public statements, op-eds in the *L'Osservatore Romano*, or in conservative US newspapers such as *The Washington Times,* was a mirror image of the liberal critique which supported the Holy See's struggle against a "decadent" West. Even if media portrayals and dominant narratives had a distorting effect, this cannot hide the fact that there was a real and substantive political clash between two contending ethical positions: a liberal perspective on abortion which privileges the safety of the mother, and a Catholic perspective which privileges the inviolability of the life of the unborn fetus.

The Holy See mobilized its vast global network and received the support of a variety of church actors. The Latin American Episcopal Council, in a letter to the ICPD's Secretary General rejected a new "contraceptive imperialism" that rich Western countries wanted to impose to "control the poor population." It demanded that international funds earmarked for family planning be redirected toward education.[64] Lobbying efforts of US bishops put domestic pressure on the Clinton administration. In April 1994, the Holy See's delegation to PrepCom III recommended the Holy See's Secretariat of State to contact Archbishop Keeler, the President of the US Bishops' Conference, "to encourage him to instruct the competent offices of the Episcopal Conference to get in touch with the Delegation, in order to coordinate any messages or responses to the American authorities."[65] A month later, a letter signed by six US cardinals and Archbishop Keeler on the eve of a visit to the Vatican by President Clinton urged his administration "to shun the advice of those who would apply pressure on developing nations to mandate abortion as a condition for receiving aid from other countries."[66] "We worked hard, we fought, we brought together 43 delegatations," Archbishop Martino remembers. He highlights that they came from "Africa, Latin America, and Asia, *not* from Europe and North America."[67]

64. Latin-American Episcopal Council, "Letter of the Latin-American Episcopal Council (CELAM) to Mrs. Nafis Sadik," 783.

65. Unsigned memorandum, "Appunto," April 17, 1994. Box "2108/C398–1992, ONU.Conferenze, International Conf. on Population and Development, Il Cairo 5–13.9.1994 (Documenti vari della Conferenza, Interventi della Delegazione Vaticana, ICPD Newsletter)," Folder "Cairo (and regional confs) Holy See Statements," PCJP.

66. "United States Cardinals and Conference President's Letter to President William Clinton," 788.

67. Personal interview with Cardinal Renato Martino, President-Emeritus of the Pontifical Council for Justice and Peace, Vatican, March 17, 2012.

The opening session in Cairo increased the Holy See's alert. The Norwegian Prime Minister, Gro Harlem Brundtland, implicitly criticized the Holy See by categorizing religion as a "major obstacle. This happens when family planning is made the moral issue." She contended that, "morality becomes hypocrisy if it means accepting mothers suffering or dying in connection with unwanted pregnancies and illegal abortions—and unwanted children living in misery."[68] In his opening speech, Archbishop Martino pushed back. He warned that if "current bracketed texts be approved, they would endorse 'pregnancy termination' without setting any limits, any criteria or any restrictions on such practices, as integral parts of reproductive health services." A "right to abortion," he argued, would be a dangerous legal innovation that would be contrary to most constitutional and legislative positions and alien to the sensitivities of vast numbers of persons, believers and unbelievers alike."[69]

As the Holy See's ethical stance on abortion, contraception, and family values was non-negotiable, the question in Cairo was not whether the Holy See would change its teachings but how far it would push to advance them in the face of powerful adversity. In fact, the Holy See did not attach equal importance to all three issues. Above all, its strategy prioritized ruling out abortion as a means of family planning by upholding the agreement of the 1984 Mexico City Population Conference that "[i]n no case should abortion be promoted as a method of family planning." Once this goal was achieved, the Holy See was willing to remove the brackets around the term "family planning." It did, however, reserve its right to interpret this ambiguous concept in accordance with Catholic teaching.

The EU suggested a compromise solution that ruled out abortion as a family planning method while urging that governments deal with "abortion as a major public health concern."[70] Together with Honduras, El Salvador, Guatemala, Ecuador, and Malta, the Holy See was able to op-

68. "Prime Minister Gro Harlem Brundtland, Key Note Address to the International Conference on Population and Development, Cairo, 5 September 1994," Box "ONU.Conferenze International Conference on Population and Development, Il Cairo: 5–13 Sett. 1994 (Draft Final Document, Documenti vari della Conferenza, Report of the International Conference)," Folder "Cairo, Conference Statements," PCJP.

69. Martino, "Statement by His Excellency Archbishop R. Martino, Apostolic Nuncio, Permanent Observer of the Holy See to the United Nations and Head of the Delegation of the Holy See to the International Conference on Population and Development, Cairo, 7 September 1994."

70. Maddox and Nicholson, "EU Delegates Battle to Head off Abortion Row," *Financial Times*, September 5, 1994.

pose the compromise for a while.[71] At this phase of the negotiations the much evoked "alliance" between the Holy See and Muslim governments broke down as Indonesia, Pakistan, Iran, and Egypt supported the compromise.[72] While the delegations of these predominantly Muslim countries shared the Holy See's stance on family and religious values, they supported the use of contraceptives and the use of abortion in well-defined situations.[73]

"Does the Vatican rule the world?" the Egyptian population minister asked. "If they are not going to negotiate, why did they come?"[74] The "Vatican's willingness to delay an international forum in order to make a point on abortion," *The New York Times* reported, "has isolated it from several large Islamic nations where it might have expected to find some support."[75] An ICPD spokesperson even threatened to drop the UN's traditional quest for unanimity in favor of a "general agreement" by the majority of UN member states. Lionel Hurst of Antigua, the Vice-Chairman of the committee who was in charge of the abortion negotiations predicted that, in such a scenario, the Vatican would be "voted down" with an "overwhelming majority."[76]

Ultimately, the Holy See decided to only give its partial assent to the Cairo final document. It went for a "pick and choose" approach by joining the consensus only on the chapters with which it agreed.[77] Among the

71. Murphy, "Shaky Compromise on Abortion Unravels at Population Conference," *The Gazette*, September 8, 1994.

72. Lancaster and Rensberger, "Abortion Objections Stall Forum," *The Washington Post*, September 7, 1994; Crossette, "Vatican Holds up Abortion Debate at Talks in Cairo," *The New York Times*, September 8, 1994.

73. Bowen, "Abortion, Islam, and the 1994 Cairo Population Conference."

74. Nicholson, "Vatican Makes Waves at Cairo Conference," *Financial Times*, September 8, 1994.

75. Crossette, "Vatican Holds up Abortion Debate at Talks in Cairo," *The New York Times*, September 8, 1994.

76. "U.N. Says Vatican Camp may be 'Voted Down' on Abortion." *Deutsche Presse-Agentur*, September 9, 1994.

77. The Holy See did join the consensus on: Principles, Chapter V (Family), Chapter III (Population, Sustained Economic Growth and Sustainable Development), Chapter IV (Gender Equality, Equity and Empowerment of Women), and Chapters IX and X (Migration Issues). The Holy See did not join the Consensus on Chapter VII (Reproductive Rights and Reproductive Health), Chapter VIII (Health, Morbidity, and Mortality), and the operative chapters XII-XVI, which deal with research, national action, international cooperation, partnership with the NGO community, and follow-up activities. See Martino, "Statement by His Excellency Archbishop R.

"good" outcomes of the conference, Archbishop Martino's closing speech mentioned the recognition of the importance of marriage, women's advancement through education, the consensus on migration, increased respect for religious and cultural beliefs, and a general new appreciation for women's health. However, he strongly deplored that the draft recognized "abortion as a dimension of population policy, and, indeed of primary health care, even though it does stress that abortion should not be promoted as means of family planning." Moreover, the Holy See feared that the chapters on reproductive rights and health could be seen as "accepting extra-marital sexual activity, especially among adolescents" and as supportive of the view "that abortion services belong within primary health care as a method of choice."[78]

The Holy See submitted lengthy reservations and asked for their inclusion into the final conference report, along with its closing speech. The Holy See strictly limited its understanding of the terms "sexual health," "sexual rights," "reproductive health," and "reproductive rights" to married couples only, as opposed to individuals, adolescents, or nonmarried couples. The Holy See also stressed that it does not consider abortion or access to abortion as a dimension of these terms. With regard to family planning services, the Holy See defined terms such as "contraception," "family planning," or "widest range of family planning services" exclusively in relation to the natural cycle method of contraception.[79]

The Holy See's decision to withhold assent rather than preventing a compromise highlights both the freedom and the constraints the Holy See possesses in living out Catholic social doctrine. Even on a topic that seemingly does not allow for any compromise, the Holy See had different policy options available. By attending the conference in the first place rather than boycotting it, as Saudi Arabia did, the Holy See retained and exercised the possibility of shaping the agenda and the outcome of the ICPD. Looking back, Cardinal Martino adamantly defends this pragmatic decision: "We would not have made an impact if we had boycotted the conference." By actively engaging and shaping the Cairo process, he says, "we got more than reservations, we helped create substantial change." The change was successful as, at major international UN conferences, the

Martino, Apostolic Nuncio, Permanent Observer of the Holy See to the United Nations and Head of the Delegation of the Holy See at the Concluding Session," 783.

78. Ibid., 783.

79. Holy See, "Reservations of the Holy See," 321.

"abortion language has never been re-opened."[80] Its insistence that abortion not be an integral part of family planning was a real achievement for the Holy See. However, by realizing when the moment had come that continued principled opposition would no longer serve a useful purpose, the Holy See demonstrated it also acted pragmatically rather than simply ideologically.

Fine-tuning Feminism in Beijing

The FWCW, organized under the auspices of the UN, took place in Beijing from September 4–15, 1995. Its theme was "Action for Equality, Development and Peace." Previous world conferences had taken place in Mexico City (1975), Copenhagen (1980), and Nairobi (1985). These conferences marked the beginning, middle, and end of the 1976–1985 UN Decade for Women.[81] The purpose of the FWCW was to discuss women's rights, empowerment of women, and violence against women. The preparation phase for the Beijing process included interregional conferences and expert group meetings. The Holy See attended the numerous preparatory conferences with a view to following and shaping the drafting of the final action plan. While the most divisive issue of the Cairo process had been abortion, controversies during the Beijing process focused on the concept of gender. The relevant group of international stakeholders remained similar even though the relationship between their interests had changed.

The US delegation continued maintaining close relations with the international women's movement. The feminist leader Bella Abzug, for example, was a paid consultant on the team of Timothy Wirth who remained the main US negotiator during the Beijing process.[82] This time, given the forthcoming 1996 presidential elections, the Clinton administration did not want to alienate Catholic voters. Hence, there were no prominent public clashes between the US and the Holy See during the Beijing process. The US ambassador to the Holy See, Raymond Flynn,

80. Personal interview with Cardinal Renato Martino, President-Emeritus of the Pontifical Council for Justice and Peace, Vatican, March 17, 2012.

81. Pietilä, *Unfinished Story*, 42–45.

82. Archibald, "Feminists Win Word War in Conference Platform," *The Washington Times*, August 2, 1995.

argued that this was largely due to successful diplomatic groundwork done by his embassy in Rome.[83]

Ambassador Flynn claims that he had "lobbied heavily" for the appointment of Harvard law professor Mary Ann Glendon as head of the Holy See Delegation to the Beijing conference.[84] Timothy Wirth viewed her appointment as a "symbol of a Vatican that wants to work things out."[85] Cardinal Martino cannot support this claim. Pope John Paul II had asked Martino twice if he was willing to represent the Holy See in Beijing. Realizing the symbolic difference which a female appointment would make, the Holy See diplomat responded: "Holy Father, this time, it has to be a woman!" The pope was surprised. "But there was never a woman leading a Holy See delegation," he countered. "Holy Father, you've made so many things for the first time, surely you can appoint a woman," Archbishop Martino replied. Pope John Paul II agreed but not without getting Archbishop Martino's agreement to serve as co-head of delegation. Martino submitted a list with the names of three suitable women coming from "Indonesia, Africa, and the US." The Holy Father ended up choosing Glendon "due to her competence, reputation, and human rights philosophy."[86]

The Holy See resented the concept of gender that was promoted by feminist groups, and rejected the view that sexual identity boiled down to social constructions. The Holy Father rather emphasized the "complementary characteristics of that which is feminine and masculine," which includes a strong emphasis on the role of motherhood.[87] The Holy See was "perplexed by the tendency throughout the [draft] document to impose a certain specific Western model of the 'promotion of women' . . . which ignores the values of women who for the most part live in other regions of the world."[88] Whereas the concept of gender appeared over 300 times

83. Flynn, "Letter from the Vatican," 149–50.

84. Tagliabue, "Vatican Attacks U.S.-Backed Draft for Women's Conference," *The New York Times*, August 26, 1995.

85. Tofani, "Vatican Taking a Softer Line at U.N. Conference," *Philadelphia Inquirer*, September 14, 1995.

86. Personal interview with Cardinal Renato Martino, President-Emeritus of the Pontifical Council for Justice and Peace, Vatican, March 17, 2012.

87. John Paul II, "Message of His Holiness Pope John Paul II to Mrs. Gertrude Mongella," 420.

88. Tauran, "Statement by His Excellency Archbishop Jean-Louis Tauran, Secretary for Relations with States of the Holy See: The Position of the Holy See on the Draft Platform for Action for the Fourth World Conference on Women," 498.

in the draft platform for action, the Holy See criticized that the concept of mother/motherhood only surfaced ten times. Moreover, it deplored that the description of the family as "fundamental unit of society" remained bracketed throughout the draft document, as was the right of parental control over the education of adolescents.[89] Nevertheless, the Holy See made no general attacks on the UN and did not try to re-open the abortion debate. In fact, the Holy See pragmatically considered it "dangerous to re-open on statements and texts on which it proved possible to find a balanced understanding after long months of difficult negotiations."[90]

The international women's movement was a major force in the Beijing process which it viewed as the culmination of a long feminist struggle. The influential Women's Environment and Development Organization, led by Bella Abzug, coordinated the "Linkage Caucus" that was composed of "some 1,320 NGO representatives from seventy-three countries covering all regions of the world." Its efforts included networking, the distribution of advocacy papers, and lobbying for specific language changes during the drafting process.[91] The Caucus's main position paper, "A Pledge for Gender Justice," called upon governments to "commit to women's programmes 50 percent of all resources and funds needed to eradicate poverty, illiteracy, disease," to "ensure women's rights to education, health care and bodily integrity," to integrate "gender perspectives into all policy-making," and to "assure gender balance in all governmental bodies, including elected and appointed positions."[92]

During the Cairo process, many Muslim leaders had called for boycotting the conference. A new tendency now emerged as international Islamist associations promoted active participation rather than mere denunciation.[93] The Holy See and Muslim governments shared a concern for a more positive appreciation of the role of motherhood and family. The Holy See organized a workshop in Rome held in June 1995 that

89. Navarro-Valls, "Briefing by Dr. Joaquín Navarro-Valls, Director of the Press Office of the Holy See on the topic of the United Nations Fourth World Conference on Women," 508, 510.

90. Tauran, "Statement by His Excellency Archbishop Jean-Louis Tauran, Secretary for Relations with States of the Holy See: The Position of the Holy See on the Draft Platform for Action for the Fourth World Conference on Women," 503.

91. Archibald, "Abzug Network rules U.N. Women's Agenda," *The Washington Times*, August 10, 1995.

92. "A Pledge to Gender Justice."

93. El-Hadi, "Islamic Politics in Beijing."

brought together the Pontifical Council for Interreligious Dialogue with several influential Muslim organizations. The workshop's goal was to "exchange their views on the place of women in society." Its participants expressed their shared "apprehension regarding the draft Document for Beijing which ignores the positive role of religion in this process."[94]

The Western liberal press quickly insinuated that the Vatican and Islam were once again constructing an "unholy alliance" to relegate women to their traditional roles as housewives and mothers.[95] The Holy See's spokesman, Joaquín Navarro-Valls, explicitly rejected such accusations. While the Holy See did listen to the concerns of Muslim representatives with great interest, there were "some substantial differences between Christianity and Islam on themes such as women, family, etc."[96] Contrary to prevailing Muslim interests, the Holy See did not have a problem with the empowerment of women and supported a greater presence of women in the public sphere as long as society and the state equally supported a woman's personal decision to stay at home and support her family if she prefers to do so. Also, as opposed to the Catholic stress on equality under the law, Islamist associations demanded "equity" rather than "equality" when it came to women's inheritance rights in order to guarantee traditional privileges of the oldest son.[97]

While the Holy See did not push for a re-consideration of the abortion issue, it did successfully defend the sub-clause of the Cairo consensus that in "no case should abortion be promoted as a method of family planning."[98] In the draft Platform for Action this phrase initially had been bracketed. The wish not to re-open the abortion question was shared by both the US and the Holy See. Keeping a low profile on abortion did not, however, prevent the Holy See from vigorously defending traditional

94. "Bolletino N. 248–29.06.1995, Dichiarazione del Direttore della Sala Stampa, Dr. Joaquín Navarro-Valls." Box "2108/C382–1993, ONU.Conferenze, 4th World Conference on Women, Pechino (Beijing), 4–15.9.1995 (Scatola I)," Folder "Incontro tra Ponf. Cons. per il Dialogo Interreligioso e 3 organizzazioni islamiche internazionali al Centro Islamico di Roma in vista della IV conf. Mond. sulla Donna, 23.6.1995," PCJP.

95. Field, "Women Face an Unholy Alliance," *The Observer*, September 3, 1995.

96. Navarro-Valls, "Briefing by Dr. Joaquín Navarro-Valls, Director of the Press Office of the Holy See on the topic of the United Nations Fourth World Conference on Women," 513.

97. El-Hadi, "Islamic Politics in Beijing," 50–51.

98. Navarro-Valls, "Briefing by Dr. Joaquín Navarro-Valls, Director of the Press Office of the Holy See on the topic of the United Nations Fourth World Conference on Women," 508.

Catholic teaching *vis-à-vis* intra-Catholic dissent. The group "Catholics for a Free Choice" had already irritated the Holy See during the Cairo process by supporting pro-abortion policies in the name of Catholicism. In March 1995, the Holy See officially disapproved the group's request for accreditation at the FWCW during the 39th Session of the Commission on the Status of Women, claiming that the NGO's use of the name Catholic in its title was misleading as the organization promoted positions fundamentally different to church teaching.[99]

The Holy See's support for strengthening family life and motherhood made it easy for critics to suggest the Holy See, "in step with several fundamentalist Muslim countries," aims to "keep women in the home."[100] Such a critique overlooks, however, that the Holy See fully supports equality of women in every area: "equal pay for equal work, protection for working mothers, fairness in career advancements, equality of spouses with regard to family rights and the recognition of everything that is part of the rights and duties of citizens in a democratic State." Pope John Paul II claimed that the presence of the female "genius" in the public sphere was of special importance. He deplored that, throughout history, women had been "relegated to the margins of society and even reduced to servitude" and admitted that, historically, the church had been complicit in this process.[101]

Criticizing violence against women was another crucial area of concern for the Holy See. Papal diplomats particularly criticized sexual exploitation, domestic violence, female feticide, and violence against women during military conflict.[102] Promoting education, especially for girls and young women was another integral part of the Holy See's wider agenda. In his send-off message to the Holy See delegation to the FWCW, the Holy Father committed "all Catholic caring and educational institutions to adopt a concerted and priority strategy directed to girls and young women, especially to the poorest."[103]

99. Holy See, "Holy See Mission Press Release."

100. Manthorpe, "UN Conference on Women," *The Ottawa Citizen*, August 31, 1995.

101. John Paul II, "Letter of His Holiness Pope John Paul II to Women," 831.

102. Martino, "Statement of His Excellency Archbishop Renato R. Martino, Apostolic Nuncio, Permanent Observer of the Holy See to the United Nations at the 39th Session of the Commission on the Status of Women."

103. John Paul II, "Message of His Holiness Pope John Paul II to the Delegation of the Holy See to the Fourth World Conference on Women," 426.

The Holy See defended a traditional understanding of gender which defined the term as the generic concept that distinguishes "male" from "female." It criticized the argument that sexual identity could be fluid or legitimately encompass homosexuality, transsexuality, or bisexuality. The Holy See's opposition to the concepts of "sexual orientation" or "lifestyle" even went so far that its Secretary for Relations with States, Archbishop Jean-Louis Tauran, expressed his fear that "it could for example happen in the future that pedophilia might be considered a 'sexual orientation.'"[104] The Holy See bracketed all references to the concept of gender in the draft Platform of Action[105] and perceived the draft document as "extraordinarily unbalanced" for privileging the concept of "gender" (300 references) over the concept of motherhood (ten references) as well as health problems related to sexual life (forty references) over tropical diseases (two references).[106]

The Holy See's strategy was to cast itself as the real defender of the interest of women and to portray mainstream feminism as outdated. The Holy See affirmed the equal dignity of women, the rights of motherhood, and women's freedom to choose whether to become mothers, to pursue a career; or to find the right mix between these two vocations. The Holy See's criticism of feminism, Doris Buss explains, smartly played on "existing tensions and concerns among feminist scholars and activists," especially the concern that mainstream feminism reflected mostly the interests of white, Western women who do not appreciate the differences between men and women, between the developed and the developing world, and between religious and non-religious women.[107]

The FWCW was attended by delegations of 189 governments and some 17,000 participants, including 6,000 government delegates, 4,000 accredited NGO representatives, and 4,000 journalists.[108] In her opening statement as head of the Holy See delegation, Mary Ann Glendon emphasized the values of "marriage, motherhood, and the family" as well as religion. The Holy See supported "the right of women to effectively

104. Tauran, "Statement by His Excellency Archbishop Jean-Louis Tauran, Secretary for Relations with States of the Holy See: The Position of the Holy See," 502.

105. Buss, "Robes, Relics and Rights," 348.

106. Navarro-Valls, "Briefing by Dr. Joaquín Navarro-Valls, Director of the Press Office of the Holy See on the topic of the United Nations Fourth World Conference on Women," 508.

107. Buss, "Robes, Relics and Rights," 354.

108. Pietilä, *Unfinished Story*, 70.

enjoy equal opportunities with men in the workplace as well as in the decision-making structures of society." The Holy See's strongest objection was the draft action program's "tendency to focus privileged attention and resources on the consideration of health problems related to sexuality." On the abortion issue, Glendon defended the "clear consensus" that "abortion should not be promoted as a means of family planning." All "who are genuinely committed to the advancement of women can and must offer a woman or a girl who is pregnant, frightened and alone a better alternative than the destruction of her own unborn child."[109]

Western media continued to show a hostile attitude toward the Holy See. There were frequent accusations that the Holy See wanted to re-open the Cairo consensus,[110] and that it was siding with fundamentalist Muslim states such as Iran to "block financial aid and an improvement in women's legal status."[111] Against the backdrop of these expectations, the Holy See's decision not to re-open the abortion issue came as a surprise to many observers. Despite its misgivings about the Cairo consensus, the Holy See prudently believed it had more to lose than to gain by raising the abortion question, especially the important disclaimer that abortion was not to be promoted as a means of family planning. "Our position has been to stick to Cairo and fight against any going back on the Cairo language. We want to make a constructive and positive effort," Glendon clarified.[112]

As the US kept a lower profile during the FWCW than it had during the ICPD process, the main clash in Beijing pitched the Holy See against the EU. At the heart of the conflict were contending visions on family, the role of religion in the public sphere, motherhood, and parental authority. The Holy See opposed efforts "to change 'family' to the politically correct and ambiguous word 'families'—which lends itself to the interpretation that any group of unrelated people may call itself a family." If alternative lifestyles were placed on the same legal footing as traditional families, the Holy See feared that legal privileges given to child-raising families could be undermined. It also objected to the EU's attempt to remove all

109. Glendon, "Statement of Professor Mary Ann Glendon, Head of the Delegation of the Holy See to the Fourth World Conference on Women, Beijing."

110. "Vatican Denies 'Hard Line' on Reproductive Issues," *The Irish Times*, September 5, 1995.

111. Field, "Women Face an Unholy Alliance," *The Observer*, September 3, 1995.

112. Mufson, "Vatican will not Contest Language on Abortion," *The Washington Post*, September 7, 1995.

references to religion, morals, ethics, or spirituality.[113] Its delegation was particularly shocked by a remark made by a representative of the EU delegation during a negotiation session on women's health that suggested that there was "no place for ethics in medicine."[114]

Mary Ann Glendon and her delegation were instructed by Archbishop Jean-Louis Tauran to "go to Beijing and be witnesses."[115] Cardinal Martino adds that the delegation was not only "a witness, but a strong actor."[116] There is no doubt that the Holy See delegation lived out this mission faithfully and authentically. The Holy See had to face a tricky challenge. On the one hand, it needed to defend traditional Catholic teaching on family values and sexual ethics. On the other hand, the Holy See wanted to demonstrate to the world its commitment to the UN system and its desire to enable an international compromise. In Beijing, as in Cairo, the Holy See had to live out the tension between defending Catholic orthodox teaching while presenting the Holy See as a constructive international actor. Putting too much emphasis on defending traditional teaching could sabotage the creation of international consensus whereas too much compromise could undermine deeply held Catholic principles.

It was the latter concern that pushed conservative Catholics to lobby the Holy See to abstain from joining the consensus even in a partial manner. Representatives of the movement Neocatechumenal Way, for example, urged Glendon to reject the entire document.

> The Declaration and Program of Action were, in their view, so permeated with a false anthropology, so obsessed with sexuality to the exclusion of other issues, so profoundly subversive of the good for women, that the best way for the Church to witness to the truth would be to denounce them and decline to join the Conference consensus.[117]

Cardinal Martino denies, however, that there was any internal ecclesial pressure on the delegation to abstain from joining the Beijing consensus even partially. The delegation's strategy of "accepting the good

113. Holy See, "Press release issued by the Delegation of the Holy See during the Fourth World Conference on Women, Beijing," 537.

114. de Lucia, "Sconcertante Affermazione della Rappresentante dell'Unione Europea."

115. Glendon, "What Happened at Beijing," n.p.

116. Personal interview with Cardinal Renato Martino, President-Emeritus of the Pontifical Council for Justice and Peace, Vatican, March 17, 2012.

117. Glendon, "What Happened at Beijing," n.p.

where it appears" received "full agreement by the Secretariat of State and the Holy Father." Neither in Cairo nor in Beijing did the Holy See delegation receive any other instructions.[118] At both conferences, the Holy See showed its commitment to internationalism by pragmatically opting for a "pick and choose strategy."

In her closing statement, Glendon praised the sections "on the needs of women in poverty, on strategies for development, literacy and education, violence and peace, access to employment, land, capital and technology." The issues on which the Holy See "strongly disagree[d]" with the final documents included "an exaggerated individualism, in which key, relevant provisions of the Universal Declaration of Human Rights are slighted—such as the obligation to provide 'special care and assistance' to motherhood." This selectivity, Glendon deplored, "marks another step in the colonization of the broad and rich discourse of universal rights by an impoverished, libertarian rights dialect. Surely this international gathering could have done more for women and girls than to leave them alone with their rights!"[119]

As in Cairo, the Holy See submitted detailed reservations and asked for their inclusion in the final conference report. These reservations served both international and intra-Catholic purposes. Internationally, it enabled the Holy See to advance its own perspective of the Beijing conference, by laying down its interpretation of ambiguous terms and concepts. Thus, the reservation provided a helpful instrument for future diplomatic references to the FWCW. Moreover, the Holy See also submitted a statement of interpretation of the term "gender," which defended its traditional understanding of the concept and the distinctiveness and complementarity of women and men.[120] Hence, in terms of intra-Catholic debate, the Holy See used the occasion to immediately counter claims that its decision to partially join the consensus implied a softening of its traditional teaching on abortion, contraception, and family values.

118. Personal interview with Cardinal Renato Martino, President-Emeritus of the Pontifical Council for Justice and Peace, Vatican, March 17, 2012.

119. Glendon, "Statement by Professor Mary Ann Glendon, Head of the Holy See Delegation, at the concluding session of the Fourth World Conference on Women, Beijing, 15 September 1995," 531–32.

120. Holy See, "Statement of Interpretation of the Term 'Gender' by the Holy See Delegation," 536.

Conclusion

Protecting unborn life, defending Catholic sexual ethics, and promoting Catholic family values were the overarching themes of Catholic social doctrine that Holy See diplomacy staunchly lived out during the Cairo and Beijing processes. Despite hostile Western public opinion in general, and liberal Catholic expectations in particular, Pope John Paul II made the conferences in Cairo and Beijing pastoral and diplomatic priorities to prevent a liberalization of international abortion norms and to denounce a spreading "culture of death." Defending orthodox Catholic teaching was imperative for the Holy See. In order to do so, it created flexible diplomatic coalitions with like-minded governments from the global South and the Muslim world. Nevertheless, even on such sensitive and controversial topics as abortion or contraception, Catholic teachings provide a normative framework but do not dictate policy options. In fact, the Holy See took its commitment to multilateralism, the UN system, and international law seriously and refused to boycott the conferences or thwart a consensus. Pragmatically, the Holy See gave its partial assent to the final conference outcomes.

Affirming orthodox Catholic teaching was a crucial mediating factor. From a liberal or feminist point of view, this commitment came across as fundamentalist, inflexible, and outdated. From a Catholic point of view, however, it was simply a prophetic exercise of reminding the world of time-honored values and principles. The indirect, yet crucial, domestic audience of the Holy See's diplomatic interventions was the Catholic Church. Liberal Catholics who believed that the Second Vatican Council would usher in a modernization of the Catholic Church were disappointed. Critics like Hans Küng deplored that the pope was "more rigorous on contraception than Islamic fundamentalists" and "had long since lost his battle over sexual morality, even in his own church."[121]

Contrary to Küng's assessment, the immediate result was the opposite. The Holy See's involvement in the Cairo and the Beijing conferences in the mid-1990s helped to reify the normative status of traditional Catholic teaching on abortion and contraception given the sheer number of strongly worded encyclicals, messages, and speeches John Paul II dedicated to these topics. The Cairo and Beijing conferences illustrated how Pope John Paul II shifted the church's approach away from a liberal Catholic emphasis on concessions to worldly expectations toward an

121. Küng, "P.S: Lonely Power of Vatican City," *The Guardian*, September 16, 1994.

evangelical stress on converting the world. Once the overarching bipolar world of the Cold War had disappeared, differences between Catholic values and Western liberalism became much more visible than in the previous decade.

Unlike Saudi Arabia, which boycotted both the ICPD and the FWCW, the Holy See never considered such a boycott but saw itself as an active yet critical shaper of both processes. The Holy See's rhetoric also differed tremendously from socially conservative religious US actors and movements that coalesced around a shared opposition to a "global liberal agenda," "international feminism," and "secular humanism."[122] On the one hand, there was a strong convergence of interests between the Holy See and America's Christian Right based on a common opposition to abortion and a promotion of traditional family values.[123] On the other hand, the Christian Right tended to demonize the UN for imposing an anti-Christian "New World Order" based on socialism, feminism, and environmentalism. Generally speaking, the American Christian Right tends to be very suspicious of supranational organizations such as the UN and accuses them of promoting multinational armed forces, feminism, and anti-Christian values.[124]

In contrast, the Holy See's commitment to internationalism and UN principles has deep historical and normative roots. They have to do with the Catholic Church's transnational nature and go back to a historical suspicion of the sovereign Hobbesian nation-state whose modern origins had challenged the authority of the papacy. This internationalism distinguishes the Holy See from both the Christian Right as well as from mainstream US evangelical Christianity. According to Archbishop Renato Martino, UN-Holy See relations are "based on a tradition of mutual collaboration while respecting each other's role." The Holy See's criticism of the Cairo draft was "not directed at the United Nations per se." Rather, the Holy See believed its role was to make "a sound, democratic argumentation which can be found in any parliament when attempting to formulate and elaborate a final document that must be agreed upon by all."[125]

122. Buss and Herman, *Globalizing Family Values*, xviii–xx.

123. Witham, "Population Plan Draws Interfaith Fire," *The Washington Times*, August 24, 1994.

124. Herman, "Globalism's 'Siren Song,'" 60–62.

125. Martino, "Interview Given to Vatican Radio," 328.

"You can't get all that you want in international diplomacy," Martino argues. This did not mean that the Holy See would relish in a state of splendid isolation by passively acquiescing with whatever the dominant powers could agree to. "If you're alone and isolated," Cardinal Martino explains, "other states would simply have told us: put a reservation on whatever section you're unhappy with." By forging coalitions with like-minded states and using the leverages of the Holy See's power in global politics, the Holy See retained the possibility of shaping the diplomatic outcomes in Cairo and Beijing.[126] Once the Holy See achieved its primary goal of ruling out abortion as a means of family planning, however, its delegation pragmatically opted for a "pick-and-choose approach," giving its assent only to those sections of the final conference reports with which it fully agreed.

To conclude, Catholic teaching on abortion, sexual ethics, and family values provides a very helpful general understanding of the Holy See's motivations and interests at the UN conferences in Cairo and Beijing, and the emerging conflict with the liberal Western stress on individual autonomy. Spelling out these normative interests during the preparatory phases and conferences required, however, a careful calibration of the normative imperative to promote the church's traditional teaching with a pragmatic wish to be a constructive member of the international community.

126. Personal interview with Cardinal Renato Martino, President-Emeritus of the Pontifical Council for Justice and Peace, Vatican, March 17, 2012.

7

Criticizing Capitalism during the International Debt Crisis

Introduction

The Cold War was never confined to a geopolitical confrontation, nuclear arms race, or quest for influence in the Third World. It was also an ideological competition about an issue "almost as big as that of human survival: how best to organize human society."[1] The East's answer was the promotion of Marxist collectivism whereas the West staunchly defended capitalism and liberalism. While Pope John Paul's challenge to communism is widely known, it is often overlooked that the pope never uncritically rejoiced in the victory of liberal capitalism. As early as late 1987, before the transformations of 1989 were foreseeable, the pope argued that it was not only Marxist collectivism, but also the West's liberal capitalist socioeconomic vision that was "imperfect and in need of radical correction."[2] The pope's critique of capitalism did not stem from a neutralist impulse to carve out a third way between the East and the West, but was embedded in an alternative Catholic vision of the common good, social justice, and international order.

From the late 1980s onwards, papal engagement with capitalism focused on two pillars. Pope John Paul's social encyclicals provided a general moral evaluation of capitalism that identified both its positive

1. Gaddis, *Cold War*, 84.
2. John Paul II, *Sollicitudo Rei Socialis*, para. 21.

and negative aspects. On a policy-oriented and diplomatic level, the Holy Father prioritized debt relief as a substantial issue where papal interventions could make a real and meaningful impact. His 1994 Apostolic Letter *Tertio Millennio Adveniente* proposed spiritual preparations for the celebration of the Great Jubilee Year 2000 in commemoration of the 2000th anniversary of the birth of Jesus Christ. The pope called upon "Christians to raise their voice on behalf of all the poor of the world, proposing the Jubilee as an appropriate time to give thought, among other things, to reducing substantially, if not canceling outright, the international debt which seriously threatens the future of many nations." For the Holy Father, this policy goal was the contemporary application of the biblical tradition of the "Jubilee Year," as described in the Old Testament book Leviticus. Every fifty years, slaves were freed and all Israelites could regain possession of their ancestral land if they had lost it due to falling into slavery. Such a biblical commitment to justice and peace was a "necessary condition for the preparation and celebration of the Jubilee," the pope argued.[3]

Whereas liberal secular movements had vehemently fought against the Vatican during the Cairo and Beijing UN conferences, the pope's critical stance on capitalism and his call for debt forgiveness now offered helpful support. The Holy See was especially supportive of the Jubilee 2000 movement, which was made up of both secular and religious organizations. The movement gathered millions of signatures, lobbied creditor governments, and put public pressure on IFIs (international financial institutions) to deepen and widen existing debt relief efforts. While the UN conferences in Cairo and Beijing had brought to the forefront great tension between the Holy See and liberal secular movements, the Great Jubilee highlighted a strong convergence on the issue of debt relief. The Holy See's diplomatic practice consistently lived out the Catholic norms on capitalism and debt relief. Due to the Holy See's primary focus on the moral sphere, together with the Vatican's typical diplomatic restraint, the Holy See's style and rhetoric remained more restrained, however, than the voices of more radical critics of globalization.

3. John Paul II, *Tertio Millennio Adveniente*, paras. 12–13, 51.

Catholic Teaching on Capitalism

Pope Leo XIII published *Rerum Novarum* in the context of the Industrial Revolution that had torn apart the former feudal socioeconomic system and left the newly created working classes in a very precarious situation. Socialism, the German *Kulturkampf* under Chancellor Otto von Bismarck, and the Italian nationalist victory over the Papal States jeopardized the church's authority.[4] *Rerum Novarum* provided a strong critique of socialism, a rejection of its promotion of class struggle, and a forceful defense of private property. Neither "capitalism" nor the "free market" featured yet as such in the encyclical. Rather, the pope laid out the "relative rights and mutual duties of the rich and of the poor, of capital and of labor."[5] He was moved by the depressing condition of the working classes and deplored that "working men have been surrendered, isolated and helpless, to the hardheartedness of employers and the greed of unchecked competition."[6]

While using the Marxist concept of class as an analytical tool, the pope's overarching concern was to foster harmony rather than struggle between classes. The Holy Father asserted that the church had the authority and ability to draw "the rich and the working class together" by reminding each group of their respective duties and "obligations of justice."[7] Leo XIII did not condemn the pursuit of profit but insisted on the importance of using profit and wealth in a virtuous way, especially by giving alms to the poor. Beyond charity, the pope sketched out an important series of deeper obligations of "justice" that employers owe their workers such as granting sufficient time for leisure and rest, especially for religious duties on Sundays, making sure that work corresponds to the sex and age of people, and, above all, fixing wages at a level that is sufficient to comfortably support workers and their families.[8] *Rerum Novarum* also validated the role of the state in intervening in the economy by arguing that "wage-earners . . . should be especially cared for and protected by the government."[9]

4. Shannon, "Commentary on *Rerum novarum*," 128–31.
5. Leo XIII, *Rerum Novarum*, para. 2.
6. Ibid., para. 3.
7. Ibid., para. 19.
8. Ibid., paras. 42, 46.
9. Ibid., para. 37.

Pope Pius XI's *Quadragesimo Anno* was published at the beginning of the Great Depression as international economic relations deteriorated and unemployment was on the rise. Pius XI displayed more ideological passion than Leo XIII when he identified "Liberalism" and unequal distribution of wealth as the key problems to be overcome.[10] The encyclical was very skeptical toward the liberal capitalist mantra that unrestrained free markets will help poor people. The pope argued that the

> immense multitude of the non-owning workers on the one hand and the enormous riches of certain very wealthy men on the other, establish an unanswerable argument that the riches which are so abundantly produced in our age of "industrialism" . . . are not rightly distributed and equitably made available to the various classes of the people.[11]

Unbridled capitalism made the "concentration of power and might" the "characteristic mark . . . of contemporary economic life" and resulted in a form of economic Darwinism "which lets only the strongest survive."[12]

The major innovation that Pope John XXIII and Pope Paul VI brought to Catholic teaching on capitalism in the second half of the twentieth century was a new emphasis on international economic relations. In an era marked by decolonization and Cold War superpower competition, the papacy called for solidarity between rich and poor countries. In his 1961 encyclical *Mater et Magistra*, Pope John XXIII defended a thick role for the state and moved Catholic social doctrine closer to the modern welfare state. He suggested that workers share in the ownership of their companies. He welcomed social security, price regulation, and under certain conditions even state ownership of productive goods.[13] Such moves, together with continued papal critique of unrestricted competition did not go down very well with US conservative Catholic circles. They questioned papal authority to talk about social questions and found it easier to accept the church's role as mother (*mater*) rather than teacher (*magistra*).[14] Up to the current day, conservative American interpretations

10. Hinze, "Commentary on *Quadragesimo anno*," 167.
11. Pius XI, *Quadragesimo Anno*, para. 60.
12. Ibid., para. 107.
13. John XXIII, *Mater et Magistra*.
14. William Buckley, quoted in Mich, "Commentary on *Mater et magistra*," 211.

of social encyclicals have continued to harbor an entrenched skepticism toward state intervention and overly critical remarks of capitalism.[15]

Pope Paul VI dedicated his 1967 encyclical *Populorum Progressio* to the question of authentic development that he defined as the "new name for peace."[16] He argued that development "cannot be restricted to economic growth alone."[17] The Holy Father did not criticize industrialization, yet took issue with "unbridled liberalism" and "a type of capitalism" that is characterized by an uncritical attitude toward profit-seeking, an acceptance of free competition as the guiding norm of economics, a one-sided understanding of the right to property as something "absolute and unconditional," and a naïve assumption that free trade will necessarily result in fair prices.[18] Paul VI recast development as a spiritual rather than economic challenge. Wealthier nations were obliged to give aid to developing nations, to put trade relations on a fairer level and to support global charity efforts.[19]

In sum, modern Catholic teaching is skeptical toward unbridled capitalism and excessive individualism that loses sight of the demands of the common good, social justice, and personal virtues. The Catholic Church outlines a vision of the good life that goes beyond the conceptual and ideological limitations of both Marxism and liberalism. This does not mean that Marxism and liberalism are considered equally bad ideologies with Catholic social doctrine carving out a third path. Catholicism praises significantly more aspects of capitalism than it does of communism, especially personal initiative and free enterprise. As an autonomous tradition, however, Catholic social doctrine insists on the observance of deeper criteria of justice, subsidiarity, and solidarity.

John Paul II on Capitalism

In 1991, when the Cold War reached its end, John Paul II issued his encyclical *Centesimus Annus* in commemoration of the 100th anniversary of *Rerum Novarum*. Reflecting upon 1989—the "year of miracles"—the pope welcomed the demise of communism, the end of Central and

15. See, for example, Weigel and Royal, *Building the Free Society*.

16. Paul VI, *Populorum Progressio*, para. 76.

17. Ibid., para. 14.

18. Ibid., paras. 23, 26.

19. Ibid., para. 44.

Eastern Europe's oppressive regimes, and the spread of freedom and democracy.[20] However, unlike neoliberals, the pope held the view that it was "unacceptable to say that the defeat of so-called 'Real Socialism' leaves capitalism as the only model of economic organization."[21] With a view to influencing economic reconstruction in Central and Eastern Europe and economic thinking in the entire world, the pope warned against the risk of seeing in the collapse of communism as a "one-sided victory" for the West.[22] The pope's major social encyclicals written in the 1980s reveal the issues he had with capitalism.

The Holy Father argued that capitalism fails to provide an ethically satisfying understanding of labor and work. Capitalist market economics generally regards labor as a factor of production among others. It exhibits a tendency to objectify work, as the common usage of the phrase "human resources" reflects. Work is defined in terms of the production of goods and services. Labor is treated as an instrumental factor in this process. The purpose of work is the maximization of efficiency and shareholder value. In the view of Nobel Prize winner Milton Friedman, companies are even duty-bound to serve no other purpose than the increase of profits.[23] The pope did not accept such propositions. He resented the portrayal of work as "a special kind of 'merchandise' or as an impersonal 'force' needed for production."[24] In addition to its prevailing "objective" understanding, work also has the deeper "subjective" dimension of providing man with creative opportunities and a sense of accomplishment and purpose. In *Laborem Exercens,* John Paul argued that "man is . . . the subject of work" and work must help humans to realize their full personal vocation. Drawing upon the principle of the primacy of man, the pope stressed that "work is 'for man' and not man 'for work.'"[25] Capitalism is unjust whenever it reverses this moral order and treats man primarily as "an instrument of production whereas he—he alone . . . ought to be treated as the effective subject of work and its true maker and creator."[26]

20. John Paul II, *Centesimus Annus*, paras. 22–29.

21. Ibid., para. 35.

22. Ibid., para. 56.

23. Friedman, *Capitalism and Freedom*.

24. John Paul II, *Laborem Exercens*, para. 7.

25. Ibid., para. 6.

26. Ibid., para. 7.

In clear terms, Pope Wojtyła warned that unbridled capitalism threatens justice and human dignity.

> The Marxist solution has failed, but the realities of marginalization and exploitation remain in the world, especially the Third World, as does the reality of human alienation, especially in the more advanced countries . . . Vast multitudes are still living in conditions of great material and moral poverty. The collapse of the Communist system in so many countries certainly removes an obstacle to facing these problems in an appropriate and realistic way, but it is not enough to bring about their solution. Indeed, there is a risk that a radical capitalistic ideology could spread which refuses even to consider these problems, in the *a priori* belief that any attempt to solve them is doomed to failure, and which blindly entrusts their solution to the free development of market forces.[27]

John Paul II stressed that the consequence of "economistic" thinking can be severe. While the problem was most acute in the nineteenth century, the same errors may be repeated in contemporary times.[28] The international community needs to be aware that the "human inadequacies of capitalism and the resulting domination of things over people are far from disappearing."[29]

The Holy Father conceded that the "*free market* is the most efficient instrument for utilizing resources and effectively responding to needs." It allows people to enjoy economic initiative and free exchange.[30] He warned, however, that there are many "collective and qualitative needs which cannot be satisfied by market mechanisms."[31] At the very minimum, these needs imply "the possibility to survive, and, at the same time, to make an active contribution to the common good of humanity."[32] If an economy fails to satisfy these needs, this is a gross violation of the moral principle of the universal destination of goods which holds that the material goods of this world are intended to satisfy the needs of all humankind.

27. John Paul II, *Centesimus Annus*, para. 42.
28. John Paul II, *Laborem Exercens*, para. 13.
29. John Paul II, *Centesimus Annus*, para. 33.
30. Ibid., para. 34.
31. Ibid., para. 40.
32. Ibid., para. 34.

While the pope did not deny the right to private property, including the right of private possession of means of production, he stressed that this right was subordinated to the principle of the universal destination of material goods. For this reason, John Paul II regarded as "unacceptable" the "position of 'rigid' capitalism . . . that defends the exclusive right to private ownership of the means of production as an untouchable 'dogma' of economic life." The right to private ownership of the means of production "should undergo a constructive revision" to ensure the primacy of man over capital. In contrast to neoliberal economic thought, the pope suggested "proposals for joint ownership of the means of work" by both labor and capital.[33]

From the Catholic point of view of Pope John Paul II, unrestrained capitalism needs to be tamed, both morally and politically. Responding to the question whether capitalism should be the model for restructuring the economies of the newly independent Central and Eastern European states, he asserted that

> if by "capitalism" is meant an economic system which recognizes the fundamental and positive role of business, the market, private property and the resulting responsibility for the means of production, as well as free human creativity in the economic sector, then the answer is certainly in the affirmative, even though it would perhaps be more appropriate to speak of a "business economy," "market economy" or simply "free economy."[34]

His answer came with the important caveat, however, that

> if by "capitalism" is meant a system in which freedom in the economic sector is not circumscribed within a strong juridical framework which places it at the service of human freedom in its totality, and which sees it as a particular aspect of that freedom, the core of which is ethical and religious, then the reply is certainly negative.[35]

The pope's vision of the good economy was reformist rather than revolutionary as it aimed at making capitalism more humane. Politically, he demanded a strong role for the state to coordinate the market and to set its institutional and juridical framework to protect the weak, and

33. John Paul II, *Laborem Exercens*, para. 14.

34. John Paul II, *Centesimus Annus*, para. 42.

35. Ibid., para. 42.

to provide a stable currency and efficient public services.[36] Morally, he exhorted businessmen and society as a whole to think less economically and more ethically. This did not mean that profit had no legitimate role to play as an indicator for the functioning of business. However, the Holy Father saw profitability as only one among other factors. His critique of capitalism was a reflection of Catholic social doctrine's core propositions about the primacy of man and the moral principle of the universal destination of goods. What ultimately marks a departure "from mainstream economists and other advocates of the market system," Edward J. O'Boyle highlights, is "that human beings are far more consequential than economic systems . . . what matters the most is not how efficiently an economic system allocates resources, but how well it meets human needs."[37] The following part of this chapter will analyze how the Holy See, particularly through the PCJP, lived out this general vision of a just economy in relation to the problem of international debt.

The Jubilee 2000 Global Debt Relief Campaign

The International Debt Crisis

The debt crisis caught the world's attention in 1982 when Mexico, followed by Brazil, defaulted on the foreign debt it owed to Western commercial banks. Initially, the debt crisis affected middle-income countries in Latin America whose debt burden exceeded their economic capacity to repay debts and interests. The ensuing politicized blame game focused on identifying who bore responsibility for the situation: the Latin American middle-income countries, the rich lending states, or Western banks?

The countries suffering from unserviceable debt blamed systemic factors and external shocks: the rise of the oil price in 1973 and 1979, the explosion of interest rates in the late 1970s, deterioration in the exchange rate with the US dollar, the global recession in the late 1970s and early 1980s, irresponsible lending following the glut of "petrodollars," and ill-guided advice by the IMF and the World Bank that encouraged developing countries to shift their production from agriculture to export crops before prices would later fall substantially in the early 1980s. Rich countries and Western banks, on the other hand, blamed Latin American

36. Ibid., para. 48.

37. O'Boyle, "John Paul II's Vision of the Social Economy," 535.

countries for their bad economic policies, lack of reforms, and irresponsible borrowing. Cold War competition between the superpowers exacerbated the problem as development aid became a useful political tool for attracting poorer countries' ideological allegiances and support during UN General Assembly resolution votes.[38]

A second kind of debt crisis became acute in the late 1980s and early 1990s. This time low-income African countries were affected, especially in Sub-Saharan Africa. They were unable to pay back bilateral and multilateral loans that they owed to Western governments and IFIs. The causes of the debt crisis were similar. Yet due to the nature of the loans, the African debt dependence was more political, whereas Latin America's dependence was more financial. The African debt crisis remained unsolved for almost fifteen years because creditors refused to forgive debt, debtors failed to unite to challenge their creditors to forgive them, and because the industrialized economies benefited from the glut of cheap imports of raw material from Africa.[39]

Third World debt rose from approximately $100 billion in the 1970s to $1,450 billion in the early 1990s.[40] By 1990, Mexico ($96.8 billion) and Brazil ($116.2 billion) were the largest debtors.[41] Nominally, the Sub-Saharan African debt was much smaller than the Latin American debt. The 1990 Human Development Report put the regional share of Sub-Saharan African debt at 11.6 percent, as opposed to Latin America's 38.5 percent share of worldwide total debt of developing countries. However, in terms of human costs, the African debt crisis was more catastrophic as it aggravated entrenched preexisting poverty. The number of Africans living below the poverty line increased by two-thirds in the first half of the 1980s—a decade that threatened to reverse much of the progress that had been achieved previously. Income per person declined in Africa more than 25 percent for the entire region during the same time period.[42]

Martin Dent, one of the founders of Jubilee 2000, argues that there was an "intimate connection between the presence of absolute poverty . . . and that of unpayable sovereign debt." While debt is not the sole cause

38. Dent and Peters, *Crisis of Poverty*, 1–6; Haynes, *Third World Politics*, 77–78; Teunissen "Introduction," 1–4.

39. Haynes, *Third World Politics*, 82–83.

40. Ibid., 77–83.

41. See Ferraro and Rosser, "Global Debt and Third World Development," n.p.

42. United Nations Development Programme, "Human Development Report 1990," 34.

of poverty and while its removal provides no magic recipe for its elimination, "it is a great contributory factor of lasting poverty of low-income countries."[43] The debt crisis led to a "capital hemorrhage," worsening terms of trade, and increasing poverty. World Bank statistics revealed in 1989 that highly indebted countries received about 2 percent of GNP from abroad before 1982. Afterwards, they transferred 3 percent in the opposite direction.

Until the mid-1990s, the West's response to the debt crisis was based on two pillars. First, most measures involved adjusting either the timing and/or the method of repayment. The so-called "menu" approach to debt repayment provided a wide variety of options such as debt-equity swaps, debt-for-debt swaps, exit bonds, and cash buyback. These complex financial measures aimed to tailor the repayment procedure to the specific conditions, assets, and constraints of a particular country. This approach underpinned the 1985 Baker plan that was named after the US Secretary of the Treasury, James Baker.[44] The plan fell through as private lenders largely refused to participate. The 1989 Brady plan, named after Baker's successor, Nicholas F. Brady, was more successful. It provided modest debt reduction together with US securities in order to collateralize the new bonds that participating governments from the global South issued to their private Western lenders in return.[45]

Second, the IMF acquired a new role as provider of liquidity for countries overwhelmed by their debt. As part of the Brady plan, the IMF was now charged to create conditions which would assure repayments of creditor countries to private institutions. The IMF's main tools were Structural Adjustment Programs (SAPs) that provided a tightly managed process in order to organize just enough liquidity through bank loans, the rescheduling of debt, and the provision of multilateral loans by both the IMF and the World Bank. Austerity packages aimed at extracting the maximum amount of money from indebted countries, reducing current account deficits, fostering liberalization and privatization, and encouraging private foreign investment. Budget cuts also led to decreased spending on social welfare, unemployment, and the collapse of domestic

43. Dent and Peters, *Crisis of Poverty*, 1.

44. Ferraro and Rosser, "Global Debt and Third World Development," n.p.

45. Shelledy, "Legions Not Always Visible," 107.

industries. All this made the promise of "long-term gain" for "short-term pain" sound rather empty for the people living in the affected countries.[46]

The 1980s were shaped by the ascent of Margaret Thatcher and Ronald Reagan and their unapologetic belief in free-market capitalism. Their economic philosophy—which owed much to Milton Friedman—was built upon the idea that the efficiency of free markets would reduce poverty and increase wealth for all. The human consequences of the international debt crisis and the inability of the free market to solve the problem in an adequate and fair way provided a moral challenge to the conservative revolution of the 1980s. How would the Holy See position itself *vis-à-vis* the debt crisis given Catholic social doctrine's skeptical attitude toward that kind of capitalism?

An Ethical Approach to the Debt Crisis

At the end of 1986, at a time when debt relief was still conspicuously absent from the existing menu of options, the Pontifical Commission for Justice and Peace[47] published a paper entitled "At the Service of the Human Community: An Ethical Approach to the International Debt Crisis." This document became the normative blueprint that would inform the Holy See's engagement with the debt crisis over the next fifteen years. It viewed the debt crisis as a "serious, urgent and complex problem" that cannot be solved by the force of economics alone but requires the application of ethical principles of "justice and solidarity."[48]

The document specified six applicable principles that all touch upon central concepts of Catholic social doctrine: the creation of new forms of solidarity, the acceptance of co-responsibility by creditors and debtors alike, the establishment of relations of trust, the sharing of efforts and sacrifice, the participation of all, as well as the identification of emergency and long-term measures, including a general "reform of financial and monetary institutions." The document warned that in some cases the

46. Ferraro and Rosser, "Global Debt and Third World Development," n.p.; Haynes, *Third World Politics*, 85–90.

47. In 1988, the Apostolic Constitution *Pastor Bonus* changed its name into Pontifical Council for Justice and Peace (PCJP).

48. Pontifical Commission "Iustitia et Pax", "At the Service of the Human Community: An Ethical Approach to the International Debt Crisis," 9–10.

debt payments were so high that they were causing "severe damage" to local living standards, especially for the poor.[49]

An "ethics of survival" should guide the attitudes and decisions of both creditors and debtors. Such an ethic should "avoid breaches between creditors and debtors as well as any unilateral termination of prior commitments, respect the insolvent debtor and do not burden him with immediate and intolerable demands which he cannot meet."[50] Even if such demands were legal, they would be morally wrong and abusive. With regard to the IMF, the document notes that its

> decisions have been ill-received by the leaders and the general public of countries in difficulty; the decisions in question may seem to have been imposed in an authoritarian and technocratic way without due consideration for urgent social requirements and the specific features of each situation.[51]

The document addressed four groups: First, industrialized countries must adopt economic policies which do not hurt developing countries, get rid of protectionist measures, and bring interest rates down to "a more reasonable level." Second, developing countries must deal with domestic causes of the debt problem such as dealing with tax fraud and corruption, reducing public spending for armament and prestige projects, supporting agrarian reforms, and creating jobs. Third, the responsibility of creditors includes respecting the debtor state's ability to meet its basic needs by making concessions such as decreasing interest rates, rescheduling debt on a longer-term basis, or, in the case of the poorest countries, turning loans into grants. And fourth, multilateral financial organizations are called upon to reexamine the IMF's loan conditions, foster dialogue on the rescheduling and reduction of debt, and make special provisions for unforeseen financial difficulties due to natural disasters, excessive variations in prices of raw materials, or exchange-rate fluctuations.[52]

According to Flaminia Giovanelli,[53] complaints about the debt problem reached the Holy See after the Latin American crisis through two principal pathways. First, South American PCJP members brought this issue to the attention of the Council during their annual assemblies

49. Ibid., 11–13.

50. Ibid., 13–14.

51. Ibid., 13–14.

52. Ibid., 16–31.

53. She worked on the debt issue as PCJP desk officer in the 1980s. In 2010, she was appointed the Council's Under-Secretary.

in Rome. Second, Latin American bishops also played a very important role in bringing this issue to the forefront of the attention of the Holy Father and the PCJP during their *ad-limina* visits.[54] Pope John Paul II had personally instructed the PCJP to draft "An Ethical Approach to the International Debt Crisis" in order "to deepen the reflection on the problem."[55] Hence, the Holy See's engagement with the international debt crisis was not simply theoretically deduced from Catholic social doctrine or unilaterally prioritized by the Vatican. It was the result of complaints by local bishops and a sympathetic reception by the Holy See given its resonance with existing Catholic teaching on making unbridled capitalism more humane.

"At the Service of the Human Community" identified the debt crisis as an ethical problem. It did not yet, however, call for debt cancellation as the most appropriate response. Flaminia Giovanelli explains that the PCJP underwent a learning experience:

> At the beginning we couldn't demand outright debt cancellation. The role of the PCJP was to explain that the debt problem was not a technical but a moral issue. At the beginning everybody understood the debt problem in strictly legal terms as obligations that had to be met. However, we started to see how poor people rather than governments were paying the biggest price. We then began to understand that debt reduction might not be sufficient to solve the problem.[56]

With the 1994 apostolic letter, *Tertio Millennio Adveniente*, in which the pope laid out the church's preparations for the celebration of the new millennium, the Holy See's approach changed from debt reduction to debt cancellation. In his letter, the pope described the Old Testament tradition of the Jubilee. For the tribe of Israel, every seventh year was a special "sabbatical" year dedicated to God during which "the earth was left

54. Personal interview with Flaminia Giovanelli, Under-Secretary of the Pontifical Council for Justice and Peace, Vatican, March 20, 2012. *Ad-limina* visits refer to the obligation of diocesan bishops to visit the Vatican every five years in order to "to make a report . . . on the state of the diocese entrusted to him," "to venerate the tombs of the Blessed Apostles Peter and Paul," and to present themselves to the Roman Pontiff. See Catholic Church, *Code of Canon Law*, Can. 399 and Can. 400. Usually, diocesan bishops will visit several Holy See dicasteries to discuss specific problems.

55. Pontifical Commission "Iustitia et Pax", "At the Service of the Human Community," 5.

56. Personal interview with Flaminia Giovanelli, Under-Secretary of the Pontifical Council for Justice and Peace, Vatican, March 20, 2012.

fallow" and "slaves were set free." There were detailed regulations about the cancellation of all debts. Every fiftieth year—following seven "sabbatical" years—a special "Jubilee" year was celebrated in a broader and more solemn way.[57] Even though the ancient jubilee tradition was "more a hope than an actual fact" in order to restore social justice and offering new hope, the tradition was driven by the idea that God alone possessed ultimate dominion over the goods of the earth which he had willed for the common good.[58] In this spirit, Pope John Paul II asserted that

> a commitment to justice and peace in a world like ours, marked by so many conflicts and intolerable social and economic inequalities, is a necessary condition for the preparation and celebration of the Jubilee . . . Christians will have to give thought, among other things, to reducing substantially, if not cancelling outright, the international debt which seriously threatens the future of many nations.[59]

With this politically salient paragraph, the Holy Father committed the Catholic Church to push more vigorously for reduction, if not cancellation, as an appropriate reaction to the international debt crisis. Referring to the year 2000, the pope also identified a specific time-frame for such a campaign which would neatly converge with the underlying philosophy and deadline of the Jubilee 2000 campaign.

The Jubilee 2000 Campaign

Jubilee 2000 was the most visible, prominent, and biggest umbrella organization of a variety of international NGOs that were involved in lobbying efforts for debt relief. It was made up of seventy national coalitions which, in turn, were composed of constituent organizations. Launched in 1997, the name of this global social movement took its inspiration from the biblical jubilee theme. Its symbol, a chain, drew a parallel between the enslaving nature of the debt burden and the international campaign against the slave trade in the nineteenth century. Its record-breaking petition was signed by twenty-four million people from over sixty countries.[60]

57. John Paul II, *Tertio Millennio Adveniente*, para. 12.

58. Ibid., para. 13.

59. Ibid., para. 51.

60. Mayo, "'The World Will Never Be the Same Again,'" 144.

The founding fathers of Jubilee 2000 were Martin Dent, a retired politics lecturer from the University of Keele, and Bill Peters, a retired British diplomat and former High Commissioner in Malawi. Together with the help of Ann Pettifor, an experienced lobbyist and director of the Debt Crisis Network, they set up Jubilee 2000. The campaign adopted a "coalition" model. The founders realized that as a single individual organization they would lack the necessary strength for a sustained worldwide campaign. Jubilee 2000 opted for what was dubbed a "highlander" organizational model. This approach allowed numerous organizations, small and big, secular and religious, to "be enlisted in a great common cause" while fighting individually "in his or her clan identity and with their own clan head. This sort of organisation requires considerable skill to create and to maintain, but it has great potential for mass mobilisation and contact with key decision makers." In order to attract religious organizations such as the Catholic Church, the original Jubilee 2000 committee rejected a proposal to change the name of the campaign from Jubilee 2000 to Debt-Free 2000.[61] Its biblical name made the campaign more attractive to Christian actors in general and the PCJP in particular, especially because "jubilee" was the key concept of the relevant paragraph in *Tertio Millennio Adveniente* that contained the papal call for debt cancellation.[62]

The Jubilee 2000 coalition pursued two sets of interests. In the short term, it pushed for "specific, achievable goals in terms of debt relief for the most heavily indebted countries." In the long term, it aspired to challenge "predominant neo-liberal constructions of indebtedness and development more generally." Among its members, the movement was divided by those who thought that capitalism was inherently inimical to the interests of the poor and those who believed that globalization could be reshaped in favor of the poor.[63] The broadness of its constituent organizations helped Jubilee 2000 to present itself as a broader and more representative campaign than those of "the usual suspects" of anti-capitalist protesters. Jubilee 2000 members included faith-based groups, trade unions, business people, academics, artists, and media stars such as Bono. Campaign events deliberately were not described as demonstrations. Organizers did

61. Dent and Peters, *Crisis of Poverty*, 27–33.

62. Personal interview with Flaminia Giovanelli, Under-Secretary of the Pontifical Council for Justice and Peace, Vatican, March 20, 2012.

63. Mayo, "'The World Will Never Be the Same Again,'" 145.

not want to deter potential supporters who usually do not join public protests or campaigns.[64]

In October 1996, several industrialized countries, the World Bank, and the IMF took a first step in going beyond merely rolling over debt by adopting the Debt Initiative for Heavily Indebted Poor Countries (HIPC). This initiative was innovative as the World Bank broke with its previous principle of not writing off multilateral debt. The 1995 election of the World Bank's new President, James Wolfensohn, had been a crucial reason behind this policy shift. HIPC provided some $8 billion of debt relief and "represented a great advance in the acceptance of a new principle of the forgiveness of debt"[65] even though Jubilee 2000 criticized that HIPC "was not fast, broad or deep enough" and was still "insufficiently attentive to basic human needs."[66]

The coalition also questioned HIPC's commitment to achieving a "sustainable debt" burden rather than aspiring to total debt relief. Moreover, it challenged the prevailing definition of what constitutes a sustainable level of debt. Martin Dent and Bill Peters criticized HIPC's official definition of sustainability as not more than 80 percent of annual GNP, 220 percent of a year's export of goods and services (XGS) or a maximum of 25 percent of the yearly income from XGS as an "impossibly" high level. Also, they criticized the HIPC process for being too slow as it took at least six years from first consideration to final debt relief.[67] Only Uganda had qualified for debt relief under the HIPC initiative by July 1998.[68] Finally, with only forty-one eligible states, HIPC arguably covered not enough countries. Dent and Peters reckoned that a total of fifty-one countries urgently needed debt relief.[69]

Through public campaigning, lobbying, and extensive public relations efforts, Jubilee 2000 kept up pressure for deepening and widening the scope of the HIPC initiative. During the May 1998 G8 summit in Birmingham, Jubilee 2000 mobilized a human chain of 70,000 people.[70] The electoral replacement of German Chancellor Helmut Kohl by Ger-

64. Ibid., 148.

65. Dent and Peters, *Crisis of Poverty*, 53.

66. Busby, "Bono Made Jesse Helms Cry," 257.

67. Dent and Peters, *Crisis of Poverty*, 54–55.

68. Busby, "Bono Made Jesse Helms Cry," 257.

69. Dent and Peters, *Crisis of Poverty*, 10–13.

70. Mayo, "'The World Will Never Be the Same Again,'" 145.

hard Schröder in late 1998 created a new lobbying opportunity as the social-democratic Schröder administration reversed Kohl's skeptical stance on debt relief.[71] Surrounded by 30,000 protesters, international leaders at the 1999 G8 Summit in Cologne decided to expand the HIPC initiative by providing an additional $27 billion for debt relief (HIPC-II).[72] Jubilee 2000 presented a petition with 17 million signatures to Chancellor Schröder. The Cologne summit lowered the criteria for debt sustainability to 150% of XGS, proposed to the IMF to sell some of its gold to finance debt relief, and requested that donor countries increase their funding of IFIs in order to support the same goal.[73]

The Guardian deemed Jubilee 2000 to be "the most successful mass movement of the past 25 years."[74] Even though the coalition was "far from achieving all of its supporters' goals," it brought unprecedented public scrutiny to a rather complex and non-transparent issue. Public pressure helped to increase the available amount for debt cancellation from $55 billion prior to the Cologne Summit to $111 billion by the end of 1999. Moreover, Jubilee 2000 won "the battle over basic messages" as the summit leaders borrowed heavily from the campaign's language by making repeated references to expressions such as "faster, deeper, and broader debt relief," "poverty reduction plans for the effective targeting of savings derived from debt relief," or "consultation with civil society."[75]

What was remarkable about Jubilee 2000 was the dynamic interconnectedness between religion and politics. Even if it may not have been shared by all activists, the biblical theme of restoring God's justice through debt relief provided a politically effective moral framework for raising the issue of unsustainable debt. At the G8 summits in Birmingham and Cologne, "the majority of protestors were from church groups and church-linked charities."[76] The religious symbolism was particularly important in the United States. President Clinton had agreed in September

71. *Süddeutsche Zeitung*, "Schröder's teures Versprechen," June 14, 1999, Box "4241/C2781999 AA.VV. Fascicolo di Documenti sul Debito Internazionale, 1990–1999," Folder "Vertice G8 di Colonia (giugno 1999); commenti sul 'dopo Colonia,'" PCJP.

72. Busby, "Bono Made Jesse Helms Cry," 257.

73. G7 Information Center, "G7 Statement"; Shelledy, "Legions Not Always Visible," 108.

74. Elliott, "Candle lit for debt relief's unfinished business," n.p.

75. Collins et al., "Jubilee 2000," 135–41.

76. Busby, "Bono Made Jesse Helms Cry," 264.

1999 to cancel 100 percent of bilateral debts, perhaps partly motivated by a wish to seek personal "redemption through virtuous public politics" in the aftermath of the Lewinsky affair.[77] The Clinton administration encountered some difficulties, however, securing the funding from a Republican-controlled Congress.

The religious symbolism provided an effective tool for lobbying influential Republican gatekeepers. The religious case for debt relief differed from the financial or technical argument that most debt by heavily indebted countries simply was "bad" debt that should be written off for the sake of good accounting. Rather, the religious argument stressed that debt relief was the right thing to do from a biblical point of view. The religious argument particularly impressed Jesse Helms, the leading conservative and deeply religious Chairman of the Senate Foreign Relations Committee from 1995–2001. Following a visit by Bono, Senator Helms accepted the argument for debt relief. "I was deeply impressed," with Bono, Helms remembered. "He has depth that I didn't expect. He is led by the Lord to do something about the starving people in Africa."[78] By October 2000, congressional resistance had been overcome and Congress approved by a wide margin the full amount asked for by President Clinton. As Representative Sonny Callahan, a Republican from Alabama, put it: "We've got the pope and every missionary in the world involved in this thing, and they persuaded just about everyone that this is the noble thing to do."[79]

The Holy See and the Jubilee 2000 Campaign

The Holy See's contribution to the Jubilee 2000 campaign was based on personal support by Pope John Paul II and the effective use of transnational church advocacy. The pope instructed the PCJP to "update and develop suggestions and guidance in the spiritual and cultural context of the Great Jubilee Year 2000."[80] The relevant contact person at the PCJP was Bishop Diarmuid Martin.[81] He had helped represent Holy See inter-

77. Peterson, "The Rock Star, the Pope and the World's Poor," n.p.

78. Quoted in Busby, "Bono Made Jesse Helms Cry," 248.

79. Kahn, "Leaders in Congress Agree to Debt Relief for Poor Nations," n.p.

80. John Paul II, "Discorso di Giovanni Paolo II ai Membri dell'Assemblea Plenaria del Pontificio Consiglio della Giustizia e della Pace," para. 4.

81. Monsignor Diarmuid Martin (born in 1945) was Under-Secretary of the

ests during the Cairo and Beijing UN conferences. Martin's first assignment upon his appointment as PCJP's Under-Secretary in 1986 was to read the proofs of "At the Service of the Human Community."[82] In the late 1990s, having been promoted to the position of Secretary, Bishop Martin worked on debt relief by attending numerous conferences, seminars, and meetings that brought him in close dialogue with leading churchmen from the South, representatives of IFIs, and Jubilee 2000.

The Holy See's strategy was primarily directed at political and economic leaders. Martin was aware that it was "difficult to win elections with debt relief issues." He aimed to convince Western leaders that it was in their self-interest to find effective solutions to the debt problem.[83] The Holy See established working relations with the World Bank at the highest level. In November 1997, Pope John Paul II received the Bank's President, James Wolfensohn, for a personal audience at the Vatican. In a press statement published after the visit, Wolfensohn explained that the Holy Father and the World Bank shared the "primary aim to change the lives of the poor in the world." He further revealed that discussions between the World Bank and the church had been going on for the past eighteen months and asked for the pope's "blessing" for the ongoing collaboration between the World Bank and the Catholic Church.[84] In Wolfensohn's view, Pope John Paul's biblical call for debt relief helped to kickstart the entire Jubilee campaign "in the most unlikely way."[85]

The PCJP was involved in the organization of a series of important conferences. In February 1998, it organized a meeting at its headquarters

---

Pontifical Council for Justice and Peace from 1986 to 1994 when he was promoted to the rank of Secretary. He had a leading role in representing the Holy See both during the Cairo and Beijing processes. In 2004, he was appointed Archbishop of Dublin.

82. "The Holy See and International Debt, Speaking notes of the Most Rev. Diarmuid Martin, Secretary of the Pontifical Council for Justice and Peace, National Gathering on Jubilee Justice, Los Angeles, 18 July 1999," Box "4241/C186–2000 AA.VV. Fascicolo di Documenti sul Debito Nell'Ottica Della Chiesa Cattolica," Folder "Santa Sede—interventi a Conferenze int.li/ interventi a simposi e seminari," PCJP.

83. "Cancellare il debito, dare fiato alla vita," Interview between Fulvio Muzi and Bishop Diarmuid Martin, *Mondo e Missione* (August-September 1998), p. 52, Box "4241/C186–2000 AA.VV. Fascicolo di Documenti sul Debito Nell'Ottica Della Chiesa Cattolica," Folder "Santa Sede—interventi a Conferenze int.li/ interventi a simposi e seminari," PCJP.

84. "Radiogiornale," November 18, 1997, Box "4241/C186–2000 AA.VV. Fascicolo di Documenti sul Debito Nell'Ottica Della Chiesa Cattolica," Folder "Testi di Giovanni Paolo II sul debito dal 1983," PCJP.

85. Wolfensohn, *Global Life*, 290.

in the Palazzo San Calisto in the Roman quarter of Trastevere. Representatives from the World Bank, the IMF, Caritas Internationalis, Sant'Egidio, the Archdiocese of Westminster, the second section of the Holy See's Secretariat of State, the Holy See's central organizing committee for the Jubilee, the Pontifical Commission for Latin America, the Pontifical Council *Cor Unum*, and the Pontifical Council for the Laity all attended the meeting. The second part of the meeting was held behind closed doors and only included representatives of the World Bank, the IMF, and representatives of various dicasteries of the Holy See. The seminar was an opportunity for various Vatican and Catholic Church stakeholders to get an inside briefing on the HIPC initiative.

A second important seminar was cosponsored by the PCJP and Seton Hall University, a private Catholic university based in New Jersey. The high-level meeting took place in October 1998. Participants included World Bank President James Wolfensohn, IMF Managing Director Michel Camdessus, the US Secretary of the Treasury Lawrence Summers, finance ministers from Zambia, Honduras, and Uganda, leading directors from Caritas Internationalis, the charities Cafod, and Oxfam, as well as several Catholic archbishops, including Theodore McCarrick (Archbishop of Washington), Medardo Mazombwe, (Archbishop of Lusaka/Zambia), and Óscar Rodríguez Maradiaga (Archbishop of Tegucigalpa/Honduras).[86] The conference was funded by a grant received by the US National Conference of Bishops from the Raskob Foundation.[87] It was "strictly off the record,"[88] but unpublished documents from the PCJP's public archive reveal some insights.

"We in the fund are mainly economists, particularly attentive to macroeconomic realities," IMF Managing Director Michel Camdessus argued during his speech, while churches and NGOs "have on your side a unique wealth of grass-roots experience . . . Please help us to perceive the

86. "The Ethical Dimensions of Debt," *NewsNotes*, November/December 1998, pp. 22–23, Box "4241/C186–2000 AA.VV. Fascicolo di Documenti sul Debito Nell'Ottica Della Chiesa Cattolica," Folder "Lettere pastorali, dichiarazioni e appelli di conferenze episcopali e commissione G&P dal 1984 al 1999," PCJP.

87. Founded in 1945, the organization has distributed more than $150 million in grants to Catholic organizations and programs around the world. It is named after John J. and Helena S. Raskob, two wealthy Catholic philanthropists.

88. Shelledy, "Legions Not Always Visible," 108. Shelledy claims the Seton Hall Conference took place in "March 1999." However, archival material from the Documentation Centre of the Pontifical Council for Justice and Peace suggest that the meeting took place from October 22 to 23, 1998.

message of the voiceless." The IMF was clearly interested in obtaining the church's blessing to legitimize its debt relief projects. Camdessus asked the church to encourage poor countries to seize the HIPC initiative. At the same time, he defended SAPs. Even if "they can be painful, they are vital for long-term economic development." At a time when Catholic NGOs still were debating whether HIPC was simply a thinly disguised form of SAPs, the IMF wanted to sell the HIPC initiative to the Holy See. Indeed, the IMF's Managing Director wanted to harness the lobbying power of the Vatican to put increasing pressure on creditor nations. Camdessus suggested that the church "join us in urging the donor community to fulfil—and to go beyond—its pledges" so that both the SAP and the HIPC initiatives are fully funded.[89]

Did the Holy See become co-opted by the World Bank and the IMF? As long as official diplomatic archives and the Vatican's own files remain closed, it is impossible to provide a detailed account of any deals that may or may not have been struck. Interestingly, in August 2000, Pope John Paul II appointed Michel Camdessus to be an official member of the PCJP. Some six months after Camdessus's resignation from the IMF, he joined a larger body of ecclesiastical, academic, political, and economic high-level advisors. This position includes, however, mostly symbolic as opposed to financial rewards.

Existing public sources suggest that the Holy See did not become an uncritical ally of the World Bank and the IMF. While the Holy See refrained from publicly blessing the HIPC initiative, it toned down the intensity of its diplomatic criticism and instead opted to engage the IFIs in dialogue. It was international Catholic NGOs and church leaders from the South whose advocacy reports or public statements were more outspoken than the Holy See's prudent and diplomatic approach.

Caritas Internationalis, together with CIDSE, an international alliance of sixteen Catholic development agencies from Europe and North America, argued that the HIPC initiative was "failing to provide an adequate solution." It provided "too little debt relief, too slowly, to too few countries" and continued to overlook "the human cost of debt

89. "Concerns for the Poor and Justice in Debt Relief and Adjustment Programs" by Michel Camdessus/IMF, October 22, 1998, Seton Hall conference on international debt, sponsored by the PCJP and the US Catholic Bishops Conference, Box "4241/C186–2000 AA.VV. Fascicolo di Documenti sul Debito Nell'Ottica Della Chiesa Cattolica," Folder "Lettere pastorali, dichiarazioni e appelli di conferenze episcopali e commissione G&P dal 1984 al 1999," PCJP.

repayments." The same report also criticized that HIPC "relies on decision-making processes that do not adequately involve poor and powerless people."[90]

A 2000 CIDSE-Caritas Internationalis background paper further questioned the IMF's "attitude" and suggested that its centralized organizational culture is "reluctant to adapt its core policies, its mandate and modus operandi to a policy environment where Poverty Reduction Strategies are shaped according to the particular conditions of individual low-income countries." The paper argued that the IMF and World Bank should accept responsibility for the human costs of their structural adjustment policies and give up their status as sole judges of nationally developed Poverty Reduction Strategy Papers (PRSPs).[91]

This new initiative was started by the World Bank and the IMF in 1999 to create greater national ownership of debt relief and to ensure that debt relief would actually translate into poverty reduction. PRSPs were prepared under the guidance of national governments through civil society participation.[92] A PCJP-sponsored conference held in Rome in December 2000 was influential in shaping the Catholic Church's critical evaluation of the PRSP process. There was a growing consensus that the PRSP initiative was disappointing. Representatives of national bishops' conferences from twenty of the poorest countries from Latin America, the Caribbean, and Asia as well as experts from Catholic NGOs discussed how to move "from debt relief to poverty reduction."[93]

Bishop Diarmuid Martin, in his opening speech, admitted that he was "horrified" to realize that he was "partly responsible" for the seminar's focus on poverty reduction. While this was the politically correct term, Christians should strive for nothing less than poverty elimination,

90. "Proclaim Jubilee: An urgent appeal for debt relief for the world's poor by the year 2000," A CIDSE and Caritas Internationalis Position Paper, January 1999, Box "4241/C278–1999 AA.VV. Fascicolo di Documenti sul Debito Internazionale, 1990–1999," Folder "CAFOD, CIDSE, CIDSE + Caritas Internationalis, Christian Aid," PCJP.

91. "PRS—Poverty Reduction or Public Relations Strategies? By Henry Northover. A CIDSE-Caritas Internationalis Background Paper, September 2000," Box "4241/C14–2001," PCJP.

92. International Monetary Fund, "Poverty Reduction Strategy in IMF-supported Programs."

93. Undated and unsigned summary, "From Debt Relief to Poverty Reduction," Box "090/C93–2001, PCJP Seminario 'Dalla riduzione del debito alla riduzione della povertà,' Roma 3–6 dicembre 2000," PCJP.

Martin argued. The purpose of the conference was not to "canonise or to condemn the new policies proposed by the International Financial Institutions but to discuss how far these PRSP's are really something new, rather than being structural adjustment with a social veneer." The objective was to determine the church's response, i.e., "how much of our resources it is useful to invest in PRSPs [and] how much we should align our policies with PRSPs."[94]

Skeptical voices prevailed at the conference. The final document recommended that "the Church should not endorse a Poverty Reduction Strategy Paper that has excluded meaningful participation of civil society." The World Bank and the IMF were urged "to set out transparent criteria on the minimum standards required for participation." While the church should speak out against bad governance and corruption and cooperate with other religious and civil society actors it should not jeopardize "the confidence of the poor in their Church" by becoming "manipulated by other institutions as it participates in political and economic programmes." The nature and extent of the church's engagement in the PRSP process should depend on the "political, social and ecclesial context" of each country. Participants expressed a concern that the church's participation in the PRSP process would merely serve to rubber-stamp preexisting agendas by the World Bank and the IMF. Feedback revealed that the consultation process had been "disappointing," "superficial," and "carried out too hastily." In one case, church representatives had only been given three days of notice before a major consultation.[95]

Conferences, lobbying, and debates on the debt crisis took place not only in Rome but around the Catholic world. On the whole, the church's voices from the Global South tended to strike a more critical tone than their Northern counterparts. In the Philippines, Cardinal Ricardo Vidal "demand[ed] the unconditional, immediate, and total cancellation of Third World debts, beginning with the illegitimate debts, and oppose[d] the International Monetary Fund-World Bank (IMF-WB) debt relief

94. "From Debt Relief to Poverty Reduction. Opening Address by Bishop Diarmuid Martin, Secretary of the Pontifical Council for Justice and Peace, Vatican City, 3 December 2000," Box "090/C93–2001, PCJP Seminario 'Dalla riduzione del debito alla riduzione della povertà,' Roma 3–6 dicembre 2000," PCJP.

95. Undated and unsigned summary, "From Debt Relief to Poverty Reduction," Box "090/C93–2001, PCJP Seminario 'Dalla riduzione del debito alla riduzione della povertà,' Roma 3–6 dicembre 2000," PCJP.

plan for highly-indebted poor countries."[96] At a seminar in the Honduran capital of Tegucigalpa, the local archbishop warned that foreign debt was hovering "like a funeral stone over Honduras."[97]

Bishops' conferences from Northern developed countries, especially from the G7, played a different role. Their task was to put pressure on their respective governments to grant debt relief more willingly. US bishops helped by lobbying the Republican-controlled Congress to agree to far-reaching debt cancellations. In April 1999, the Committee on International Policy of the US Conference of Catholic Bishops (USCCB) argued that the US government had a "special responsibility to help find a solution," especially as its lending practices and economic policies "contributed" to the debt crisis.[98] In an op-ed published in *The Washington Post*, the chairman of the USCCB's Committee on International Policy, Cardinal Bernard Law, wrote that he was "disturbed by the woefully inadequate allocation for poor country debt relief." By the time of Cardinal Law's intervention, the Senate had only approved $75 million and the relevant House Committee "a meager $69 million" compared to the $435 requested by the Clinton administration. Cardinal Law found it "very difficult to explain to Catholic bishops, missionaries and relief workers in Africa and Latin America why the United States, blessed with such wonderful resources and such a powerful economy, is reluctant to commit such a relatively small amount."[99]

The personal support of Pope John Paul II played the most visible role of the Holy See's contribution to the Jubilee 2000 campaign. When the Holy Father received a group from Jubilee 2000 on September 23, 1999—exactly one hundred days before the start of the Great Jubilee—religion and popular entertainment joined forces to call for debt relief. With the words "Holy Father, this is Mr. Bono, and he is a singer, and has done a lot for the campaign," Bishop Martin introduced Bono to the Holy

96. "Cancel Debt Payment, Church Leaders Urge," *Manila Standard*, June 7, 1999.

97. *ENI Bulletin* (Number 02) "Churches and activists plan strategy to win debt forgiveness for poor, by Paul Jeffrey, 28 January 1999," February 3, 1999, p. 3, Box "4241/C186–2000 AA.VV. Fascicolo di Documenti sul Debito Nell'Ottica Della Chiesa Cattolica," Folder "Lettere pastorali, dichiarazioni e appelli di conferenze episcopali e commissione G&P dal 1984 al 1999," PCJP.

98. Administrative Board of the United States Catholic Conference, "A Jubilee Call for Debt Forgiveness," n.p.

99. Law, "Forgiving Debts of the Poor," *The Washington Post*, September 20, 2000.

Father. Bono gave John Paul II his famous dark sunglasses. The pope immediately put them on while grinning mischievously.[100]

The Holy Father gave Jubilee 2000 his blessing and asserted that the "law of profit alone cannot be applied to that which is essential for the fight against hunger, disease and poverty." He wished that poorer countries had "a fuller share at the banquet of life."[101] Expressing the Holy See's concern about the slowness of the debt relief process, the Holy Father encouraged Jubilee 2000 to keep up the pressure:

> Debt relief is, however, urgent. It is, in many ways, a precondition for the poorest countries to make progress in their fight against poverty. This is something which is now widely recognized, and credit is due to all those who have contributed to this change in direction. We have to ask, however, why progress in resolving the debt problem is still so slow. Why so many hesitations? Why the difficulty in providing the funds needed even for the already agreed initiatives? It is the poor who pay the cost of indecision and delay.[102]

The papal audience was a very welcome publicity act for Jubilee 2000. "The pope has enormous influence," Bono argued, "he has a lot of fans . . . He's a big live attraction. All over the world people listen to him, billions of people listen to him . . . He's going to be telling the world that the most important thing for him as we go into the next millennium is that we do something about the one billion people who are in dire need."[103] As an entertainer, Bono understood that it took "a picture of me with the pope or a president to get debt cancellation on the front pages. Otherwise it's just too obscure a melody line. Unless these types of issues become pop, they don't become political."[104]

100. Agnew, "The Day the 'Funky' Pope Met 'Mr. Bono,'" *The Irish Times*, September 24, 1999.

101. John Paul II, "Message of the Holy Father to the group 'Jubilee 2000 Debt Campaign,'" n.p.

102. Ibid., n.p.

103. Donnelly, "Bono Puts Pope in the Shade," *The Mirror*, September 24, 1999.

104. Martin, "U2: Day 2," *The Mirror*, August 27, 2011.

Conclusion

Catholic teaching on capitalism provided the Vatican with a moral framework for tackling the problem of debt relief and legitimated subsequent calls for outright debt cancellation in the lead-up to the year 2000. While there was no formal alliance with Jubilee 2000, the Holy See supported the same interests in fighting for poverty reduction and challenging capitalism's mantra that free markets are a panacea for growth and justice.

Since the late nineteenth century, Catholic social doctrine has been committed to the idea that capitalism can be reformed through the infusion and dissemination of ethics and morality. Such a reformist attitude enabled the Holy See to act in a double role—as a moral voice for reform as well as a constructive interlocutor of political and international financial leaders. Yet the Vatican's commitment to gradual reformism is likely to disappoint those who promote more revolutionary solutions in order to transcend capitalism, rather than mitigate its social consequences. While the Holy See called for debt relief, it did so with diplomatic restraint rather than prophetic zeal and with a stress on a moral as opposed to a political message. Both mediating factors help us understand how and why the Holy See lived out the underlying Catholic teaching on capitalism in the form of a prudent dialogue with, rather than radical criticism of, the World Bank and the IMF.

To the skeptical political observer, the Holy See's claim to be a moral rather than a political actor sounds like mere rhetoric, if not hypocrisy. However, this distinct role understanding has a profound effect on the way Holy See diplomacy lives out Catholic social doctrine. The Holy See believes that its responsibility and duty are to highlight the moral boundaries within which legitimate good politics can take place. It does not believe it has the right to lay out concrete policy proposals or technical blueprints. Such direct political engagement is entrusted to lay Catholics rather than the clergy or the magisterium.[105]

In today's pluralized world, the Holy See's Catholic differentiation between morality and politics is either easily misunderstood or rejected. Today's postmodern societies have a profound general skepticism toward religious or moral truth claims. This explains why the Holy See's moral opposition to abortion, for example, is dismissed as undue religious interference into politics by pro-choice supporters. The clash of different

105. Pontifical Council for Justice and Peace, *Compendium*, paras. 565–74.

moral visions—particularly between liberals' emphasis on individual freedom and autonomy and the Catholic tradition's stress on truth and justice—is a major challenge both for Catholic social doctrine and for Holy See diplomacy.

The Holy See's aspiration to be a moral rather than political actor already had a strong impact on its diplomacy toward Poland. In the case of the Jubilee 2000 debt relief campaign, this role conception helps us understand why the Holy See continuously pushed for debt relief and poverty reduction. The Holy See's overarching argument was that development in general, and debt relief in particular, cannot and should not be seen as purely economic or political questions, but must be addressed as moral problems. The PCJP and Catholic bishops across the world emphasized the fight against poverty, defended the priority of human development over profit, and critically evaluated SAPs. By linking debt relief to the church's religious celebration of the Great Jubilee, Pope John Paul II personally threw the Holy See's support behind the Jubilee 2000 cause and encouraged bishops around the world to lobby their respective governments.

When it came to specific policy details, however, the Holy See refrained from offering concrete suggestions about the HIPC process, eligibility criteria for debt relief, or how to provide additional funding. "It is not the role of the church to give technical advice," explains Flaminia Giovanelli from the PCJP.[106] The pope, in his audience with Jubilee 2000 leaders, stressed that existing initiatives were inadequate and that more decisive action was necessary. He did not go into specifics. The kind of Catholic actors that were more forthcoming with concrete policy advice were international NGOs such as CIDSE or Caritas Internationalis. In contrast to the Holy See's preference for close dialogue with other governments and international institutions, these NGOs tended to draw upon a more critical language. They did not shy away from making more specific policy suggestions.

The Holy See's prudential restraint makes its moral interventions into global economic problems different from the more explosive fervor of contemporary groups such as Attac or Occupy Wall Street. The Holy See respects diplomatic etiquette and protocol and prefers to engage with IFIs such as the IMF or the World Bank in close and respectful dialogue, as evidenced by the series of seminars that brought together leading

106. Personal interview with Flaminia Giovanelli, Under-Secretary of the Pontifical Council for Justice and Peace, Vatican, March 20, 2012.

representatives of the Vatican, the World Bank, and the IMF. Contrary to more zealous international social movements, the Holy See refrained from demonizing the IFIs. This prudent approach, we have seen throughout this book, is very much part of the Holy See's diplomatic identity.

The Holy See's restraint can easily disappoint those Christians who wish for more confrontational or prophetic messages from the Vatican. Close diplomatic collaboration makes the Holy See vulnerable to becoming used, if not manipulated, by outside players. In the case of the international debt crisis, the IMF and the World Bank were clearly interested in using the Catholic Church's global legitimacy and credibility for their own purposes, particularly in the global South. The Holy See tends to be highly aware of this dynamic though and did its best not to become coopted. In fact, both the Holy Father and the PCJP pushed global opinion, creditor states, and international financial institutions to do more on debt relief rather than merely bless existing HIPC programs.

8

Conclusion

The 2013 apostolic exhortation *Evangelii Gaudium*—written "on the proclamation of the Gospel in today's world"—was the first major papal document entirely drafted by Pope Francis, the first pope from the global South. In this document, Pope Francis set a couple of new and refreshing accents for Catholic social doctrine. He admonished Catholic Christians to go back to the essentials: a personal relationship with Jesus in the community of the church and a strong concern for helping the poor. Pope Francis particularly called for internal examination of conscience not with a view to liberalize, protestantize, or modernize the church. Rather, he encouraged all Catholics to more authentically live the gospel by overcoming unhealthy manifestations of excessive clericalism, spiritual elitism, internal church polarizations, and forms of spiritual worldliness that privilege human glory over a radical Christian concern for others, especially for the most needy.

With regard to Catholic social doctrine, Francis insisted that Christians "cannot help but be concrete—without presuming to enter into details—lest the great social principles remain mere generalities which challenge no one. There is a need to draw practical conclusions" so that they can have a real impact in the world.[1] The Holy Father identifies the heart of the challenge that religious actors like the Holy See face if they want to faithfully live out their underlying traditions in the world of global politics. To fully unfold their meaning and their emancipatory potential, it is not sufficient to simply preach religious doctrines or norms. General principles have to be interpreted and applied to concrete circumstances.

1. Francis, *Evangelii Gaudium*, para. 182.

If religious traditions are to be more than vague banalities, this process is full of ethical dilemmas, difficult decisions, and political repercussions.

Based upon Alasdair MacIntyre's concept of tradition as a "historically extended, socially embodied argument,"[2] I set out to inquire how the Holy See, in its diplomatic practices, lives out its own normative tradition of Catholic social doctrine in global politics. The concluding chapter aims to bring together the findings of this book and will address both theoretical and practical implications that arise from this study.

Theoretical Implications

The Tradition Paradox

A MacIntyrean approach to the study of religious traditions is underpinned by the assumption that these traditions serve as a principled basis for action that cannot be overlooked. Catholic social doctrine provides such a principled basis for Holy See diplomacy. In global politics, the Holy See practices what it preaches. However, due to their living nature, Catholic social norms never determine the Holy See's diplomatic practice. They rather provide advice, reasons for action, constraints, and shape the Holy See's perception of global politics. They do not serve as an efficient cause for Holy See diplomacy in a mechanistic sense. Evidence from this study suggests the impact of tradition on religious activism in global politics is stronger when it comes to understanding the broader picture, but weaker in relation to explaining specific decisions.

During the Cold War era, fear of communism overshadowed the Holy See's criticism of liberal capitalism which only came to the forefront in the post-Cold War era. Catholic social doctrine's emphasis on the primacy of the human person, the centrality of morality, the promotion of peace, and the support for an international community among states constitutes the normative framework that both connects and underpins the Holy See's criticism of communism, liberalism, and capitalism. Few, if any, other religious traditions, political ideologies, or worldviews criticized all of the twentieth century's major ideologies—capitalism, liberalism, and communism. The distinct breadth of the Holy See's agenda in global politics provides the strongest and clearest evidence that the

2. MacIntyre, *After Virtue*, 22.

contours of its diplomacy cannot be understood without reference to the underlying normative tradition of Catholic social doctrine.

On the other hand, once we focus on specific decisions or positions, the impact of tradition on Holy See diplomacy is more difficult to pinpoint. On the whole, specific actions are the result of a complex interplay between traditional aims, historical circumstances, and prudential considerations. The decision not to publicly criticize the escalation of US warfare in South Vietnam in 1965, for example, was driven both by a fear of a communist victory and a wish to project the image of a neutral arbiter. During the protracted Polish crisis in the 1980s, the Holy See prudently balanced its call for moral reform with a concern for political stability. The partial assent which the Holy See delegations gave to the Cairo and Beijing final documents, to mention another example, was a compromise between a normative wish to defend traditional teaching and a pragmatic internationalist commitment to the UN system.

This paradox reveals a deeper tension of tradition-driven understanding of religious activism in global politics. Tradition is a necessary but not sufficient explanatory factor. It is necessary to understand the bigger picture, to create a set of expectations that constitutes a normal position on a given issue, and to broadly compare the agenda of a specific religious actor with those of other key actors. Tradition is insufficient, on the other hand, to explain or predict specific decisions, especially in situations of conflict, crisis, or political contestation. Agency and free will make prediction impossible. To fully understand this process, it is inescapable that we must closely examine contextual, institutional, and historical factors that mediate the way tradition is interpreted and applied.

Mediating Factors

If religious traditions are to be socially embodied in the real world rather than simply studied from sacred books, circumstances will inevitably influence how tradition affects practice. Certain mediating factors prioritize particular aspects of a specific tradition at the expense of others.

In the case of the Vietnam War, fear of communism and concern for South Vietnamese Catholics resulted in cautious peace diplomacy. The Holy See neither called for a withdrawal of US forces from South Vietnam nor endorsed the positions of Saigon and Washington despite considerable papal sympathies for their struggle against the communist

North. In the Polish case, the Holy See's desire to play a moral rather than political role, its commitment to prudence, and the personality of Pope John Paul II help us understand why the Holy See wanted to promote moral change without undermining domestic stability or deteriorating East-West relations.

In Cairo and Beijing, the Holy See's commitment to defending orthodox teaching as well as its Catholic internationalism led the Holy See to vigorously defend traditional teaching against both internal and external criticism. At the same time, the Holy See did not want to prevent an international consensus at the ICPD and the FWCW, even if their outcomes were not optimal from a Catholic point of view. In the case of the Jubilee 2000 anti-debt campaign, Catholic social doctrine encouraged the Holy See to support its international campaign for debt relief. During this process, the Holy See's self-restriction to moral interventions, with its deep-rooted prudent style of diplomacy resulted in the articulation of broad moral visions rather than political blueprints for action. Both factors help us understand why and how the Holy See preferred to engage with international financial institutions in close dialogue rather than subject them to harsher criticism.

Compared to the initial review of possible mediating factors, as discussed in Chapter 3, legal neutrality and political nonalignment have not featured very prominently in the case studies. This does not necessarily mean these two factors had no influence on Holy See diplomacy. Both factors are so deeply embedded in the Holy See's diplomatic identity that neither the Holy See nor its political partners or opponents feel a need to explicitly cite these factors in their conversations or analyses. Fear of communism also did not feature in the initial list. It played a crucial role during the Vietnam War but, interestingly enough, not so much during the Polish crisis. In Poland, the Holy See was more worried about the prospects of Soviet intervention and civil unrest. While encouraging moral and social change, both the Holy See and local church leaders refrained from demonizing communism and lived out Catholic teaching on communism rather pragmatically—without ever condoning it.

The single most influential aspect of the Roman Curia's organizational culture, as it pertains to its diplomatic relations, is its strong commitment to prudence that played a key role in both Poland and during the Jubilee 2000 campaign. This prudential dimension toned down the prophetic intensity of the Holy See's statements and positions for the sake of enabling dialogue with the Polish government and, in the Jubilee 2000 case, with the World Bank and the IMF.

In sum, contrary to Cold War communist rhetoric that portrays the Vatican as moral cheerleader for the capitalist West or the post-Cold War liberal and feminist critique that dismiss the Vatican as a fundamentalist, obscurantist actor, this study points toward the overriding importance of pragmatism and prudence as key features of the way the Holy See lives out Catholic norms in global politics.

Merits and Limits of a Tradition-Focused Approach

A tradition-based approach to the study of religious practice means to adopt an insider approach that accepts a particular religious normative vision as it is, with a view to inquire how a religious actor has lived up to its own normative standards and to examine the dilemmas it encounters in the process of doing so. Such an approach opens up the black box of religious agency by raising deeper questions about the normative sources of religious interests and practices. Indeed, understanding religiously motivated action in global politics requires a scholar to go deeper than imposing her or his favorite variables and explanatory models upon a given religious actor. It means to critically adopt a religious actor's worldview, arrive at an understanding of how its religious tradition specifies a particular political problem, and then examine the process of how the religious actor arrives at concrete policies and decisions. Such an approach is demanding as it presupposes substantive and detailed knowledge about a specific religious tradition, religious organization, and its prevailing culture. However, it promises to lead to a much richer and detailed account by creatively combining the study of theology, politics, and history.

The difficulty of using Catholic social doctrine to fully understand concrete specific decisions and positions of Holy See diplomacy raises the question, though, of how a tradition-focused approach compares to theoretical alternative framework. A conventional realist approach would attempt to explain Holy See diplomacy with reference to an overriding concern to protect the security of the Catholic Church as a transnational institution, i.e., to protect and promote its membership and financial resources. Indisputably, the commitment to protect Catholic interests, especially the safety and religious freedom of local Catholics is a key motivating factor for the Holy See. After all, it is the only sovereign actor that has the capacity, explicit will, and authority to watch over and protect Catholic interests across the world. This interest is imperative in situations of international conflict, civil war, domestic discrimination, religious persecution, or mass migration.

If the security of Catholics was the overriding concern, it is problematic, however, to explain why the Holy See does not choose more obvious and effective strategies for pursuing this goal. A realist explanation would imply that the Holy See should frequently be making deals with revolutionaries, despots, and authoritarian leaders (providing moral legitimacy in turn for security guarantees) or bandwagon with outside forces (providing moral legitimacy in turn for military intervention). While such strategies were not unheard of in previous centuries, both the Vietnam and Poland cases suggest the Vatican was strongly committed to a just peace. In accordance with Catholic social doctrine, this conception of justice did not allow for the indiscriminate support of US warfare in Vietnam, or turning a blind eye to the injustices committed by the North Vietnamese or Polish governments.

Moreover, the protection of local Catholic interests is by no means extraneous to Catholic social doctrine. Ever since the Second Vatican Council, religious freedom has been part and parcel of the Catholic worldview. Above and beyond, the Roman Pontiff, in his role as successor to Saint Peter, has historically claimed both authority and responsibility toward the global Catholic Church. Hence, Holy See diplomacy is not simply the function of a narrow interest in promoting local Catholic interests, important as they may be, but also the translation of a broader normative tradition into the realities of global politics.

A second plausible alternative to my key argument is that Holy See diplomacy is purely driven by an instrumental desire to safeguard its moral reputation, which is a key component of its broader "soft power" in global politics.[3] Put differently, concern about its public reputation rather than its social doctrine shapes and drives Holy See diplomacy. Admittedly, the Vatican frequently displays a strong desire to project a moral role and is hesitant to become overtly involved in party politics or geopolitical conflict. If possible, it certainly has a preference to be a neutral moral arbiter. This dynamic has been particularly noticeable in the Poland and Jubilee 2000 cases during which the Holy See displayed a

3. See Nye, *Soft Power*; Troy, "Die Soft Power des Heiligen Stuhls."

preference for gradual reformism in contrast to the more radical, revolutionary approaches displayed by the Polish workers' movement Solidarity or by contemporary anti-globalization movements.

The fact that the Holy See views itself as a moral as opposed to a political actor does not undermine, however, this book's overarching argument. This is because the Holy See's distinction between politics and morality is not the result of *ad hoc* calculations about what decision represents the best public relations move. Rather, it is the consequence of Catholic social doctrine's deeper philosophical roots in the natural law tradition. If the imperative had been a concern with its reputation, it is difficult to see why the Holy See did not simply change its controversial teachings on abortion, sexual ethics or family values in order to more effectively reach a Western, liberal audience. Critics of the tradition-focused approach have to explain why such doctrinal changes were not even contemplated even though they probably would have made the Vatican more popular at the UN and to the modern liberal world at large.

The Catholic understanding of natural law recognizes only few moral absolutes. Its general principles such as the common good or its reflections on a just economy operate at a higher level of abstraction. This prevents Catholic social doctrine from denigrating into a fundamentalist vision that regulates every aspect of human life, thus depriving humans of freedom, responsibility, and choice. Rather, the Holy See consistently displays respect for the autonomy of the political sphere and recognizes that—within moral limits—individuals may legitimately disagree with each other about the best political strategies to promote positive political or economic change.[4] In today's highly pluralistic world, however, it is precisely this distinction between flexible political issues and absolute moral issues that no longer enjoys widespread assent. The precise categorization of specific issues such as economic relations or abortion into one of the categories, as well as the Holy See's claim to act as the divinely willed interpreter of natural law, have become highly controversial—and hence politicized—questions.

The third and most serious challenge comes from a more idealistic and theological perspective. Given the importance which the Holy See attaches to prudence, pragmatism, and caution across the case studies, do its policies not lack the prophetic idealism that religious people ought to expect from their leaders? Noticeably, the Holy See is the most prominent

4. George, "Natural Law and International Order," 56.

yet not the most prophetic actor of the Catholic Church. Its status as a sovereign actor and its active, century-long presence in the international system make the Holy See an "inside" actor with great respect for diplomatic conventions, protocol, and the necessity of compromises. "Outside" Catholic actors can speak much more freely and prophetically. The American Trappist monk Thomas Merton and the Catholic anti-Vietnam War movement in the 1960s, individuals such as the assassinated Polish priest Father Jerzy Popiełuszko,[5] very liberal or very conservative associations of Catholics in the cases of the UN conferences in Cairo or Beijing, or Catholic NGOs during the Jubilee 2000 anti-debt campaign, all spoke a more direct language, expressed more passionate criticism, or made bolder proposals than the Holy See.

The Holy See's commitment to prudence does not imply, however, the adoption of an amoral relativistic view of politics or a readiness to draw upon immoral means if necessary. It rather means that the Holy See is well aware of the inevitable tensions between ideals and reality, between the morally desirable and the politically possible, as well as between general principles and the concrete case. The Vatican insists on objective moral principles while pragmatically realizing that practical realities frequently result in suboptimal outcomes. Indeed, Holy See diplomacy displays many characteristics of a classical realist approach to global politics in the line of thinkers such as E.H. Carr, Hans Morgenthau, or Reinhold Niebuhr.[6] The Holy See's attachment to prudence does not contradict, however, this book's central argument as realism does not have a theoretical monopoly on prudence. After all, it is a virtue which has already been praised by Scripture and which the Catechism of the Catholic Church lists among the four cardinal virtues.[7] Prudence is very much a part of lived Catholic social doctrine, especially in global politics.

Practical Implications

Creating Pragmatic Coalitions

There is more than sufficient evidence to debunk the frequent invocations of various "holy alliance" arguments as political myths that serve no deeper analytical purpose. In fact, the relationship between the interests

5. He was officially declared "Blessed" in 2010.

6. On classical realism in IR, see Lebow, *The Tragic Vision of Politics*.

7. Catholic Church, *Catechism*, paras. 1805–6.

of the Holy See and the interests of other international actors, particularly the United States, fluctuates greatly. The Holy See is too committed to political nonalignment and too prudent to engage in lasting strategic alliances. The reasons for this prudential rejection of deeper alliances with other states remain understudied. Evidence of this study suggests, however, that the Holy See is driven by a sober realization that only limited faith can be put into the intentions and interests of other governments. Their ideological preferences quickly can change due to democratic transitions. In any event, they are unlikely to ever fully converge with Catholic social doctrine, whose aims transcend the conventional battle lines between liberals and conservatives. When push comes to shove, historical experience suggests that other governments will be more concerned about their own national interests as opposed to the safety and well-being of the global Catholic community. At the end of the Vietnam War, for example, US diplomats and military troops simply left the country while millions of Catholics had to stay behind, facing a challenging life under socialist rule.

While strategic alliances are neither holy nor helpful explanatory tools, the Holy See remains open to the option of engaging in *ad hoc* coalitions to promote its interests on specific issues. Indeed, the Holy See is not deterred from creating pragmatic coalitions even when its partners have vastly different political, moral, or religious outlooks and, at times, may even try to manipulate the Holy See.

During the Vietnam War there was a considerable overlap of United States and Holy See interests based on shared anti-communist beliefs and a concern about the territorial integrity and independent future of a noncommunist South Vietnam. Pope Paul VI presented himself as a friend of the US government who believed in the underlying justice of America's cause in South Vietnam even as he failed to be more forthcoming with public expressions of support. Rather than listening to the Vatican's moral advice, the White House was more interested in trying to politically use the Vatican by enlisting the pope as a moral cheerleader for the war. Time and again, the White House overlooked or neglected papal peace initiatives for arbitration, peace negotiations, and bombing halts.

The Polish case reveals a politically significant friendship between the Vatican and the Reagan administration. However, the Holy See's style and diplomatic tone *vis-à-vis* the Eastern bloc was considerably less ideological than the Reagan administration's "peace through strength" approach. The Holy See not only refused to demonize the Soviet Union but, contrary to the expectations and interest of the White House, the pope refused to publicly endorse US economic sanctions against Poland and the Soviet Union.

The abrupt deterioration of US-Holy See relations in the post-Cold War era proves there was no deep and lasting "holy alliance" between them. Given the pro-choice stance of the Clinton administration as well as of many EU member states, it was commonsensical that the Holy See would look for like-minded partners elsewhere. In governments from predominantly Muslim states as well as from Central and South America, the Holy See found such partners. Due to theological and political differences, however, there could not be a "holy alliance" with Muslim states. In Cairo, the Holy See was much stricter on abortion and artificial contraception than most Muslim governments, whereas in Beijing it supported a more far-reaching role for women in the public sphere.

Although the Holy See had become an object of aversion for the liberal Western press during the ICPD in Cairo and the FWCW in Beijing, it became an important partner of the progressive campaign for international debt relief in the lead-up to the Great Jubilee. The Holy See vigorously supported Jubilee 2000 and even blessed it during a well-publicized papal audience with Bono, without ever formally adhering to the campaign. At the same time, the Holy See also maintained close relations with the IMF and the World Bank to engage in a dialogue about its activities in the fields of debt reduction, debt cancellation, and civil society participation, while refraining, however, from providing public legitimacy for these programs.

In sum, the Holy See is best-suited to choose its partners pragmatically, according to the issue under consideration. Journalists, diplomats, and Vatican observers are advised to understand the relationship between the Holy See and other political actors in terms of temporary divergences or convergences of interests rather than speculating about enduring holy alliances or lasting ideological enmity. A state's relationship with the Holy See is unlikely to ever fully converge on all key issues. Serious differences of opinion on some issues can simultaneously be complemented by a strong convergence of interests on other issues. To make the most of diplomatic relations with the Vatican, foreign governments or ambassadors to the Holy See are advised to mitigate or downplay tensions, and play up cooperation on shared interests, preferably on concrete projects. They will have to be careful, however, not to come across as too pushy or exaggerating lest they provoke a potentially embarrassing counter-reaction on the part of the Holy See. To protect itself from such attempts to entice moral support for political purposes, the Holy See, for its part, needs to prudently yet publicly distance itself whenever its partners overplay the nature or extent of cooperative initiatives.

Taking Catholic Social Doctrine More Seriously

If lived out authentically, Catholic social doctrine provides a prudent yet powerful countercultural challenge to hegemonic ideologies of global politics and to the international *status quo* with its many wars, economic injustices, dictatorships, and threats to life. A key challenge, however, inherent in any effort to taking Catholic social doctrine more seriously in global politics resides in the very nature of diplomacy.

Diplomacy can be a rather bureaucratic practice with a technocratic focus on the transmission of messages or the negotiation of agreements. Furthermore, diplomacy usually has a cooperative and rational, as opposed to an antagonistic or passionate, style. Its protocol and conventions aim to minimize friction and maximize understanding rather than facilitate prophetic calls for moral and political conversion. Moreover, foreign ambassadors are bound to respect the duty of noninterference in the domestic affairs of the home-country. Papal nuncios and officials in the Secretariat of State do not have to worry about economic or consular affairs even though they do play a distinct role in the management of relations between the Holy See and the local churches, which includes the important responsibility of nominating local bishops.

This study has shown that, despite these structural limits, the Holy See succeeded in conveying its key messages in each case: a just peace for Vietnam, order and moral progress for Poland, traditional sexual and family ethics for the United Nations, and fair economic relations during the international debt crisis. In contrast to other more passionate or radical Catholic actors, however, the Holy See tends to err on the side of caution. Its prudent, diplomatic, and detached approach of bringing peace to Vietnam appears in glaring contrast to the bloody and barbaric images of the war such as the My Lai Massacre, the humanitarian and ecological costs associated with the military use of Agent Orange, or the widespread use of terror by the Vietcong.

How may the Holy See and the Catholic Church better promote Catholic social doctrine, both in its diplomatic endeavors and beyond?

To begin with, Catholic social doctrine needs to be promoted at all levels of the church, beginning with local dioceses and parishes. It cannot be an elitist instrument to be left solely in the hands of popes, bishops, and priests. Otherwise it is bound to always remain the church's "best-kept secret."[8] If it is truly to be a living tradition, all Catholics ought to know its essential contours and embody it in their everyday lives. If it is truly to serve as an authoritative tradition, the Catholic Church will also have to rethink the reasons for studying, promoting, and embodying Catholic social doctrine. In an increasingly pluralistic and secularized modern world, a legalistic stress on obligation will not suffice. The challenge is to convince baptized Catholics and all people of good will that Catholic social doctrine offers a powerful, countercultural way of seeing and engaging with the modern world that is a direct consequence of the Christian faith rather than an optional add-on feature.

To bolster the authoritativeness of Catholic social doctrine it is essential to maintain and protect its coherence and balance which provides a unique challenge to the conventional political division into liberal and conservative camps. The Catholic community is not immune to such political divisions even though they tend to assume a more complex form inside the church. As John L. Allen notes, contemporary Catholicism suffers from a sort of "tribalism" in which various Catholic subcultures—such as progressive reformers, peace and justice activists, pro-lifers, or neoconservatives—tend to their own by reading their own publications, worshiping mainly with each other, glorifying their own theological or ecclesial heroes, and having only limited interaction with other "tribes."[9] Selective readings, interpretations, and applications of Catholic social doctrine are part and parcel of this Catholic tribalism.

Considering the distinct breadth of Catholic social doctrine, it is not surprising that different aspects will have greater or lesser appeal to different Catholics. In some cases, a personal interest in protecting migrants, the environment, or the unborn, may even lead to a pastorally fruitful intensified contact with the church. Moreover, Catholic individuals or groups should have both the freedom and the right to define their own priorities when it comes to Catholic social doctrine. Yet ignoring secular problems for the benefit of focusing on sacred issues, for example, cannot be an appropriate option. A Christian commitment has political,

8. Magliano, "Surprise! Catholic Social Teaching is the Church's Best-Kept Secret," n.p.

9. Allen, *Future Church*, 84, 454.

social, and economic consequences as it is evident when the church struggles with wars, political ideologies, family values, or just economic relations. This does not mean that all members of the church have to engage in excessive political activism. On a basic level it means, however, that Christians cannot view such issues as being separate from their faith.

Church leaders, for their part, have to guard themselves against becoming manipulated or used for selective purposes. If the church becomes exclusively associated with the conservative war against abortion, same-sex marriage, and euthanasia, or with the progressive struggle for justice, peace, and the environment, the broader and autonomous authority of Catholic social doctrine will get lost in the trenches of party politics or international culture wars. The social gospel and the gospel of life have to go hand in hand, otherwise Catholic social doctrine will lose its attractive and challenging uniqueness. Given its preeminent position, the Holy See has a special responsibility to keep together what both liberal and conservative Catholics try to divide.

Finally, Holy See diplomacy could be made more accountable to Catholic social doctrine. For a community that puts so much emphasis on individual sin it is astounding that there exists neither a formal nor an informal process of institutional self-reflection. If sin is as pervasive in individual life as the church teaches, the complexities of global politics surely provide just as much, if not more, opportunity for institutional mistakes, errors, and shortcomings. The recurring tension between speaking out and remaining silent continues to be a major dilemma of Holy See diplomacy. No template or best practice guidelines can put this dilemma to rest. "If the church sticks to abstract principles," John L. Allen explains, "it's accused of being pie in the sky and irrelevant. If it endorses specific policy proposals, it's accused of exceeding its competence, blurring the lines between church and state, and confusing prudential judgment with dogmatic certainty."[10]

Horizontal accountability could be increased by increasing the relevant training of Holy See diplomats abroad and officials employed in the Vatican. A handbook could be drafted that explains the normative value of diplomacy in relation to promoting moral change in general and Catholic social doctrine in particular. In a similar vein as a recent document written for Catholic businessmen,[11] such a *vademecum* for Holy

10. Allen, "A Vatican Document to Make Socrates Proud," n.p.

11. Pontifical Council for Justice and Peace, "Vocation of the Business Leader."

See diplomats could be written in an interrogatory rather than dogmatic manner, raising pertinent examinations of conscience such as whether concern for the poor and the underprivileged dominates decision-making and whether the same moral standards are applied equally both geographically and in terms of religious affiliation.

There is even a stronger need for vertical accountability in which the Holy See's engagement with global politics should be subject to more discussion, debate, and critical scrutiny both within the wider church community and beyond. Catholic universities and intellectuals should be particularly active in this process. It is imperative that the Vatican opens up access to its archives beyond the pontificate of Pius XI (1922–39) as soon and as completely as possible. It is difficult to even fully understand its engagement with the Vietnam War, for example, while mainly relying on Vatican-related files of other states.

The recent phenomenon of popes making public apologies for past shortcomings and mistakes committed on behalf of the church is also an encouraging phenomenon which deserves further support and should ideally be concrete rather than general. Finally, all Christians—in fact, all people of good will—need to reflect more on what it means to live an authentic life not only on Fridays in mosques, Saturdays in synagogues, or Sundays in churches, but also with respect to how they think, talk, and pray about global politics on a daily basis.

Religious ideas have to be defined and interpreted; religious practices have to be lived out one way rather than another, faithfully or not so faithfully; religious actors have to make choices about how much or little they engage with the outside world, and they have to decide how much or how little they tolerate internal dissent on a given issue. Every state and political community arrives at a more or less contested common understanding about how expansive or limited the place of religion should be in the public sphere. Any political conflict, event, issue, institution, or debate has repercussions for the common good. It may conform to—or be in tension with—the social vision of a specific religious tradition. Even relatively powerful religious actors have to be cautious about becoming manipulated by outside political actors. Politics then is inherently religious and religion is inherently political, whether religious and political leaders are willing to admit it or not.

At a time when the liberal secular West remains perplexed by the resilience, if not resurgence, of religion, the question of how people with different, if not conflicting, theological and political commitments ought to live with each other, both domestically and internationally, remains as important as ever. Any attempt to address this question should pay attention to the joys, hopes, and concerns expressed in religious traditions and to the moral and political processes through which people inherit, interpret, and incarnate them in global politics.

Bibliography

Abdullah, Yasmin. "The Holy See at United Nations Conferences: State or Church?" *Columbia Law Review* 96 (1996) 1835–75.

"About John C. Ford, S.J." http://www.twotlj.org/Ford.html.

Administrative Board of the United States Catholic Conference. "A Jubilee Call for Debt Forgiveness." April 1999. http://www.usccb.org/issues-and-action/human-life-and-dignity/debt-relief/jubilee-debt-forgiveness.cfm.

Agnew, Paddy. "The Day the 'Funky' Pope Met 'Mr. Bono.'" *The Irish Times*, September 24, 1999. https://www.irishtimes.com/news/the-day-the-funky-pope-met-mr-bono-1.230689.

Alberigo, Giuseppe, and Alberto Melloni. *Storia del Concilio Vaticano II*. Bologna: Il Mulino, 1995.

Alexiev, Alex. *The Kremlin and the Pope*. Santa Monica, CA: RAND Corporation, 1983.

Allen, John L. *All the Pope's Men: The Inside Story of How the Vatican Really Thinks*. New York: Doubleday, 2004.

———. *The Future Church: How Ten Trends are Revolutionizing the Catholic Church*. New York: Doubleday, 2009.

———. "A Vatican Document to Make Socrates Proud." *National Catholic Reporter*, April 13, 2012. http://ncronline.org/blogs/all-things-catholic/vatican-document-make-socrates-proud.

Appleby, R. Scott. *The Ambivalence of the Sacred: Religion, Violence, and Reconciliation*. Lanham, MD: Rowman & Littlefield, 2000.

———. "Rethinking Fundamentalism in a Secular Age." In *Rethinking Secularism*, edited by Craig J. Calhoun et al., 225–46. New York: Oxford University Press, 2011.

Araujo, Robert John, and John A. Lucal. *Papal Diplomacy and the Quest for Peace: The United Nations from Pius XII to Paul VI*. Philadelphia: Saint Joseph's University Press, 2010.

———. *Papal Diplomacy and the Quest for Peace: The Vatican and International Organizations from the Early Years to the League of Nations*. Naples, FL: Sapientia Press of Ave Maria University, 2004.

Archibald, George. "Abzug Network rules U.N. Women's Agenda; Seeks 'Gender Justice,' Empowerment," *The Washington Times*, August 10, 1995.

———. "Feminists Win Word War in Conference Platform; Vatican Agrees to 'Universal' Rights." *The Washington Times*, August 2, 1995.

Ascherson, Neal. *The Polish August: The Self-Limiting Revolution*. Harmondsworth, UK: Penguin, 1981.

Augustine. *The City of God Against the Pagans*. Translated by R. W. Dyson. Cambridge: Cambridge University Press, 1998.

BBC Summary of World Broadcasts. "Vatican Radio Criticism of Polish Coverage, Part E, Eastern Europe, Ee/6135/C/12," June 7, 1979.

Baden, Sally, and Anne Marie Goetz. "Who Needs [Sex] When You Can Have [Gender]? Conflicting Discourses on Gender at Beijing." *Feminist Review* 56 (1997) 3–25.

Barbato, Mariano. "A State, a Diplomat, and a Transnational Church: The Multilayered Actorness of the Holy See." *Perspectives* 21 (2013) 27–48.

Benedict XVI. *Caritas in Veritate*. June 29, 2009. http://w2.vatican.va/content/benedict-xvi/en/encyclicals/documents/hf_ben-xvi_enc_20090629_caritas-in-veritate.html.

Bernstein, Carl. "The Holy Alliance." *Time*, February 24, 1992. http://www.carlbernstein.com/magazine_holy_alliance.php.

Bernstein, Carl, and Marco Politi. *His Holiness John Paul II and the Hidden History of Our Time*. London: Bantam, 1997.

Biskupski, Mieczysław B. *The History of Poland*. Westport, CT: Greenwood, 2000.

Boscia, Teri. "The United States' Vietnam War: A Selective Annotated Bibliography." *Reference Services Review* 30 (2002) 160–68.

Bowen, Donna Lee. "Abortion, Islam, and the 1994 Cairo Population Conference." *International Journal of Middle East Studies* 29 (1997) 161–84.

Burleigh, Michael. *Sacred Causes: Religion and Politics from the European Dictators to Al Qaeda*. London: HarperPress, 2006.

Busby, Joshua William. "Bono Made Jesse Helms Cry: Jubilee 2000, Debt Relief, and Moral Action in International Politics." *International Studies Quarterly* 51 (2007) 247–75.

Buss, Doris E. "Robes, Relics and Rights: The Vatican and the Beijing Conference on Women." *Social & Legal Studies* 7 (1998) 339–63.

Buss, Doris, and Didi Herman. *Globalizing Family Values: The Christian Right in International Politics*. Minneapolis: University of Minnesota Press, 2003.

Califano, Joseph A., Jr. "The President and the Pope: L. B. J., Paul VI and the Vietnam War." *America* 165 (1991) 238–39.

Campbell, Francis. "The UK, the Holy See, and Diplomacy." Zenit, October 30, 2010. https://zenit.org/articles/ambassador-s-address-on-uk-holy-see-relations.

"Cancel Debt Payment, Church Leaders Urge," *Manila Standard*, June 7, 1999.

Cardinale, Hyginus Eugene. *The Holy See and the International Order*. Gerrards Cross, UK: Colin Smythe, 1976.

Casaroli, Agostino. *Il Martirio della Pazienza: La Santa Sede e i Paesi Comunisti (1963–89)*. Turin: Einaudi, 2000.

Catholic Church. *Catechism of the Catholic Church*. New York: Doubleday, 1995.

———. *Code of Canon Law*. Vatican: Libreria Editrice Vaticana, 1983.

Cavanaugh, William T. *The Myth of Religious Violence: Secular Ideology and the Roots of Modern Conflict*. Oxford: Oxford University Press, 2009.

———. *Theopolitical Imagination*. London: T. & T. Clark, 2002.

———. "What Is Religion?" In *Religion and International Relations: A Primer for Research*, edited by Michael C. Desch and Daniel Philpott, 56–67. Mellon Initiative on Religion Across the Disciplines, University of Notre Dame. http://rmellon.nd.edu/assets/101872/religion_and_international_relations_report.pdf.

Central Intelligence Agency. "Poland's Prospects Over the Next Six Months: Special National Intelligence Estimate." January 27, 1981. https://www.cia.gov/library/readingroom/docs/DOC_0000273319.pdf.

———. "Poland's Prospects Over the Next 12 to 18 Months: Special National Intelligence Estimate." August 30, 1982. https://www.cia.gov/library/readingroom/docs/DOC_0000273321.pdf.

Chadwick, Owen. *Britain and the Vatican during the Second World War*. Cambridge: Cambridge University Press, 1986.

Chong, Alan, and Jodok Troy. "A Universal Sacred Mission and the Universal Secular Organization: The Holy See and the United Nations." *Politics, Religion & Ideology* 12 (2011) 335–54.

Clodfelter, Mark. *The Limits of Air Power: The American Bombing of North Vietnam*. New York: Free Press, 1989.

Coleman, John A. "Raison d'Église: Organizational Imperatives of the Church in the Political Order." In *Secularization and Fundamentalism Reconsidered*, edited by Jeffrey K. Hadden and Anson Shupe, 252–75. New York: Pragon House, 1989.

Collins, Carole J. L., et al. "Jubilee 2000: Citizen Action across the North-South Divide." In *Global Citizen Action*, edited by Michael Edwards et al., 135–48. Boulder, CO: Lynne Rienner, 2001.

Crossette, Barbara. "Vatican Holds up Abortion Debate at Talks in Cairo." *The New York Times*, September 8, 1994. http://www.nytimes.com/1994/09/08/world/vatican-holds-up-abortion-debate-at-talks-in-cairo.html.

Cruise O'Brien, Conor. "A Holy and Explosive Alliance." *The Independent*, August 26, 1994. http://www.independent.co.uk/voices/a-holy-and-explosive-alliance-1385817.html

Davies, Norman. *God's Playground: A History of Poland*. Oxford: Oxford University Press, 2005.

Davis, Sid. "When LBJ took a Flying Leap at Peace." *The Washington Post*, December 24, 2007. http://www.washingtonpost.com/wp-dyn/content/article/2007/12/23/AR2007122302188.html.

Dent, Martin J., and Bill Peters. *The Crisis of Poverty and Debt in the Third World*. Burlington, VT: Ashgate, 1999.

Dobson, Alan P. "The Reagan Administration, Economic Warfare, and Starting to Close Down the Cold War." *Diplomatic History* 29 (2005) 531–56.

Domenico, Roy Palmer. "America, the Holy See and the War in Vietnam." In *Papal Diplomacy in the Modern Age*, edited by Peter C. Kent et al., 203–19. Westport, CT: Praeger, 1994.

Donnelly, Claire. "Bono Puts Pope in the Shade; He Hands Pontiff His Sunglasses." *The Mirror*, September 24, 1999.

Duc, Nguyen Phu. *The Viet Nam Peace Negotiations: Saigon's Side of the Story*. Edited by Arthur J. Dommen. Christiansburg, VA: Dalley, 2005.

Duffy, Eamon. *Saints & Sinners: A History of the Popes*. New Haven: Yale University Press, 1997.

Dunn, Dennis J. *Détente and Papal-Communist Relations, 1962–1978*. Boulder, CO: Westview, 1979.

Dziwisz, Stanisław. *Mein Leben mit dem Papst: Johannes Paul II. wie er wirklich war*. Leipzig: Benno, 2007.

El-Hadi, Amal Abd. "Islamic Politics in Beijing: Change of Tactics but Not Substance." *Reproductive Health Matters* 4 (1996) 47–54.

Elliott, Larry. "Candle Lit for Debt Relief's Unfinished Business." *The Guardian*, November 27, 2000. https://www.theguardian.com/business/2000/nov/27/debt.development.

Essig, Andrew M., and Jennifer L. Moore. "U.S.-Holy See Diplomacy: The Establishment of Formal Relations, 1984." *The Catholic Historical Review* 95 (2009) 741–64.

Ferraro, Vincent, and Melissa Rosser. "Global Debt and Third World Development." In *World Security: Challenges for a New Century*, edited by Michael Klare et al., 332–55. New York: St. Martin's, 1994.

Field, Catherine. "Women Face an Unholy Alliance." *The Observer*, September 3, 1995.

Fisk, Robert. "'Holy Alliance' tries to Wreck Birth-Control Conference," *The Independent*, August 31, 1994. http://www.independent.co.uk/news/world/holy-alliance-tries-to-wreck-birth-control-conference-fundamentalists-are-spreading-lies-about-the-1379658.html.

Flynn, Raymond L. "Letter from the Vatican: Common Objectives for Peace." *SAIS Review* 16 (1996) 143–53.

Francis. *Evangelii Gaudium*. November 24, 2013. https://w2.vatican.va/content/francesco/en/apost_exhortations/documents/papa-francesco_esortazione-ap_20131124_evangelii-gaudium.html.

Friedman, Elisabeth Jay. "Gendering the Agenda: The Impact of the Transnational Women's Rights Movement at the UN Conferences of the 1990s." *Women's Studies International Forum* 26 (2003) 313–31.

Friedman, Milton. *Capitalism and Freedom*. Chicago: University of Chicago Press, 1962.

Friedrichs, Jörg, and Friedrich Kratochwil. "On Acting and Knowing: How Pragmatism Can Advance International Relations Research and Methodology." *International Organization* 63 (2009) 701–31.

Fukuyama, Francis. *The End of History and the Last Man*. London: Penguin, 1992.

G7 Information Center. "G7 Statement." June 18, 1999. http://www.g8.utoronto.ca/summit/1999koln/g7statement_june18.htm.

Gaddis, John Lewis. *The Cold War: A New History*. New York: Penguin, 2005.

Gaillardetz, Richard R. "The Ecclesiological Foundations of Modern Catholic Social Teaching." In *Modern Catholic Social Teaching: Commentaries and Interpretations*, edited by Kenneth R. Himes et al., 72–98. Washington, DC: Georgetown University Press, 2005.

Garton Ash, Timothy. *The Polish Revolution: Solidarity*. 3rd ed. New Haven, CT: Yale University Press, 2002.

George, Robert P. "Natural Law and International Order." In *International Society: Diverse Ethical Perspectives*, edited by David Mapel and Terry Nardin, 54–69. Princeton: Princeton University Press, 1998.

Gerald R. Ford Presidential Library. "Memorandum of Conversation between the President and Ambassador John Volpe." March 25, 1975. https://fordlibrarymuseum.gov/library/document/memcons/1552999.pdf.

Gill, Anthony James. *Rendering Unto Caesar: The Catholic Church and the State in Latin America*. Chicago: University of Chicago Press, 1998.

Glendon, Mary Ann. "Statement of Professor Mary Ann Glendon, Head of the Delegation of the Holy See to the Fourth World Conference on Women, Beijing, 5

September 1995." In *Serving the Human Family: The Holy See at the Major United Nations Conferences*, edited by Carl J. Marucci, 523–30. New York: Path to Peace Foundation, 1997.

———. "Statement by Professor Mary Ann Glendon, Head of the Holy See Delegation, at the Concluding Session of the Fourth World Conference on Women, Beijing, 15 September 1995." In *Serving the Human Family: The Holy See at the Major United Nations Conferences*, edited by Carl J. Marucci, 531–35. New York: Path to Peace Foundation, 1997.

———. "What Happened at Beijing." *First Things*, January 1, 1996. https://www.firstthings.com/article/1996/01/005-what-happened-at-beijing.

Graham, Robert A. *Vatican Diplomacy: A Study of Church and State on the International Plane*. Princeton: Princeton University Press, 1959.

Gunn, T. Jeremy. *Spiritual Weapons: The Cold War and the Forging of an American National Religion*. Westport, CT: Praeger, 2009.

Gunning, Jeroen, and Richard Jackson. "What's So 'Religious' about 'Religious Terrorism?'" *Critical Studies on Terrorism* 4 (2011) 369–88.

Halliday, Fred. "Culture and International Relations: A New Reductionism?" In *Confronting the Political in International Relations*, edited by Michi Ebata et al., 47–67. Basingstoke, UK: Macmillan, 2000.

Hanson, Eric O. *The Catholic Church in World Politics*. Princeton: Princeton University Press, 1987.

Hassner, Ron E. *War on Sacred Grounds*. Ithaca, NY: Cornell University Press, 2009.

Haynes, Jeffrey. *Third World Politics: A Concise Introduction*. Oxford: Blackwell, 1996.

Hehir, J. Bryan. "Papal Foreign Policy." *Foreign Policy* 78 (1990) 26–48.

Herman, Didi. "Globalism's 'Siren Song': The United Nations and International Law in Christian Right Thought and Prophecy." *The Sociological Review* 49 (2001) 56–77.

Higer, Amy J. "International Women's Activism and the 1994 Cairo Population Conference." In *Gender Politics in Global Governance*, edited by Mary K. Meyer and Elisabeth Prügl, 122–41. Lanham, MD: Rowman & Littlefield, 1999.

Hinze, Christine Firer. "Commentary on *Quadragesimo anno (After Forty Years)*." In *Modern Catholic Social Teaching: Commentaries and Interpretations*, edited by Kenneth R. Himes et al., 151–74. Washington, DC: Georgetown University Press, 2005.

"Holy Alliance," *The Globe and Mail*, August 30, 1994

Holy See. *Actes et Documents du Saint-Siège relatifs à la Seconde Guerre Mondiale*. 9 vols. Vatican: Libreria Editrice Vaticana, 1967–81.

———. "Holy See Mission Press Release—Holy See Delegation Challenges NGO Accreditation of 'Catholics for a Free Choice' to United Nations Women's Conference, New York, 21 March 1995." In *Serving the Human Family: The Holy See at the Major United Nations Conferences*, edited by Carl J. Marucci, 853. New York: Path to Peace Foundation, 1997.

———. "National Report of the Holy See in Preparation for the International Conference on Population and Development, 23 March 1993." In *Serving the Human Family: The Holy See at the Major United Nations Conferences*, edited by Carl J. Marucci, 221–28. New York: Path to Peace Foundation, 1997.

———. "Press Release issued by the Delegation of the Holy See during the Fourth World Conference on Women, Beijing, 9 September 1995." In *Serving the Human*

Family: The Holy See at the Major United Nations Conferences, edited by Carl J. Marucci, 537–38. New York: Path to Peace Foundation, 1997.

———. "Reservations of the Holy See to the Programme of Action adopted at the International Conference on Population and Development, Cairo, 13 September 1994." In *Serving the Human Family: The Holy See at the Major United Nations Conferences*, edited by Carl J. Marucci, 321–22. New York: Path to Peace Foundation, 1997.

———. "The Secretariat of State." http://www.vatican.va/roman_curia/secretariat_state/documents/rc_seg-st_12101998_profile_en.html.

———. "Statement of Interpretation of the Term 'Gender' by the Holy See Delegation." In *Serving the Human Family: The Holy See at the Major United Nations Conferences*, edited by Carl J. Marucci, 536. New York: Path to Peace Foundation, 1997.

Hurd, Elizabeth Shakman. *The Politics of Secularism in International Relations*. Princeton: Princeton University Press, 2008.

International Monetary Fund. "Poverty Reduction Strategy in IMF-Supported Programs." September 29, 2016. http://www.imf.org/external/np/exr/facts/prsp.htm.

Jacobs, Seth. *America's Miracle Man in Vietnam: Ngo Dinh Diem, Religion, Race, and U.S. Intervention in Southeast Asia, 1950–1957*. Durham, NC: Duke University Press, 2004.

Jay, Antony, ed. *The Oxford Dictionary of Political Quotations*. Oxford: Oxford University Press, 1996.

John XXIII. *Mater et Magistra*. May 15, 1961. http://w2.vatican.va/content/john-xxiii/en/encyclicals/documents/hf_j-xxiii_enc_15051961_mater.html.

———. *Pacem in Terris*. April 11, 1963. http://w2.vatican.va/content/john-xxiii/en/encyclicals/documents/hf_j-xxiii_enc_11041963_pacem.html.

John Paul II. "Address of His Holiness John Paul II to the Diplomatic Corps Accredited to the Holy See, 12 January, 1985." http://w2.vatican.va/content/john-paul-ii/en/speeches/1985/january/documents/hf_jp-ii_spe_19850112_corpo-diplomatico.html.

———. "Angelus." December 13, 1981. http://w2.vatican.va/content/john-paul-ii/it/angelus/1981/documents/hf_jp-ii_ang_19811213.html.

———. *Centesimus Annus*. May 1, 1991. http://w2.vatican.va/content/john-paul-ii/en/encyclicals/documents/hf_jp-ii_enc_01051991_centesimus-annus.html.

———. "Ceremonia di Benvenuto. Discorso di Giovanni Paolo II." June 16, 1983. http://w2.vatican.va/content/john-paul-ii/it/speeches/1983/june/documents/hf_jp-ii_spe_19830616_arrivo-varsavia.html.

———. "Discorso del Santo Padre Giovanni Paolo II alla Delegazione del Sindacato Indipendente et Autonomo Polacco 'Solidarnosc.'" January 15, 1981. http://w2.vatican.va/content/john-paul-ii/it/speeches/1981/january/documents/hf_jp-ii_spe_19810115_solidarnosc.html.

———. "Discorso di Giovanni Paolo II ai Membri dell'Assemblea Plenaria del Pontificio Consiglio della Giustizia e della Pace." November 8, 1996. http://w2.vatican.va/content/john-paul-ii/it/speeches/1996/november/documents/hf_jp-ii_spe_19961108_giustizia-pace.html.

———. "Discorso di Giovanni Paolo II al Corpo Diplomatico accreditato presso la Santa Sede, January 14, 1984." http://w2.vatican.va/content/john-paul-ii/it/

speeches/1984/january/documents/hf_jp-ii_spe_19840114_corpo-diplomatico.html.

———. "Discorso di Giovanni Paolo II al Corpo Diplomatico accreditato presso La Santa Sede, January 16, 1982." http://w2.vatican.va/content/john-paul-ii/it/speeches/1982/january/documents/hf_jp-ii_spe_19820116_corpo-diplomatico.html.

———. *Evangelium Vitae*. March 25, 1995. http://w2.vatican.va/content/john-paul-ii/en/encyclicals/documents/hf_jp-ii_enc_25031995_evangelium-vitae.html.

———. *Familiaris Consortio*. November 22, 1981. http://w2.vatican.va/content/john-paul-ii/en/apost_exhortations/documents/hf_jp-ii_exh_19811122_familiaris-consortio.html.

———. *Laborem Exercens*. September 14, 1981. http://w2.vatican.va/content/john-paul-ii/en/encyclicals/documents/hf_jp-ii_enc_14091981_laborem-exercens.html.

———. "Letter to Families." February 2, 1994. https://w2.vatican.va/content/john-paul-ii/en/letters/1994/documents/hf_jp-ii_let_02021994_families.html.

———. "Letter of His Holiness Pope John Paul II to the World's Heads of State, Vatican, 19 March 1994." In *Serving the Human Family: The Holy See at the Major United Nations Conferences*, edited by Carl J. Marucci, 199–201. New York: Path to Peace Foundation, 1997.

———. "Letter of His Holiness Pope John Paul II to Women, Vatican, 29 June 1995." In *Serving the Human Family: The Holy See at the Major United Nations Conferences*, edited by Carl J. Marucci, 829–38. New York: Path to Peace Foundation, 1997.

———. *Love and Responsibility*. Translated by H. T. Willetts. London: Collins, 1981.

———. "Message of His Holiness Pope John Paul II for the Celebration of the Day of Peace, 1 January 1979." http://w2.vatican.va/content/john-paul-ii/en/messages/peace/documents/hf_jp-ii_mes_19781221_xii-world-day-for-peace.html.

———. "Message of His Holiness Pope John Paul II to Mrs. Gertrude Mongella, Secretary General of the United Nations' Fourth World Conference on Women, Vatican, 26 May 1995." In *Serving the Human Family: The Holy See at the Major United Nations Conferences*, edited by Carl J. Marucci, 419–24. New York: Path to Peace Foundation, 1997.

———. "Message of His Holiness Pope John Paul II to Mrs. Nafis Sadik, Secretary General of the 1994 International Conference on Population and Development and Executive Director of the United Nations Population Fund, Vatican, 18 March 1994." In *Serving the Human Family: The Holy See at the Major United Nations Conferences*, edited by Carl J. Marucci, 191–97. New York: Path to Peace Foundation, 1997.

———. "Message of His Holiness Pope John Paul II to the Delegation of the Holy See to the Fourth World Conference on Women, Vatican, 29 August 1995." In *Serving the Human Family: The Holy See at the Major United Nations Conferences*, edited by Carl J. Marucci, 425–27. New York: Path to Peace Foundation, 1997.

———. "Message of the Holy Father to the Group 'Jubilee 2000 Debt Campaign.'" September 23, 1999. http://w2.vatican.va/content/john-paul-ii/en/speeches/1999/september/documents/hf_jp-ii_mes_23091999_jubilee-2000-debt-campaign.html.

———. "Messaggio del Santo Padre Giovanni Paolo II al Primate di Polonia, Cardinale Stefan Wyszyński." March 28, 1981. http://w2.vatican.va/content/john-paul-ii/

it/messages/pont_messages/1981/documents/hf_jp-ii_mes_19810328_primate-polonia.html.

———. *Return to Poland: The Collected Speeches of John Paul II*. London: Collins, 1979.

———. *Sollicitudo Rei Socialis*. December 30, 1987. http://w2.vatican.va/content/john-paul-ii/en/encyclicals/documents/hf_jp-ii_enc_30121987_sollicitudo-rei-socialis.html.

———. *Tertio Millennio Adveniente*. November 10, 1994. https://w2.vatican.va/content/john-paul-ii/en/apost_letters/1994/documents/hf_jp-ii_apl_10111994_tertio-millennio-adveniente.html.

———. "Udienza Generale, December 16, 1981." http://w2.vatican.va/content/john-paul-ii/it/audiences/1981/documents/hf_jp-ii_aud_19811216.html.

———. "Udienza Generale, October 24, 1984." http://w2.vatican.va/content/john-paul-ii/it/audiences/1984/documents/hf_jp-ii_aud_19841024.html.

Johnson, Lyndon B. "Address at Johns Hopkins University." April 7, 1965. https://millercenter.org/the-presidency/presidential-speeches/april-7-1965-address-johns-hopkins-university.

Jütte, Robert. *Contraception: A History*. Translated by Vicky Russell. Cambridge: Polity, 2008.

———. *Lust ohne Last: Geschichte der Empfängnisverhütung von der Antike bis zur Gegenwart*. Munich: C. H. Beck, 2003.

Kahn, Joseph. "Leaders in Congress Agree to Debt Relief for Poor Nations." *The New York Times*, October 18, 2000. http://www.nytimes.com/2000/10/18/world/leaders-in-congress-agree-to-debt-relief-for-poor-nations.html.

Kaiser, Robert Blair. *The Encyclical That Never Was: The Story of the Commission on Population, Family and Birth, 1964–66*. London: Sheed & Ward, 1987.

Karnow, Stanley. *Vietnam: A History*. New York: Viking, 1983.

Karsh, Efraim. *Neutrality and Small States*. London: Routledge, 1988.

Kent, Peter C. *The Lonely Cold War of Pope Pius XII: The Roman Catholic Church and the Division of Europe, 1943–1950*. Montréal: McGill-Queen's University Press, 2002.

Kent, Peter C., and John F. Pollard. *Papal Diplomacy in the Modern Age*. Westport, CT: Praeger, 1994.

Kifner, John. "Pope will Visit Poland next June, Warsaw and Primate Announce." *The New York Times*, November 9, 1983. http://www.nytimes.com/1982/11/09/world/pope-will-visit-poland-next-june-warsaw-and-primate-announce.html?pagewanted=print.

Köck, Heribert Franz. "Sonstige Völkerrechtssubjekte." In *Österreichisches Handbuch des Völkerrechts*, edited by Hanspeter Neuhold et al., 184–88. Vienna: Manz'sche Verlags- und Universitätsbuchhandlung, 2004.

Koehler, John O. *Spies in the Vatican: The Soviet Union's Cold War Against the Catholic Church*. New York: Pegasus, 2009.

Kohan, John. "Poland. My Heart Will Stay." *Time*, July 4, 1987. http://content.time.com/time/magazine/article/0,9171,950919,00.html.

———. "Return of the Native." *Time*, June 27, 1983. www.time.com/time/printout/0,8816,953941,00.html.

Kramer, Mark. "Jaruzelski, the Soviet Union, and the Imposition of Martial Law in Poland: New Light on the Mystery of December 1981." *Cold War International History Project Bulletin* 11 (1998) 5–14.

Kratochwil, Friedrich. "How Do Norms Matter?" In *The Role of Law in International Politics: Essays in International Relations and International Law*, edited by Michael Byers, 35–68. Oxford: Oxford University Press, 2001.

———. "On the Notion of 'Interest' in International Relations." *International Organization* 36 (1982) 1–30.

Krygier, Martin. "Law as Tradition." *Law and Philosophy* 5 (1986) 237–62.

Küng, Hans. "P.S.: Lonely Power of Vatican City." *The Guardian*, September 16, 1994.

Lancaster, John, and Boyce Rensberger. "Abortion Objections Stall Forum: Vatican Rejects Cairo Compromise as Unacceptable." *The Washington Post*, September 7, 1994.

Latin-American Episcopal Council. "Letter of the Latin-American Episcopal Council (Celam) to Mrs. Nafis Sadik, Secretary-General of the International Conference on Population and Development, Santafé De Bogotá, 14 March 1994." In *Serving the Human Family: The Holy See at the Major United Nations Conferences*, edited by Carl J. Marucci, 780–85. New York: Path to Peace Foundation, 1997.

Law, Bernard. "Forgiving Debts of the Poor." *The Washington Post*, September 20, 2000. https://www.washingtonpost.com/archive/opinions/2000/09/20/forgiving-debts-of-the-poor/893d070f-3a69-4abc-92ca-70225cb3ef8f/?utm_term=.ea034f8a611f.

Lebow, Richard Ned. *The Tragic Vision of Politics: Ethics, Interests, and Orders*. Cambridge: Cambridge University Press, 2003.

Leo XIII. *Rerum Novarum*. May 15, 1891. http://w2.vatican.va/content/leo-xiii/en/encyclicals/documents/hf_l-xiii_enc_15051891_rerum-novarum.html.

Linden, Ian. *Global Catholicism: Diversity and Change since Vatican II*. London: Hurst, 2009.

de Lucia, Carlo. "Sconcertante Affermazione della Rappresentante dell'Unione Europea." *L'Osservatore Romano*, September 8, 1995.

Luxmoore, Jonathan, and Jolanta Babiuch. *The Vatican and the Red Flag: The Struggle for the Soul of Eastern Europe*. London: G. Chapman, 2000.

MacIntyre, Alasdair. *After Virtue: A Study in Moral Theory*. 2nd ed. London: Duckworth, 1985.

Maddox, Bronwen, and Mark Nicholson. "EU Delegates Battle to Head off Abortion Row: Dispute Looms at Cairo Population Conference," *Financial Times*, September 5, 1994.

Magliano, Tony. "Surprise! Catholic Social Teaching is the Church's Best-Kept Secret." *National Catholic Reporter*, April 16, 2002. http://ncronline.org/blogs/making-difference/surprise-catholic-social-teaching-churchs-best-kept-secret.

Mann, Judy. "The Front Lines of the Population War." *The Washington Post*, August 31, 1994.

Manthorpe, Jonathan. "UN Conference on Women: Human Rights, Violence Against Women Top Agenda." *The Ottawa Citizen*, August 31, 1995.

Martin, Paul. "U2: Day 2: Bono Reveals Secrets of Life on the Road." *The Mirror*, August 27, 2011.

Martino, Renato Raffaele. "Interview Given to Vatican Radio by His Excellency Archbishop Renato R. Martino, Apostolic Nuncio, Permanent Observer of the Holy See to the United Nations, Head of the Delegation of the Holy See to the International Conference on Population and Development, Cairo, 30 August 1994." In *Serving the Human Family: The Holy See at the Major United*

Nations Conferences, edited by Carl J. Marucci, 328–30. New York: Path to Peace Foundation, 1997.

———. "Statement by His Excellency Archbishop R. Martino, Apostolic Nuncio, Permanent Observer of the Holy See to the United Nations and Head of the Delegation of the Holy See at the Concluding Session of the International Conference on Population and Development, Cairo, 13 September 1994." In *Serving the Human Family: The Holy See at the Major United Nations Conferences*, edited by Carl J. Marucci, 318–20. New York: Path to Peace Foundation, 1997.

———. "Statement by His Excellency Archbishop R. Martino, Apostolic Nuncio, Permanent Observer of the Holy See to the United Nations and Head of the Delegation of the Holy See to the International Conference on Population and Development, Cairo, 7 September 1994." In *Serving the Human Family: The Holy See at the Major United Nations Conferences*, edited by Carl J. Marucci, 311–17. New York: Path to Peace Foundation, 1997.

———. "Statement of His Excellency Archbishop Renato R. Martino, Apostolic Nuncio, Permanent Observer of the Holy See to the United Nations at the 39th Session of the Commission on the Status of Women on Preparations for the Fourth World Conference on Women, New York, 16 March 1995." In *Serving the Human Family: The Holy See at the Major United Nations Conferences*, edited by Carl J. Marucci, 493–96. New York: Path to Peace Foundation, 1997.

Marx, Karl, and Friedrich Engels. *The Communist Manifesto: A Modern Edition*. London: Verso, 1998.

Mayo, Marjorie. "'The World Will Never Be the Same Again'? Reflecting on the Experiences of Jubilee 2000, Mobilizing Globally for the Remission of Unpayable Debts." *Social Movement Studies: Journal of Social, Cultural and Political Protest* 4 (2005) 139–54.

McAndrews, Lawrence J. "Lonesome Dove: The Pope, the President, the Church, and Vietnam, 1963–1969." *White House Studies* 9 (2010) 247–67.

McClory, Robert. *Turning Point: The Inside Story of the Papal Birth Control Commission, and How Humanae Vitae Changed the Life of Patty Crowley and the Future of the Church*. New York: Crossroad, 1995.

McIntosh, C. Alison, and Jason L. Finkle. "The Cairo Conference on Population and Development: A New Paradigm?" *Population and Development Review* 21 (1995) 223–60.

Mich, Marvin L. "Commentary on *Mater et magistra* (*Christianity and Social Progress*)." In *Modern Catholic Social Teaching: Commentaries and Interpretations*, edited by Kenneth R. Himes and Lisa Sowle Cahill, 191–216. Washington, DC: Georgetown University Press, 2005.

Miller, James E., ed. *Foreign Relations of the United States, 1964–1968*. Vol. 12, *Western Europe*. Washington, DC: United States Government Printing Office, 2001.

Mindszenty, József. *Memoirs*. Translated by Richard and Clara Winston. New York: Macmillan, 1974.

Morgan, Joseph G. "A Change of Course: American Catholics, Anticommunism, and the Vietnam War." *U.S. Catholic Historian* 22 (2004) 117–30.

Mufson, Steven. "Vatican will not Contest Language on Abortion," *The Washington Post*, September 7, 1995.

Murphy, Francis Xavier. "Vatican Politics: Structure and Function." *World Politics* 26 (1974) 542–59.

Murphy, Kim. "Shaky Compromise on Abortion Unravels at Population Conference," *The Gazette*, September 8, 1994.

Musto, Ronald G. *The Catholic Peace Tradition*. New York: Peace, 2002.

Nardin, Terry. "Ethical Traditions in International Affairs." In *Traditions of International Ethics*, edited by Terry Nardin and David R. Mapel, 1–22. Cambridge: Cambridge University Press, 1992.

Navarro-Valls, Joaquín. "Briefing by Dr. Joaquín Navarro-Valls, Director of the Holy See Press Office, on the Draft Program of the International Conference on Population and Development, 8 August 1994." In *Serving the Human Family: The Holy See at the Major United Nations Conferences*, edited by Carl J. Marucci, 302–5. New York: Path to Peace Foundation, 1997.

———. "Briefing by Dr. Joaquín Navarro-Valls, Director of the Press Office of the Holy See on the Topic of the United Nations Fourth World Conference on Women, Vatican, 20 June 1995." In *Serving the Human Family: The Holy See at the Major United Nations Conferences*, edited by Carl J. Marucci, 505–13. New York: Path to Peace Foundation, 1997.

Neale, Palena R. "The Bodies of Christ as International Bodies: The Holy See, Wom(B) an and the Cairo Conference." *Review of International Studies* 24 (1998) 101–18.

The New York Times. "Vatican newspaper says Wałęsa has lost his battle with regime," June 25, 1983. http://www.nytimes.com/1983/06/25/world/vatican-newspaper-says-walesa-has-lost- his-battle-with-regime.html.

Nichols, Aidan. *The Shape of Catholic Theology: An Introduction to its Sources, Principles, and History*. Collegeville, MN: Liturgical, 1991.

Nicholson, Jim. *The United States and the Holy See: The Long Road*. Edited by Giovanni Cubeddu. Rome: 30Days, 2002.

Nicholson, Mark. "Vatican Makes Waves at Cairo Conference." *Financial Times*, September 8, 1994.

Noonan, John Thomas. "Abortion and the Catholic Church: A Summary History." *Natural Law Forum* 12 (1968) 85–131.

———. *A Church that Can and Cannot Change: The Development of Catholic Moral Teaching*. Notre Dame: University of Notre Dame Press, 2005.

Nye, Joseph S. *Soft Power: The Means to Success in World Politics*. New York: PublicAffairs, 2004.

O'Boyle, Edward J. "John Paul II's Vision of the Social Economy." *International Journal of Social Economics* 32 (2005) 520–40.

O'Brien, David J. "American Catholic Opposition to the Vietnam War: A Preliminary Assessment." In *War or Peace? The Search for New Answers*, edited by Thomas A. Shannon, 119–50. Maryknoll, NY: Orbis, 1980.

O'Sullivan, John. *The President, the Pope, and the Prime Minister: Three Who Changed the World*. Washington, DC: Regnery, 2006.

Paltrow, Scott J. "Poland and the Pope: The Vatican's Relations with Poland, 1978 and Beyond." *Millennium: Journal of International Studies* 15 (1986) 1–25.

Paul VI. "Address of the Holy Father Pope Paul VI to the United Nations Organization." October 4, 1965. https://w2.vatican.va/content/paul-vi/en/speeches/1965/documents/hf_p-vi_spe_19651004_united-nations.html.

———. *Angelus Domini*. July 9, 1972. http://w2.vatican.va/content/paul-vi/it/angelus/1972/documents/hf_p-vi_ang_19720709.html.

———. *Dignitatis Humanae.* December 7, 1965. http://www.vatican.va/archive/hist_councils/ii_vatican_council/documents/vat-ii_decl_19651207_dignitatis-humanae_en.html.

———. "Discorso di Paolo VI all'Unione Cattolica della Stampa Italiana e Proposta di un Arbitrato dell'O.N.U. per la Pace nel Vietnam." January 29, 1966. http://w2.vatican.va/content/paul-vi/it/speeches/1966/documents/hf_p-vi_spe_19660129_stampa-vietnam.html.

———. "Discours du Pape Paul VI à un Pèlerinage du Vietnam." May 24, 1967. https://w2.vatican.va/content/paul-vi/fr/speeches/1967/may/documents/hf_p-vi_spe_19670524_pellegrinaggio-vietnamiti.html.

———. *Gaudium et Spes.* December 7, 1965. http://www.vatican.va/archive/hist_councils/ii_vatican_council/documents/vat-ii_cons_19651207_gaudium-et-spes_en.html.

———. *Humanae Vitae.* July 25, 1968. http://w2.vatican.va/content/paul-vi/en/encyclicals/documents/hf_p-vi_enc_25071968_humanae-vitae.html.

———. *Mense Maio.* April 29, 1965. http://w2.vatican.va/content/paul-vi/en/encyclicals/documents/hf_p-vi_enc_29041965_mense-maio.html.

———. *Populorum Progressio.* March 26, 1967. http://w2.vatican.va/content/paul-vi/en/encyclicals/documents/hf_p-vi_enc_26031967_populorum.html.

Peterson, Jonathan. "The Rock Star, the Pope, and the World's Poor." *Los Angeles Times*, January 7, 2001. http://articles.latimes.com/2001/jan/07/news/cl-9258.

Philpott, Daniel. "The Catholic Wave." *Journal of Democracy* 15 (2004) 32–46.

———. "Explaining the Political Ambivalence of Religion." *American Political Science Review* 101 (2007) 505–25.

———. "Has the Study of Global Politics Found Religion?" *Annual Review of Political Science* 12 (2009) 183–202.

Pietilä, Hilkka. *The Unfinished Story of Women and the United Nations.* Edited by Beth Peoc'h. Geneva: United Nations Non-Governmental Liaison Service, 2007.

Pius IX. *Qui Pluribus.* November 9, 1846. https://w2.vatican.va/content/pius-ix/it/documents/enciclica-qui-pluribus-9-novembre-1846.html.

Pius XI. *Casti Connubii.* December, 31, 1930. https://w2.vatican.va/content/pius-xi/en/encyclicals/documents/hf_p-xi_enc_19301231_casti-connubii.html.

———. *Divini Redemptoris.* March 19, 1937. https://w2.vatican.va/content/pius-xi/en/encyclicals/documents/hf_p-xi_enc_19370319_divini-redemptoris.html.

———. *Mit brennender Sorge.* March 14, 1937. http://w2.vatican.va/content/pius-xi/en/encyclicals/documents/hf_p-xi_enc_14031937_mit-brennender-sorge.html.

———. *Quadragesimo Anno.* May 15, 1931. https://w2.vatican.va/content/pius-xi/en/encyclicals/documents/hf_p-xi_enc_19310515_quadragesimo-anno.html.

"A Pledge to Gender Justice." July 28, 1995. http://www.affection.org/sante/asvc/www.igc.apc.org/womensnet/beijing/ngo/wedo/pldg.html.

Pontifical Commission "Iustitia et Pax." "At the Service of the Human Community: An Ethical Approach to the International Debt Crisis." December 27, 1986. http://www.justpax.va/content/dam/giustiziaepace/pubblicazioni/Textson-line-only/The%20International%20Debt%20Question_ENG.pdf.

Pontifical Council for Justice and Peace. *Compendium of the Social Doctrine of the Church.* Vatican: Libreria Editrice Vaticana, 2004.

———. *John Paul II and the Family of Peoples: The Holy Father to the Diplomatic Corps (1978–2002).* Vatican: Libreria Editrice Vaticana, 2002.

———. "Vocation of the Business Leader: A Reflection." http://www.iustitiaetpax.va/content/dam/giustiziaepace/VBL/Vocation_ENGLISH_4th%20edition.pdf.

"Pope Sings a Hymn for His Poland." *The New York Times*, August 21, 1980.

Porter, Jean. "Tradition in the Recent Work of Alasdair MacIntyre." In *Alasdair MacIntyre*, edited by Mark C. Murphy, 38–69. New York: Cambridge University Press, 2003.

Reagan, Ronald. "The President's News Conference." January 19, 1982. https://www.reaganlibrary.archives.gov/archives/speeches/1982/11982b.htm.

———. "Remarks at the Annual Convention of the National Association of Evangelicals in Orlando, Florida." March 8, 1983. https://reaganlibrary.archives.gov/archives/speeches/1983/30883b.htm.

———. "Statement on the Lifting of Economic Sanctions against Poland." February 19, 1987. https://www.reaganlibrary.archives.gov/archives/speeches/1987/021987a.htm.

———. "Statement on U.S. Measures Taken against the Soviet Union Concerning Its Involvement in Poland." December 29, 1981. https://reaganlibrary.archives.gov/archives/speeches/1981/122981m.htm.

"Report on the 4th Session of the Commission Set Up by the Holy See to Study the Problems of Population, Family, and Birth-Rate. (Rome. 25th to 28th March 1965)." http://www.twotlj.org/25-28%20March%201965%20Session.pdf.

Reus-Smit, Christian. "Constructivism." In *Theories of International Relations*, edited by Scott Burchill et al., 209–30. 2nd ed. New York: Palgrave, 2001.

Reus-Smit, Christian, and Duncan Snidal. "Between Utopia and Reality: The Practical Discourses of International Relations." In *The Oxford Handbook of International Relations*, edited by Christian Reus-Smit and Duncan Snidal, 3–37. Oxford: Oxford University Press, 2008.

Rossi, Fabrizio. *Der Vatikan: Politik und Organisation*. Munich: C. H. Beck, 2005.

Roy, Olivier. *Secularism Confronts Islam*. New York: Columbia University Press, 2007.

Ryall, David. "The Catholic Church as a Transnational Actor." In *Non-State Actors in World Politics*, edited by Daphné Josselin and William Wallace, 41–58. Basingstoke, UK: Palgrave, 2001.

———. "The Cross and the Bear: The Vatican's Cold War Diplomacy in East Central Europe." In *Deconstructing and Reconstructing the Cold War*, edited by Alan P. Dobson et al., 181–201. Aldershot, UK: Ashgate, 1999.

———. "How Many Divisions? The Modern Development of Catholic International Relations." *International Relations* 14 (1998) 21–34.

Schuck, Michael L. "Early Modern Roman Catholic Social Thought, 1740–1890." In *Modern Catholic Social Teaching: Commentaries and Interpretations*, edited by Kenneth R. Himes et al., 99–124. Washington, DC: Georgetown University Press, 2005.

Shannon, Thomas A. "Commentary on *Rerum novarum* (*The Condition of Labor*)." In *Modern Catholic Social Teaching: Commentaries and Interpretations*, edited by Kenneth R. Himes et al., 127–50. Washington, DC: Georgetown University Press, 2005.

Shelledy, Robert B. "Legions Not Always Visible on Parade: The Influence of the Vatican in World Politics." PhD diss., University of Wisconsin-Madison, 2003.

———. "The Vatican's Role in Global Politics." *SAIS Review* 24 (2004) 149–61.

Singh, Jyoti Shankar. *Creating a New Consensus on Population: The Politics of Reproductive Health, Reproductive Rights and Women's Empowerment*. London: Earthscan, 2009.

Slevin, Gerald. "New Birth Control Commission Papers Reveal Vatican's Hand." *National Catholic Reporter*, March 23, 2011. http://www.ncronline.org/news/vatican/new-birth-control-commission-papers-reveal-vaticans-hand.

Smith, Steve. "Positivism and Beyond." In *International Theory: Positivism and Beyond*, edited by Steve Smith et al., 11–44. Cambridge: Cambridge University Press, 1996.

Smith, Steve, et al. "Introduction." In *International Theory: Positivism and Beyond*, edited by Steve Smith et al., 1–8. Cambridge: Cambridge University Press, 1996.

Smith, Thomas W. *History and International Relations*. London: Routledge, 1999.

Sodano, Angelo. "Address by His Eminence Angelo Cardinal Sodano, Secretary of State, on the Position of the Holy See Regarding the International Conference on Population and Development at the Special Assembly for Africa of the Synod of Bishops, Vatican, 21 April 1994." In *Serving the Human Family: The Holy See at the Major United Nations Conferences*, edited by Carl J. Marucci, 229–37. New York: Path to Peace Foundation, 1997.

Staniszkis, Jadwiga. *Poland's Self-Limiting Revolution*. Edited by Jan T. Gross. Princeton: Princeton University Press, 1984.

Stepan, Alfred. "The World's Religious System and Democracy: Crafting the 'Twin Tolerations.'" In *Arguing Comparative Politics*, edited by Alfred Stepan, 213–53. Oxford: Oxford University Press, 2002.

Stummvoll, A. Alexander. "John Paul II, the Cold War, and the Catholic Tradition of International Relations, 1978–1991." MPhil diss., University of Oxford, 2007.

———. "A Living Tradition: The Holy See, Catholic Social Doctrine, and Global Politics, 1965–2000." PhD diss., European University Institute, 2012.

Tagliabue, John. "Vatican Attacks U.S.-Backed Draft for Women's Conference," *The New York Times*, August 26, 1995. http://www.nytimes.com/1995/08/26/world/vatican-attacks-us-backed-draft-for-women-s-conference.html.

———. "Vatican Seeks Islamic Allies in U.N. Population Dispute." *The New York Times*, August 18, 1994. http://www.nytimes.com/1994/08/18/world/vatican-seeks-islamic-allies-in-un-population-dispute.html.

Tauran, Jean-Louis. "Statement by His Excellency Archbishop Jean-Louis Tauran, Secretary for Relations with States, at a Meeting with Ambassadors Accredited to the Holy See, Vatican, 25 March 1994." In *Serving the Human Family: The Holy See at the Major United Nations Conferences*, edited by Carl J. Marucci, 251–60. New York: Path to Peace Foundation, 1997.

———. "Statement by His Excellency Archbishop Jean-Louis Tauran, Secretary for Relations with States of the Holy See: The Position of the Holy See on the Draft Platform for Action for the Fourth World Conference on Women, Vatican, 26 May 1995." In *Serving the Human Family: The Holy See at the Major United Nations Conferences*, edited by Carl J. Marucci, 497–504. New York: Path to Peace Foundation, 1997.

Teunissen, Jan Joost. "Introduction." In *HIPC Debt Relief: Myths and Reality*, edited by Jan Joost Teunissen et al., 1–10. The Hague: FONDAD, 2004.

Thomas, Scott M. *The Global Resurgence of Religion and the Transformation of International Relations: The Struggle for the Soul of the Twenty-first Century*. New York: Palgrave Macmillan, 2005.

Tindal-Robertson, Timothy. *Fatima, Russia and Pope John Paul II: How Mary Intervened to Deliver Russia from Marxist Atheism, May 13, 1981–December 25, 1991*. Rev. ed. Leominster, UK: Gracewing, 1998.

Tittmann, Harold H. *Inside the Vatican of Pius XII: The Memoir of an American Diplomat During World War II*. Edited by Harold H. Tittmann III. New York: Doubleday, 2004.

Tofani, Loretta. "Vatican Taking a Softer Line at U.N. Conference." *Philadelphia Inquirer*, September 14, 1995.

Toft, Monica Duffy, et al. *God's Century: Resurgent Religion and Global Politics*. New York: Norton, 2011.

Troy, Jodok. "Die Soft Power des Heiligen Stuhls: Unsichtbare Legionen zwischen internationaler Gesellschaft und Weltgesellschaft." *Zeitschrift für Außen- und Sicherheitspolitik* 3 (2010) 489–511.

"U.N. Says Vatican Camp may be 'Voted Down' on Abortion." *Deutsche Presse-Agentur*, September 9, 1994.

United Nations. "Draft Programme of Action of the International Conference on Population and Development." May 13, 1994. https://documents-dds-ny.un.org/doc/UNDOC/LTD/N94/216/53/pdf/N9421653.pdf?OpenElement.

———. "Vienna Convention on Diplomatic Relations." http://legal.un.org/ilc/texts/instruments/english/conventions/9_1_1961.pdf.

United Nations Development Programme. "Human Development Report 1990." http://hdr.undp.org/sites/default/files/reports/219/hdr_1990_en_complete_nostats.pdf.

"United States Cardinals and Conference President's Letter to President William Clinton on the Cairo Conference." In *Serving the Human Family: The Holy See at the Major United Nations Conferences*, edited by Carl J. Marucci, 787–90. New York: Path to Peace Foundation, 1997.

Vallier, Ivan. "The Roman Catholic Church: A Transnational Actor." *International Organization* 25 (1971) 479–502.

Van Staaveren, Jacob. *Gradual Failure: The Air War Over North Vietnam 1965–1966*. Washington, DC: Air Force History and Museums Program, 2002.

Vatican City State. "Treaty Between the Holy See and Italy." http://www.vaticanstate.va/content/dam/vaticanstate/documenti/leggi-e-decreti/Normative-Penali-e-Amministrative/LateranTreaty.pdf.

"Vatican Denies 'Hard Line' on Reproductive Issues." *The Irish Times*, September 5, 1995.

Wałęsa, Lech. *A Way of Hope*. New York: H. Holt, 1987.

Walsh, Michael J. "Introduction." In *Proclaiming Justice and Peace: Documents from John XXIII to John Paul II*, edited by Michael Walsh and Brian Davies, xi–xxiii. London: CAFOD, 1984.

Weigel, George. *The Final Revolution: The Resistance Church and the Collapse of Communism*. Oxford: Oxford University Press, 1992.

———. *Witness to Hope: The Biography of Pope John Paul II*. New York: HarperCollins, 2005.

Weigel, George, and Robert Royal. *Building the Free Society: Democracy, Capitalism, and Catholic Social Teaching*. Grand Rapids: Eerdmans, 1993.

Wilson Center. "Stenographic Minutes of the Meeting of Leading Representatives of the Warsaw Pact Countries in Moscow." December 5, 1980. http://digitalarchive.wilsoncenter.org/document/111232.pdf?v=c23a0e92c5e2ff5fdd2652d7ac411fd3.

Witham, Larry. "Population Plan Draws Interfaith Fire; U.N. Accused of Secular 'Imperialism.'" *The Washington Times*, August 24, 1994.

Wolfensohn, James D. *A Global Life: My Journey among Rich and Poor, from Sydney to Wall Street to the World Bank*. New York: PublicAffairs, 2010.

Zalewski, Marysia. "'All These Theories yet the Bodies Keep Piling Up': Theory, Theorists, Theorising." In *International Theory: Positivism and Beyond*, edited by Steve Smith et al., 340–53. Cambridge: Cambridge University Press, 1996.

Index